The Constitutionals

Peter Robinson was born in Salford, Lancashire, in 1953 and grew up mainly in Liverpool. He holds degrees from the Universities of York and Cambridge. After teaching for many years in Japan, he returned to Europe in 2007 and is currently Professor of English and American Literature at the University of Reading. The poetry editor for Two Rivers Press, author of many books of poetry, translations, prose fiction, and literary criticism, he has been awarded the Cheltenham Prize, the John Florio Prize, and two Poetry Book Society Recommendations.

POETRY
Overdrawn Account
This Other Life
Entertaining Fates
Lost and Found
About Time Too
Selected Poems 1976–2001
Ghost Characters
The Look of Goodbye
The Returning Sky
Buried Music
Collected Poems 1976–2016
Ravishing Europa

PROSE & INTERVIEWS
Talk about Poetry: Conversations on the Art
Spirits of the Stair: Selected Aphorisms
Foreigners, Drunks and Babies: Eleven Stories
The Draft Will
September in the Rain: A Novel

TRANSLATIONS
The Great Friend and Other Translated Poems
Selected Poetry and Prose of Vittorio Sereni
The Greener Meadow: Selected Poems of Luciano Erba
Poems by Antonia Pozzi

CRITICISM
In the Circumstances: About Poems and Poets
Poetry, Poets, Readers: Making Things Happen
Twentieth Century Poetry: Selves and Situations
Poetry & Translation: The Art of the Impossible
The Sound Sense of Poetry

PETER ROBINSON

The Constitutionals

A Fiction

for Ian,
plenty of crimes in Royal Berkshire
for your delectation —
Peter
20 June 2019

TWO
RIVERS
PRESS

First published in the UK in 2019 by Two Rivers Press
7 Denmark Road, Reading RG1 5PA
www.tworiverspress.com

ISBN 978-1-909747-48-7

1 2 3 4 5 6 7 8 9

Two Rivers Press is represented in the UK by Inpress Ltd
and distributed by NBNi.

Cover illustration and design by Sally Castle
Text design by Nadja Guggi and typeset in Pollen

Printed and bound in Great Britain by Imprint Digital, Exeter.

for Ornella, Matilde & Giulia

NOTE

This is a work of fiction. Although incidents, accidents, events, and the narrative shape of *The Constitutionals* are derived from experience, each living character in it—and especially its narrator—is a composite drawing upon various individuals, invented or real, and the author's imagination. Places and times have been adapted and conflated to suit the shape of the book, and with the exception of its public figures and famous, notorious, or forgotten personages, any resemblance to people living or dead is fortuitous. Opinions expressed are those of the characters, including the narrator, though some may well coincide with its writer, and perhaps even some of its readers.

'a distemper was here his favourite metaphor... it was exactly the same in the body national as in the body natural... nor was he in so much pain of a consumption from the mass of corrupted matters and ulcerated humours in our constitution—which he hoped was not as bad as it was imagined;—but he verily feared, that in some violent push, we should go off, all at once, in a state apoplexy ...'

—Laurence Sterne, *The Life and Opinions of Tristram Shandy*

1

Setting off on these constitutionals, after first slamming shut our flaked black-painted door and dropping the junk mail into a maroon recycle bin, I would cross the loose stone path—already there when we took out a mortgage on this house. Its pebbles must have been gathered by the previous owner—one of those 'if you can't paint good paint big' abstract expressionists—from his holiday beaches. Or so it would seem, for mixed in with them were shells and other seashore shards: nostalgic reminders of our distant island home.

And if that weren't enough, immediately beyond, there would be a great moat-like puddle from the flooded gutter, one no amount of attention by council contractors appeared to reduce in inclement weather. I would leap over or, today, tiptoe gingerly around it. Then the only thing remaining was to cross the road by that white-painted bump of a mini-roundabout and head off down the avenue in the direction of the cemetery, round by a columnar post-box, under a telegraph pole, beside the house opposite and its new low garden wall.

There I would slip back the triptych of ultra-art-house movies—films in which 'a marginalized individual sets out to avert global catastrophe, hoping to trigger the end of neoliberalism by going for a walk.' They had been borrowed from one of those online film clubs who send their discs out to customers, and were, at that very moment, thudding down into the little red post-box, back through its inflamed throat, as though done with forever.

Only, days later, finding myself no less haunted, I would be compelled to rent them yet once more. You see, out on these constitutionals of mine, I'm following in the footsteps of their director, Patrick ... Patrick whatever ... who also wrote that he had 'decided to cure myself by making a film about London.' Just so: some repetitive-compulsive watching of what had become his trilogy would prove an unexpectedly therapeutic experience—so much so that, as with the morphine they once gave you for pain that would do your head in, you must watch its dosage so as not to get hooked on the relief.

Returned to England after so long abroad, returned to this place in the Thames valley not far from where the first of those films was shot, overlapping in space with where the second and third begin, it was like I had been taken over by a virus, one much more metaphysical than the thing that had flattened me for six weeks or so, it being more of an electronic one, threatening to dispossess me—before you could say Jack Robinson—of myself alone. It was almost a case of identity theft, an idea that, admit it, rather depended on the assumption that you had an identity to steal.

Setting out on these constitutionals, attempting to walk myself back into a memory of health, I couldn't help thinking that the inner and outer were trying to re-establish contact with each other, struggling together, so to speak, in these attempts of mine to get out of the house, to face the world—even if only the streets and buildings, the trees and sky, of this eastern district in our Thames valley county seat. Which is why these constitutionals of mine would be taking me down the road, past the black-and-white nameplate for Eastern Avenue, noticing the late spring's wayside flowers.

Conscious as ever of the time of day, the light in the sky, the degree of cloud-cover diffusing the light, how near or far it was from sunrise or sunset, I've always been fixated on twilight, or a twilight of the mind, the moment when there emerge those spirits, the absent ones returning to their haunts, momentarily glimpsed from a corner of the eye, or as equally fixated on the way light picks out the simplest objects on the pavement, the kinds of things that a scavenger might gather to feed a fire, or construct a useful object.

Now I was once more going by that stretch of scorched-black wooden fence: for those red and blue flashing lights had, in the deep mid-winter—seen through our front bedroom window, flaring off new-fallen snow—proved to be a fire engine, just beyond the mini-roundabout daubed on the roadway where Eastern Avenue meets Addington, or maybe Erleigh Road (maps are ambiguous on this point), and whose continuance becomes Crescent Road, not infrequently flummoxing delivery truck drivers and postmen new to this round.

The red fire engine had pulled up slant-wise in the road, the men with their extinguishers promptly attending to what was doubtless a stolen car in flames and enveloped in billowing dark grey plumes. But, come daybreak, you would never have known: police, thieves, burnt car, firemen, all gone up in smoke, as it seemed, not a trace of them left from that winter night—except, of course, for those carbon footprints in the snow.

You see no sooner had we returned from our extended sojourn overseas, no sooner had we managed to take out a mortgage on our miniscule accommodation, than down I went with that terrible sickness, sickness undo death, it seemed—a very real virus of my own. It would leave me bed-ridden for weeks, and would then provide reason enough for taking these convalescent walks, to be repeating them till effective—and, further, to make them into the theme of these ashamedly autobiographical reflections. To get my own health back, I would need to take a great many of these extended walks, a series, in fact, of long-drawn-out constitutionals.

But what had got into me? It was all too painfully mysterious. The doctors couldn't put a name to it, and it seemed there might be nothing to assist in my recovery, though they did think it could be—like that film maker's central character—a virus of some kind, as if in attempting to recover lost memory, my nominal aphasia not merely nominal, the devices and desires that were me had somehow mysteriously been hacked.

For, among its many symptoms, the one that would most perplex was this problem of remembering what people are called. Almost all the surnames had, at a stroke, been vanished from my mind. What these persons had done or written—that would come back, and sometimes a vague outline or hint of how they were known, or how it was spelt. If culture is when you've forgotten what book you read it in, then I was well on my way to achieving it, not now being able to recall who said that either.

Admit it, you might remember they had the same surname as someone else equally famous, occupying a different, or a similar for that matter, area of celebrity. That's why I've done my best to describe who they are in what follows, and hope you'll be able to put a name to them—because, for me, what comes out of this general mental miasma, from which in my convalescence I've been trying to emerge, is occasionally somebody's first, their middle or second name. Yet then it will be gone again, departing as quickly as it came, leaving no more than a hazy outline. So if you can remember them, or guess who they are, then at least they won't have disappeared into the general amnesia that appears to be the fate of so much history, of all our histories now.

Luckily, I can still remember my own, and of course the nickname I've had to live with all these years, for I was given it in childhood. The character it's taken from isn't a problem either, nor his equally famous companion—the one named after a day of the week—and I can call up their author as well. At times, too, it feels like a horrid punishment for the desire possessing me in youth to be somebody, to make a name for myself, as it were, like so many have before, and so many after too. In fact, it may be that the sickness which came and did its worst for those weeks some winters back now was part of this same judgment upon it, or a dreadful psychological side effect of that youthful desire to be a name.

The doctors consulted couldn't say what was wrong, which added to the thought that there must *really* be something not merely physical amiss; and what's more, as a result of their not knowing, the medical profession, the dear old desperate NHS, couldn't prescribe anything for it either.

'You'll just have to wait till it goes of its own accord,' the GP's locum would say, 'till your immune system rallies— when things will start getting back to normal. You'll have to just grin and bear it, then we'll see.'

Sadly, though, as the weeks went by, it began to seem things never would get back to normal, and, after all, time moves on—even as you're laid up and it appears to have stopped—so when you're better it's this months-older *you* into which you must recover. You never do feel your old self again, for your old self is what's gone forever.

The virus did present physical symptoms, though, in the form of a complete nervous-system failure, a shivering fever, intolerable headache, digestive tract collapse, stabbing pains the length of the spine, and a tender prickling between the extremities of fingers and toes. There was no help for it, being inexpressibly sick in body, and much afraid in mind.

2

At more or less this very moment—and the thought would keep returning as I continued to take one unsteady step after another down the riverine slope of Eastern Avenue—at more or less the time my health collapsed in a heap from that protracted ailment, the Western world's mortgage companies, housing markets, and much of its banking system, found themselves in a game of pass the parcel, combined with one of musical chairs—where the parcels were made of non-performing debts bundled up with more desirable financial products, and the chairs, when the music stopped, meant either financial survival—if you could sit down on a government bailout (or conjure, by hook or crook, injections of external capital)—or else, if you couldn't, immediate ejection from the system.

It had come home here too, right here to this Thames-valley county town in the form of the so-called Reading Incident. This appeared to have been a bit of flagrant building-society embezzlement and accountancy fraud—which was bad enough, but then the measures taken to conceal this 'incident' meant that a financial institution of long standing with a vast hole in its balance sheets had to be sold on—the government acting as enforcer for the deal—to a still-viable bank, which required them, then, when the crisis struck, to have a vast infusion of officially syphoned-off public money to make up for that private case of fraudulent wealth creation. Something of the like, it seemed, had been happening right here in Reading, and been dubbed—by news-media outlets at that very time—*The Reading Scandal*.

Then there was this irony, another one, for me, in carrying around my desert-island-derived schoolyard nickname associated with 'anyone' or 'everyone' in that at least one of my alter-egos would be going for these constitutionals in order to overthrow the neoliberal dispensation—having been present, having fallen ill, in fact—in the very late autumn and winter of that same year when neoliberalism all but overthrew itself.

One of the things you would have to do, I told myself, when out on these constitutionals, would be, in an inversion of the current cant, to *de-monetize* the data. But walking on down Eastern Avenue amongst the real estate in the part of town where we live, however could one set about achieving that?

As suggested—and people would—you might even say I was attempting to make these things happen by going for a walk at precisely the moment when they were all but happening of their own accord. Maybe nobody needed to trigger the collapse of neoliberalism, because it was doing just this in ways that had been predicted for the era of capital so often and so many times before?

That autumn's global catastrophe in the form of a vast speculation that failed, an international banking collapse, had appeared to happen over a single weekend. The resulting necessity of saving the world—no, banks—so as to protect the savings of national populations, and prevent them from taking to the streets, had drained the national coffers of their funds in a great many of the leading economies.

But that notorious prime-ministerial slip of the tongue, was it perhaps not a mistake after all? Could it have been that now the world was none other than its interlocked financial systems and that without their continued functioning it would descend into even more chaos than it appeared to be in now?

The consequences of this crisis were not hard to predict: there would be a massive reduction in the resources of funding to stimulate growth, to massage unemployment figures, fund welfare and health services ... for public taxation had been used to plug the massive holes in the balance sheets of private, dividend-paying companies—some of whose shareholders would be employment pension providers too.

It wasn't so much the familiar complaint that public funds were invested to produce private profit, but that the private profits, once taken in the form of bonuses and dividends, were no longer there to minimize the damage of bad decisions and circumstances.

Twenty per cent of my fellow townspeople were living on some form of benefit payments, and the beggary was everywhere to be seen as I slowly began to take these walks, including all the difficulties of such supplicants, which some might flippantly compare, accompanying me on these wanderings, to being an itinerant poet—and not only those like the Buddhist monks who wrote haiku and sought alms at bridges and street corners in practically the same breath.

Each of these professions, the beggar and the poet, required an uncertainly marginal social position, one always to be granted or withdrawn by others' behaviour; and they were at one, too, in the ease with which appeals for attention from either could be ignored by anyone else.

Passing by on these constitutionals of mine, I would see such homeless rough-sleepers sitting on their pieces of cardboard, some of them reading thick popular novels of the *Les Misérables* variety—anything, of course, to pass the time as they were plaintively supplicating the likes of me, a natural touch in my casual clothing and Robinson-Crusoe beard. Though, as a matter of fact, the sight of such a mendicant reading his way through Daniel's classic piece of fiction has never actually crossed my path.

Homelessness, literal and figurative, would haunt me as I passed them by, as if a house, a roof above your head, could not be a home when there were others, the *senza tetti*, the roofless, as they're elsewhere called, on the streets without one.

The failings of our financial industries would first be visited upon the governments that had deregulated them and then they, faced with the rising cost of keeping everything running, including the financial system, would have to pass them on to *their* customers—the hapless public who had trusted these elected representatives—to pass on the long-drawn-out burdens of those failures. The whole episode would then prove one further stage in the collapse of deference and belief in those who claimed to be managing the world.

This is also why credit had to be squeezed, they said, and the overnight bank rate was reduced to almost zero, where it would stay for years and years, while mortgage payers, all those Robinsons and Fridays on their variable rates, would breathe a sigh of relief—discovering that monthly interest payments would actually go down when they came off their special enticement packages after the couple of years offered to hook them in the first place.

Like the Irishman's greatest boast, according to that immortal expatriate and *Robinson Crusoe* fan, we were all to tighten our belts and 'pay back our way.' Even the government had been doing its bit, managing, one hundred years after, finally to repay the outstanding debt incurred from the cost of the Great War, the war whose sacrifice we were being wound up through its centenary to remember and celebrate yet once more, oh ye laurel wreaths and fields of knitted poppies.

Still, it was a reassurance to know that the chancellor, a chancellor who prided himself on his fiscal probity, had at last repaid the monies borrowed for the exploding of shells, for the making of munitions planned to be un-made, monies borrowed to enable, through un-backed war credits, that four-year massacre of the imagined-to-be-innocents. Never such innocence again, as the later poets, the poets later sang. Yet there hadn't been any in the first place, for innocence and idiocy, they're not the same thing.

But those on less than a living wage, those always short at the end of the week, or month, they were being forced to borrow not from banks but from the pay-day loan sharks charging usurious rates of daily interest, rates quite legal in their then-unregulated market.

And thus it was that the financial system, correcting for self-preservation, became directly responsible for the life-destroying interest rate excesses that it mysteriously failed to denounce or outlaw.

3

Oddly enough, something similar had occurred in the very year that *Robinson Crusoe*, one of the many books I would return to during my protracted convalescence, first saw the light of day—on a Monday, the 25th of April 1719 as a matter of fact, for I can still recall dates all right. Across the Channel, where they don't always do things that differently, a Scotsman who, like the novel's author, had supported the 1707 Act of Union, and who is credited with the title of an economist, had founded in 1716 the *Banque Royale*—combining its power to print money, and relieve the embarrassments of the French Crown, with the issuing of stocks in the Mississippi Company, which bore quite some resemblance not only to our own South Sea Company of 1720 Bubble fame, but also the Florida land speculations that helped along the great crash of October 1929—the year, as chance would have it, our house had been constructed, the house for which we had mortgaged ourselves to the hilt, the one being left behind as I strolled on now, there at the corner of Addington Road.

Just as it would be for the Scots politicians in 10 and 11 Downing Street, so had it been for that French bank's founder. The inevitable occurred: first an inflationary boom and then a bursting bust. The boom was still happening—the term *millionaire* being used for the first time—in April 1719 when our desert island masterpiece first appeared in London, and the bust was as good as complete come the following spring, by which time the popularity of the first volume had generated its hasty follow-up franchise, the *Farther Adventures*, and the *Serious Reflections*.

Just as the global banking system as it had evolved since those heady days—vastly in complexity, speed of transaction, and instrumental sophistication, but barely at all, it would seem, in prudence, insight or oversight—just as this banking system was teetering like that great wave about to engulf a fishing boat in the Japanese print, teetering on the edge of collapse, I too had tumbled in a heap, with that splitting headache, gastric upset, that complete systems failure, as you might say, and a raging temperature into the bargain.

Where Northern Rock—the first of them to go—and the rest of the banks were experiencing historically nostalgic, tulip-mania-like runs, and requiring national governments to all but bankrupt themselves so as to save those banks (too big to fail) from failing, I was suffering quite another kind of run—the need to scuttle towards the bathroom without warning every five or ten minutes.

And it was then you too came to see that exactly the same distemper in the body national might also have taken over the body natural, that you might be in so much pain because consumed by the mass of corrupted matters and ulcerated humours, the overwork stress, the ill-health, the life-work imbalance which is everyone's lot round here—if it isn't the unemployment—for there was no health in us, or in our constitution.

Yet although, as you do with illnesses, the hope was it would turn out not to be as bad as imagined, there and then in my sickness I did fear that after such a violent push as was administered in our autumn of financial crisis, we too would go off, all at once, in a state apoplexy.

And at the very moment my viral collapse was making a mockery of the programme of research study-leave—the writing up of *Crusoe and the Poets*, the book of essays I'd been hoping to complete, the one I would have to abandon and, in effect, go beyond—it seemed the film trilogy and its voice-overs were either putting words into my mouth, or taking them out of it. Would we never learn, I might be asking myself, being in it for the duration? Was there any other way out? No, we wouldn't, it seemed, for we are what we are.

Those three films, the first two made while still in our extended economic migrant phase, in those remote Pacific islands, had taken a piece of my mind and turned it into what was an almost expressionless monotone, a disembodied commentary written across our dear deprecated homeland in my absence. And as with all such disembodied voices talking down to the viewer and patronizing the flora and fauna filmed, I couldn't help being resentfully haunted by the affectless tones of the voice-overs as they made what sounded like a mockery of my fondest hopes for ameliorative change in repatriation.

Not that this was their intention—quite the opposite—but the medium and message had exacted their price, and the pervading sense of defeat and lament got into the grain of the resistance portrayed. Its central figure, a Robinson too in this incarnation, was a figure of melancholy, an indefatigably resistant instance of defeated hopes, who, as it turned out, was being talked about in the form of a fictional journal, an unnamed narrator's voice-over by his companion and ex-lover, one blandly accounting for this oh-so-familiarly disenfranchised, would-be intellectual, petty bourgeois part-time lecturer at the University of Barking.

The stillness and slowness of the camera's tracking, far from suggesting some cataclysmic change, underlined that while everything was endlessly altering, the moss was growing, the brickwork crumbling, the concrete cracking and dividing, all this taking place so slowly that it was happening in sharp contrast to the vanities of power and production, the structures of freedom to exploit and control, against which the character's wanderings were aimed.

So were those films a sad, embittered joke on the aspirations of our war-baby sub-generations who had mistakenly imagined that the post-war welfare state settlement would usher in an epoch of communitarian culture? Or was the voice-over's tone no joke, just an accident of circumstance?

It was as if while one person would laugh knowingly, another would look blank, and a third might solemnly explain what the joke had been. Then you wouldn't know whether to hope the filmic experiences speeded up or went even slower, imitating sudden change or the glacial evolving of nature, though even the glaciers are shrinking, now, whatever the climate change deniers would prefer us to believe.

So, when finally out of the house that spring morning, you wouldn't know whether to laugh or cry. And this fact among others would go some way to explaining what might be involved in jotting down these journal entries of mine. I might be trying to re-appropriate the soundtrack to what remained from the thing that was once optimistically called 'my life'.

4

Nor—forgive me, I'm sure to have mentioned—did there seem anything the doctors could do for those symptoms, and especially that all but complete nominal aphasia, my problem remembering names. About which I did ask those doctors and locums what might be happening, for it felt like being struck by a symptomatic forgetting, like becoming part of this no-memory world, despite its local enthusiast historians, or even, as if they were its culture-wide compensatory specialism, precisely because of them!

Not being able to do anything for me didn't, of course, stop the doctors running their tests: blood tests, urine tests, scans and prodding—though the best of them, a lady doctor about to go on maternity leave, said, as I sat in her surgery, shivering and feverish, with my dear Friday—forgive me—at my side, that it *was* a virus and, because it was one, there was absolutely nothing to prescribe for it.

This complete collapse would simply have to take its course. All she could recommend were any painkillers available in a chemist's for the symptoms, the headaches and the aching bones. Bed rest was what she advised, and to wait for the thing to work its own way through my system.

'They left me here to die,' as Crusoe sings in the operetta spun from his story, and so it seemed at the height of that illness—being both sick of home and sick at home, and homesick for anywhere out of this world.

'They never do go away,' that nice lady doctor would explain. 'They simply lie dormant inside you, not giving you any trouble any longer, if you're lucky.'

'But how long will it take?' I managed, wincing once more, to inquire.

'Well, don't expect to get over it in twenty-four hours,' she told me. 'It ought probably to take about a fortnight, but it could be longer. You never can tell with viruses.'

Yet after more than four weeks of barely being able get out of bed, I would lie there feeling fit for nothing, nothing … and even when slightly better, all sorts of residual sensations remained—the nervous tingling, the strange prickles in between fingers and toes, and an overwhelming weakness, a mental and physical lethargy that seemed to have permanently descended. Could this be a case of what's called ME? But, if so, how could it have been contracted?

'So when will I get my life back?' you would fret and worry. 'Will I ever be me again?'

'When were you ever yourself before?' my other self would come back, just like that.

'Will I ever feel the same again?'

'Well, no, you won't, will you—you're not even what you are!' my doppelgänger would return.

Yes, as we both thought, it was all a painful mystery.

So the dull, sad days would go by. Not even able to read a book, my first resort in any situation, the only alternative was to sleep and dream. Washed up on that *Desert Island* radio show, I'm not the sort of castaway who would be able to survive with only The Bible and Shakespeare—helpful as they might be for getting through the worst of it.

No, my luxury would have to be a well-stocked library including all three volumes of *Robinson Crusoe*, of course, and I didn't doubt that what's-her-name, the presenter now, you know, about the fourth one since it was started if memory serves, would refuse so composite a luxury.

But, as it turned out, the symptoms were so bad that such a resource wouldn't have helped for a long while anyway, drugged with painkillers and feverishly sweating, unable to eat or digest what I was fatefully trying to keep down.

The sun would come up and decline in the sky. The days would follow each other, counted like clouds above the rooftops through our back-bedroom window. The distant noise of life beginning again, going by, whether inside the house or out, it would reach me like the flies upon a horse's face.

Yet among those muddled days of sleep and waking, waking in the small hours, there was nothing for it but to lie till the sky gave leave to pretend to have woken, while such thoughts as I had would come circling back, as they will, to those schoolyard taunts that always returned to my once-and-future favourite fictional character's family name.

Being taunted with the name Crusoe, it had come back yet again in those feverish dreams of wishing myself well. It hadn't exactly been among my thoughts while that nasty little virus was first coursing through me. Lying there, my head would fill with a confused pack of unlikely accusations—for the illness seemed to exacerbate those ever-ready persecutory anxieties.

It had been such a jumble of threats, of fears, and irrational angers, that all I could remember was a blur, a dispossessed smudge going on somewhere during those weeks—for by now that fever had kept me alone in our matrimonial bed, lying flat on my back, for almost two months.

At first there'd been little more to do than sleep, the effect of that being to throw out the body clock, winding down as never before, so that you would wake in the small hours and stare at the ceiling, then collapse and doze through more half-lit hours of mental twilight.

Later, when at last it was possible to sit up in bed, once more the selfishness of illness would be overwhelming. Hark at me bellowing down to my dear Friday, to our daughter, my exasperated nearest and dearest, for something to drink, another hot water bottle, or whatever might help get through another daylight hour or two.

When finally the time came to try and get out of bed, I could barely stand. The doctor had warned it might take time to recover, but even her prediction had been way off the mark. The consequence was that I had barely left our bed, or bedroom, and, aside from that trip to the doctor's, had stayed inside for so long that the long winter had faded and another springtime was almost upon us.

The end of that bitter winter had passed imperceptibly across our bedroom window. Propped up on a pillow, you had watched the light change in that patch of sky, along the slate rooflines, the chimney pots and aerials opposite—that row of terrace houses with their strangely Dutch inflection, the various attic extensions built out higgledy-piggledy above their backyards.

The sound of hung-out wet sheets being beaten about by the wind would rise from the segments of garden and yard invisible below our window frame. It was like a case of experimental cinema, or, for that matter, one of those long still shots in the Robinson films, clouds passing across the fixed window frame as on a screen, the camera unable to move or track, the astonished viewer compelled to make something of the changing light through a slowly passing day.

Without my being able to feel any of its changes, the weather had altered from a below-zero freeze to the earliest signs of a much wished-for blossoming. Then there would come the first returns of birdsong to keep me wakeful company in the pre-dawn dark.

From another fitful night with however many visits to the bathroom, I would again find myself awake before daylight, waking into a renewed sense of physical weakness, trying to relieve the morning's ache by burying my head in the much-disturbed pillow. The painkillers taken to relieve those headaches would after a while be doing even worse things to my poor digestive system—and there was nothing else for it but to wean myself off them, to put up with the pain. So there I would be, waiting for the central heating to clunk on, for strips of light to start up around the edges of the window's slatted blinds—another whole empty day before me in the dawn.

5

The look of things in our first months back had come as a perpetual surprise. Those flowering magnolia along Crescent Road, not far from where I now lay, their white petals each with a violet heart, would, flexed by a wind, blow against the raw brick front-garden walls, their petals showering across the colour-scattered pavements. How they would bring tears of nervous relief to my eyes on those first spring days of our return, oh those flowering magnolia!

Then my eyesight, as far as I could see, was still as good as ever, long trained on scanning the far horizon from a hillside on our remote Pacific shore. Now it would still give me what pleasure there is to be taken in life, and especially come springtime, when a fresh round of daffodils would flash upon the inward eye that is the bliss of … what? That's how the American poet—no, don't ask me what she's called, though it's maybe something ecclesiastical—would have her Crusoe-back-in-England make a joke about that daffodils poem, a poem written at least fifty years after the death that we might imagine for him, since, to my knowledge, the immortal Robinson is not described as dying in any of the works his author attributed to him—though his supposed model, no, sorry, that name's gone as well, died on the 13th of December 1721.

When violets appeared by mossy stones, and bluebell carpets were spread beneath the trees through woodlands, then again I would begin to think that nature, nature for those later in life, is all they have left that will not let them down—or, at least, when it does, there's no one to blame but ourselves.

Talking of mossy stones and bluebells, a conversation we had about the bluebells comes back, the local and the

Spanish kind. It was with a new-made friend—and oh how we needed friends in those first years of our return to my chilly, northern-hemisphere homeland!

Hardly surprisingly, come to think of it, we would find such friends amongst the alienated and marginalized, people whose circumstances and life histories would turn out to have included, in various forms, some stranding and marooning of their own.

'They're such a pest, the Spanish kind,' my Friday would say. 'They choke the root systems of neighbouring plants.'

'A more successful invader than the great Armada,' it came to me in a daze, my eyes fixed on a churchyard with a weeping yew across the way. And of Gresham's Law too, I thought, reminded of it by those words, which argues that in any economy it's the bad money drives out the good. Ah, the fragility of goodness, as it so often shows itself to be—at least at first.

'They're no different from the red squirrels and the American grey, or the Japanese knotweed down our alley,' she was adding to make her point.

But, as they talked, Friday—sorry—Friday and our friend, my attention would keep drifting away to rooftop and sky, for it was by no means easy to get out of the habit of searching the surroundings for any sign of help at hand.

That day, attention would alight for a moment on passers-by across the café window, or it would stray to a churchyard opposite, where, as it happened, a man was sketching, his smoking head profiled against a gravestone, the yard's copper beeches and yellow laburnum ruffled in a May morning breeze.

It kept drifting off, did attention, made newly vivid by what must have been reverse culture shock, towards the commotion of people on the street, those people with their differences, their lifestyles and ages, up-beat or down, the students, visitors from every-which-way, for the place we had agreed to meet was, after all, a university city at the start of its examination term.

Which is why, called back to their conversation, you had to admit that, no, you couldn't tell the difference, when it came to bluebells, between the Spanish and indigenous kind.

Coming back, though, and it was a pain to see, would prove far worse for my Friday. Being unable to find work in this closed shop of a society, she had been compelled to be nothing more nor less than my housekeeper—despite her host of talents, skills, languages and trades: the cultivating of our garden, home-weaving, and pet-rearing, ones she had nurtured and developed in those many years together on that far-off archipelago, no, when my dear Friday—as she naturally didn't like being called—came back to England there was nothing, it seemed, anyone needed her to do.

'It's so humiliating,' she would say, 'having to depend on you entirely all the time. I can't stand the life of an appendage!'

The economic climate didn't help, of course; but there was also the notorious suspicion of foreigners—that capitalized noun 'Foreigner', meaning my indelible nickname's own father, appearing as it does on the opening page of *Robinson Crusoe*'s first volume.

Being an invisible person, my Friday would find it far from easy to adapt to being an angel in the house—and one who for her sanity had to have reasons for getting out of that house too, yet one with few enough reasons outside our own home to feel at home in the world. Nor did it help that the place we had come to, while it might have promised to relieve my aching nostalgia, could only aggravate hers for our far-off island home.

Slates covered the roofs here, or they were clad in moss-freckled tiles. You could practically see the heat flowing out through their chimneys, the hospital incinerators, the cracks around window frame and door. You could hear the crescendo of unjust accusations, this rat race's dog-eat-dog regarded as inevitable, as natural, an expression of our human nature, and, even more absurdly, a respectable way to behave.

You would see the crime-scene tape, hear of violence in the undergrowth, and then home would come all those years of fearing strangers, dark alleys, dank canals, the public houses, and statues by remnants of factories, fetid waterways that flowed down to the sea, abscesses on the face of the flood.

Then you would hear the snuffling children, see stray dogs, sick cats with worried brows. We too would find ourselves traipsing across the autumn pavements of our first years back, pavements unfamiliarly greased with wet leaves in the rain, and on we would shuffle through a litter of sodden mulch, crowding out everything, and throwing us back upon our own resources, not a whit less than on our faraway island.

On all of us the rain and dusk descended—night skies above my homeland that would need to be defended as my own when Friday grew most restless to be gone, those night skies' verdigris and purple lights, which have become, these days, a permanent rebuke to the mistake I might have made by struggling so hard to escape from that island and return the three of us back here.

Nondescript enough, as you have seen, but if a view can be owned this one was mine. Now indeed lord of all I surveyed, if only from the bed through a back-bedroom window! But no, not even that, as things would transpire.

There's something about those rooflines and gable-ends, with their framing devices of fast-growing pines, their crisscross of washing lines, the woodwork, outhouses, something about them that keeps bringing back, keeps bringing back to mind ... well what? It might be my primal landscape, as if, though far from where I was born, this resembled it enough to seem like home.

Then, yet once more, the sound of hung-out sheets being beaten about by the wind would rise from those segments of garden and backyard invisible below. White clouds would be passing across its frame, echoing the white of the window sill, the viewer as I say compelled to make something of changing light through each slow day—enlivened by the flora and fauna that was confusing the geometries of its built environment.

And there and then, you would fix your eyes on the various birds as they were reaching or landing on the birdbaths and fence posts, would be fascinated by the skirmishes of those seasonal frequenters, their seemingly random visitations.

For this was what it felt like to be home.

6

Among the stranger experiences—and it happened in the first months after repatriation—was that very discovery of the three documentary-style films in which a figure with my name, also recently returned to these shores, who can't drive either, is doomed to become an inner émigré in the land of his birth and upbringing. The story those films fitfully, spasmodically tell was all too close for comfort, as if I had, exactly, suffered from some of that identity theft we were forever being warned about by people who wanted to sell us insurance against it. Compulsively watching the trilogy, I couldn't help feeling both intrigued and dismayed.

In a state of precarious health too, this Robinson also sets off on what are a number of implied constitutionals. He is first found wandering around in *London* (1994), the name of the film, though, since the character doesn't actually appear, his companion (also unseen, though at no point called Friday) attributes to my namesake various tendentious state-of-the-nation observations, as they haunt the blue-plaque country that signifies the metropolis's official cultural geography—this figure being generally described as evaluating all he surveys.

His creator had imagined this creature in June 1990, as I discovered from supplementary reading much later, which was barely a year, in fact, after my own shipwrecking on the far side of the planet; and this imaginary figure with my name 'was deployed as a way of allowing the films' narrators to put forward ideas that one might entertain but perhaps not wholeheartedly adopt.' His producer and director could also be faintly contemptuous of the abstract monster sprung from his own brain, observing that 'even someone as narrow-minded as Robinson' had to admit that the country he inhabited wasn't all as bad as it appeared to be painted in the films portraying his observations, with their down-in-the-mouth talk-overs.

Then this same reported-on person lights out for the English provinces, going the distance for *Robinson in Space* (1997), which is the name of the second, and not only that, but starting in the county town of Royal Berkshire, the place, by what seemed the strangest of coincidences, that happened to be where, as fate had determined, we would return from our years-long marooning to attempt some back-home-making of our own.

This same mysterious character, an invisible man for that matter, then wanders further across the country of my birth, one to which by now I had myself returned, likewise in a thoroughly dilapidated condition—as its title, *Robinson in Ruins* (2010), suggests—though it's far from clear whether he's located within a country that's in ruins or is himself ruined, the wearied and wearying character. Yet what was perhaps most surprising was that this same creature doesn't actually appear on camera in any of the films that have maybe immortalized him—for he's a little bit immortal among experimental cineastes, psycho-geographers, poets, and the like.

'His name', the film-maker explains, 'was borrowed from one of the two itinerants in Kafka's *Amerika*, though at the time I wrote that he had been born in Shropshire'—making him a Bunbury of sorts, a figure whose imaginary decease would be essential to the happiness of the main characters in the comedy by one of this town's most famous temporary residents. You know very well whom I mean.

This Robinson is, further, very much the revenant that, back home from exile, I couldn't help feeling myself to have become—the reverse culture shock making everything so much more starkly visible, visible like those magnolia petals scattered across the pavements down Crescent Road, or the passers-by gazed at through a plush café window. Yes, I would stare at them 'with the abstracted longing'—as another fan of the films has described it—'of an out-patient at a discontinued bus stop.'

Naturally this curious coincidence intrigued, yet, admit it, you couldn't help feeling faintly irritated by the thought that your own absent and invisible life had somehow been usurped, or pre-written, then shot in the terms of these three documentary politico-experimental films.

At first, for that very reason, finding them on sale in an art gallery bookshop, I remember being unable to bring myself to want to know anything about them. I had even tried pretending that they didn't exist; but then, goaded and intrigued, capitulated and subjected myself over a number of nights to the intentionally alienated, alienating style in which they had been made. For slow is not the word for the cinematic experience they offer, and it remains, at least as far as I'm concerned, an open question as to whether anybody is quite ready to be subjected to such an intensely unmoving experience, doing for the Thames valley, and then other parts of the country, what that doyen of the New York art scene had pioneered in his portrait of the Empire State Building, or his undirected screen-test portraits of celebrities.

Each of these three art-house documentary-like works is, once more, provided with a talk-over third-person narrative telling in a flatly monotonous monologue its account of this character's drift. The affectless tone is that of a famous male actor, whose name also more-than-momentarily escapes me—replaced, because death had silenced him in 2008, by that actress who is said to have turned down a Dame-hood, with her impeccably sympathetic political credentials, for the final part of the trilogy. They continue to speak even as the camera fails to move, reporting throughout the triptych on how Robinson is found to grow ever more depressed and disillusioned by the state of the country to which he has returned. For he is increasingly exasperated by the military-industrial complex, the secret state, the hidden presence of airbases and weapons sites ... and it's suggested he might be dying, or declining into addiction, and certainly living from hand to mouth.

The camera, hand-held or still, will motionlessly dwell, un-movingly, as if without purpose, rhyme, or reason, and for ever longer periods, on the unmitigated framings of mechanical reproductions, overlaying them with seemingly uninflected facts of their tendentiously slanted political and cultural history.

The effect of this haunting combination is to give an impression of detached research, research into the nature of reality, while simultaneously presenting this very detachment with a highly coloured and starkly polemical, political and cultural meaning of its own.

The additional fact that the author of one possible original for this Robinson had also written an account of a journey through the British Isles, travelling as a spy for the prime minister of the day—as the narrative points out early in *Robinson in Space*—made it as clear as daylight that the director of these films had found his Robinson lineally related to the provider of my imprinted schoolyard nickname, the founding father of the world's innumerable *Robinsonades*.

Nor were these the first Robinson films that had crossed my path and left me wondering what it had to do with us or mine. I too would try, and had started early, to 'authenticate as many Robinsons as could be found.'

At what must have been the age of seven or eight, I had, for instance, been taken to see *Swiss Family Robinson*, described on the poster as 'the Greatest Adventure Story of them All!' Though unable to recall much of it now, seeing the film in full colour and Panavision, whatever that was, had left its mark.

Remembering back, as if peering into the smoky darkness of that distant Gaumont cavern, the only frame that came again to mind was one from early on in the movie when the Robinsons' ship is caught en route to Australia in the storm that will shipwreck them on their desert island somewhere out in the dear Pacific Ocean, in the sight of which we had survived so long.

But who could say how much such childhood experiences have created my sense of what it meant to be a family in trouble? Of how a little boy might turn out to be a girl in disguise? How we'll all need to be rescued from pirates at some stage in our lives? And one day we too might even go back home to university? And hadn't I been driven by the need to try and change my own solitary stranding on that remote island to the experience of a shipwrecked family? Hadn't I done no more nor less than turn my version of *Robinson Crusoe* into *Der Schweizerische Robinson*?

Just so, we too, during those long years of isolation, would go rowing as a little family group, on boating lakes and dam-tamed rivers, reliving the adventures of *Swallows and Amazons*—another book that owes a great debt to the founding masterpiece.

Some of the details of this invisible Robinson's mysterious life couldn't help further linking together the childhood shipwreck hero who had become a part of me thanks to all that schoolyard name-calling—which had then been taken over for self-fashioning meaning formation—with the fairly washed up researcher and peripatetic teacher that in my exile I too had willy-nilly become.

When it came, then, to making sense of Patrick ... Patrick What's-his-name's experimental and politically charged, actor-less films, I had already been well enough schooled in the art of reading in not to find them, despite the visuals being on another level of patience-demand, by any means too hard going, to find them, in fact, quite relaxingly soporific ... after a while.

7

For 'Crusoe' was inevitably one of my schoolyard nicknames. I do have a name of my own, of course, a common one—as if you might have been, there but for fortune, one of those 'poor men' who 'have no name.' Yes, the majority of Robinsons in America are black. You see it has always felt that what I'm obliged to think of as mine doesn't name anyone in particular—which may be among the reasons why it has become harder and harder since that viral illness struck to remember names, to spell them right, or bring them to mind, so that there will frequently come the sensation that you're about to call the person being talked to by the name of the one we've been gossiping about. Whenever that happens—as I'm sure you can imagine—it has really been more than embarrassing.

Picture this, then, myself as a seven-year-old, on the top deck of a trolley bus or tram, having the two words pointed out by his mam. The letters were printed in large illuminated script across the front of a shop in the middle of town. Yes, from the start, I was always another—which may go some way to explaining the collecting of stories by or about those others who possess this no more than nondescript name, others with such different characters and fates, just as I'm sitting here typing away before these shelves in a large personal library containing various editions of the work that provided my oh-so-inescapable nickname.

These days, when online encyclopaedias will advise you simply to *click here* to 'disambiguate'—and it was there that the word first came to my wearied attention—one click taking you to a page that disambiguated, for instance, the Northern Irish politician from the Canadian crime writer, or the pop star from the novelist, or, for that matter the linguistics professor in Japan from the dentist with his practice in Ohio USA.

The first three and the last two of the above have the exact same name; and it's played with by that Irish writer of a seemingly invented language, linking our founding father character with the department store, for one of his portmanteau personages—'wants her wardrobe to hear from above by return with cash so as she can buy her Peter Robinson trousseau'. He's punning on the word for the clothes, linen, and other belongings that a bride would gather for her marriage associated with the department store, with which I was invited to identify myself on that tram and which had, soon after its founding, become a London outlet specializing in ladies' fashions and bridal gowns.

Still, you can disambiguate to your heart's content, but my own experience has rather tended, under the educative influence of my mother, to the confusing, and now too the forgetting of nomenclatures, and the consequent muddling of destinies.

Not feeling that you had a name, or that the name you had really named anyone in particular, such a fate didn't, unfortunately, make it possible to exist within an inviolate, an innocent, or sincere and unnamed individuality; no, on the contrary, being more nameless than unnameable had left me vulnerable to promiscuous identifications with others, whether they happened to carry around a splinter of that moniker or not.

Then perhaps it was despite or because of not having much of a name, that I've been so prone to being nicknamed and re-nicknamed, being much moved around by ... by providence, chance, or fate. Yet to this day, I don't even know what my father was called at school, what nicknames he had to endure, for my parents were of course both blessed or cursed with that same name, my mother especially since she had traded in the far more distinctive and poetical one under which she had lived when a maiden.

Crusoe wasn't the only one. There were others, many others, *Red Robbo*, after the union activist, for instance, and quite a few unprintable. It was *Dobbin* for a while, like a nag or donkey, and *Little Pig* (not one of my favourites, though another derived from the original castaway's immortal character), and *Peter Rabbit* too, when a much-harassed peripatetic teacher of the young. You will know the illustrations in the children's books: the creature caught in a cabbage patch or the figure with his telescope pointing out to sea. But that's another story—as indeed is *Piggy*, which that *Little Pig* one would sometimes be reduced to, for short as we say, and his story takes place on a different island too.

But *Crusoe* is the one they used the most, the one that stuck, like they warn you your face will—if you don't stop doing whatever it is that happens to irritate them. Then the nickname would just go round and around, like a haunting, a curse or—let's face it—a vocation.

At school, older boys with the first shadows of beards giving some shape to their chins would turn to each other in assembly, knowing the 'new boy' was standing mute in the row behind them. They would denigrate him and his own puberty-reorganized features, casting their aspersions quite loud enough to hear.

They would use those nicknames mockingly to his face, would shout them out in the playground, or down the street as we separately dragged our weary ways back home. They would mock that moody seriousness, that seven-stone weakling figure, and his camera-lens-cracking looks into the bargain.

'Ha, ha, it's *Robin Crusoe*, poor *Robin Crusoe*,' they would haplessly quote at the tops of their voices, shouting across the traffic island outside our school at home time.

I would be tardily traipsing along with my battered leather satchel, last year's grey flannels flapping about my ankles, black shoes scuffed to a cardboard grey, sporting a yellowed nylon shirt, a loosened tie, and much trodden-on cap askew. Then they would talk about 'that *Robinson*' in the third person singular to my face, poor *Robin Crusoe*, employing their chosen denigrations.

The nickname would become so ubiquitous, the not-only-verbal bullies so socially powerful, that even friends would adopt it—modifying only the tone in which it was whispered to catch your attention in a lesson, during games, or when we were dressed up on parade in our military uniforms, doing that dated rifle drill at the height of the Cold War's mutually destructive standoff.

Nicknames, as you too well know, can spread more quickly than even the Spanish Flu, and, like so many diseases, they're passed from mouth to mouth. The stray characters catching them may be quite unaware that the person designated has any other name. People would assume that my first one was *Robinson*, which they would then shorten, as if being fond or familiar.

'*Rob*, what are you trying to do?' one would ask, and I would be lost for an answer, not least because the question, when asked by an art teacher, for instance, actually meant: whatever this mess and muddle is, you would be advised to give it up, give it up immediately—as a bad job that won't get you anywhere.

Still, and for whatever reason, the one that stuck was 'Crusoe'.

8

Some years later, teenage having attacked my face with its various volcanic eruptions, there being a grey shadow around its chin line too, out-of-reach girls would pick up that schoolyard name-calling on Saturday nights at chaotically drunken parties. You might sometimes protest, and ask them to refrain. But, tell me, what would that achieve? They only laughed the more, not least at having got under my skin.

So, as you see, there was nothing else for it. I would have to take on that pandemic-like name-calling myself—since this was the only way I would be known in the schoolyard by friend and foe alike—would have to take it on as my own, to see if there wasn't an ambivalence of pitiful affection even in the hardest-faced versions of my inescapable nickname.

What reason did they have, those girls and boys from their different motivations, as it appeared, for seeming to hate me so? And, yes, I did try—and am trying now—to turn those names and their implications of alternative personas as much to my advantage as was humanly possible. That's how you could make being a 'Crusoe' into a vocation. If all the casual denigration could be transformed into a badge of honour—or shame—then that would be as good as making destiny my choice.

Yet each of those names, whatever they were, when hurled this way, would throw me back upon myself, compelling me to imagine, and doubtless exaggerate, out of what will have been the beginnings of that burgeoning persecutory anxiety, the look of myself as seen by others, by those frightened and frightening contemporaries, who surely had no reason on earth to be fearful of me. And yet this was how it happened you became habituated to seeing yourself as others saw you, as seeing yourself from outside.

'You would,' that doppelgänger would re-echo, 'you would, wouldn't you?'

And it was amongst all that idolatry of I, that execration of I, that dissipation of I, that you realized and got into the habit of thinking that your 'I' was another—and I will get to this great constitutionalist, a sufferer from 'ambulatory paranoia', as that Jack Robinson would recall, an 'homme aux semelles de vent' in good time too.

Crusoe, then, was the one that stuck; and it was what, with time, even my closest companions would call me. For, as you see, nicknames can be such ambivalent things and may readily be made into affectionate diminutives—as if they were the place in which the world's being divided about you must inevitably find its home. As if when calling out 'friend or foe' in some childish game, how could you be sure which were the affectionate uses, and which the denigrating ones?

For, perhaps unsurprisingly, Crusoe was also the most ambiguous, mocking me for my solitude—and, as at least one other writer has put it—solitude's only pride, in its most stubborn guise. Yet weren't those different uses also tempting the thought that providence had somehow singled me out for an adventure of my own, as, indeed, what else, one way or another, would our lives alone together become?

What's more, this was the one, remembered, which started these belated afterthoughts, my afterthoughts of Crusoe. These were the serious reflections growing out of what became the longest, most unexpected privacy. They came to be written down like a journal in that residential solitude, one lasting as long as those years in my original's desert island home, those years of solitude providing the time and space to fill my notebooks with raw material for what must surely come to appear as a fictionalized self-portrait.

However, written down—and I remember well the sensation staring out with my message in its bottle, staring out towards that dangerous coast, the landfall of publication—those private words of mine, this pretended autobiography, or sea voyage into the past, and return to the disappearing present, the always and never disappointing future, had left me with the usual entrapment, with a great bundle on hand, a predicament that no amount of money and influence could do anything to alter.

The blanks in that sailor's logbook, though, and proper names the worst of them, have had to be painted over with invented detail or circumlocution—as whoever has such a poor and deteriorating memory will be obliged to do, poor memory, in some cases at least, being surely caused by the need not to remember the details of one's own humiliations.

For how cruel young people can be! And how their taunts can linger!

So 'I could have been a Crusoe within myself'—as a lost, lamented poet friend once put it. For despite the intent behind all that name-calling, and like so many mocking names before—those painters, for example, the ones who were called 'wild', or the ones accused of making paintings that looked like little stock cubes—I was able to find an identity, and what started to look like a vocation, by turning their words back onto my detractors, the school-yard bullies and their snickering cohorts compelled to assert a tormenting lack of identity at anyone else's hapless expense. Yet it was to those mockers that I owed my life.

For this too can be catching, the damaged emptiness of others, passed on like a childhood malady or plague, so that those tinkling cymbals and sounding brasses can feel that little bit less empty, by reducing the painful contrast with their absent selves—or merely out of spite.

Although it was the hatred or anger in others that had done it to me, for in the first place there was nothing wrong with either my innocence or hearing, somehow I couldn't help detaching the words from those who spoke them, of taking them into myself and turning them over in my childishly troubled mind.

I would even forget who had said them, be unable to put a face to my tormentors, until the words themselves would seem to be doing the harm, lodging themselves in my distracted consciousness, ready to leap out and puncture whatever confidence might have begun to define itself, to head off any such ambition, and mute what achievements I might have been able to imagine.

Which is doubtless one thing that their name-calling was for, to keep me not in my place, but in theirs. And, as you have seen, askance as you like, my only response was to wear those nicknames, and 'Crusoe' most of all, as a badge of honour, or shame. Which, like it or not, was exactly how friends came to know me by a nickname that had started in abuse.

But then, what's in a name? Sticks and stones may break my bones ... and it's true you would get into fights when sorely provoked. Imagine me, then, being manhandled by one fellow's gang—three or four suddenly anxious boys, who saw that the taunting had got out of hand. They were restraining me from an enraged attack on one of those bullies, just as I was starting to bang his head wildly against a red brick backyard wall. He had driven me beyond the end of my tether.

There you could see the colour of his blood mingle with the crumbling brick-dust. Those gang members had saved you from doing what might have been some literal harm. Still, the bleeding-headed fellow didn't bother me ever again—though of course, and naturally enough, his mother said I was the one who had started it, and so the cycle of verbal counter-punching would continue.

And yet, indeed, what's in a name? Sticks and stones may break my bones ... though I'm not even sure about that bit of folk wisdom, since it was as if the name meant loneliness, although down the centuries it had kept such etymological company, and not only in the literary world.

For out there in the jungle, and despite the pain words can cause, it was as if I could ward off the damage with a rhyming or a rhythmical enchantment—simply by throwing as many words as possible at the stubbornly persistent problem.

I might even have been learning a style from despair, from the confusions of solitude and isolation, the one aligning them with madness (or the fear, at least, of insanity), the other with an ideal of separation from our corrupt and corrupting, our self-diluting society. And there it was again, you see, the doubling of meaning in the idea of being a Crusoe, the idea of both needing to be among people, and needing to be away from them.

It was as if exclaiming 'alone again' or 'I feel so alone', especially when naked and drenched in cooling water, emerging from a shower for instance, that there would suddenly come what felt like a false memory of being born, being hurled onto dry land from the breaking waters, as if my mother had haplessly marooned me, cast me away on this spinning desert island of a world.

Then, as though some form of consolation might be found in the history of usage, I would call up the Latin derivations. There, standing naked on the bath mat, drying myself, how they would whisper that while *solitude* required one to be alone, just as being *stranded* had need of a beach, so *isolation* demanded an island for you to find yourself cast away upon or marooned.

Perhaps that was why you would feel most yourself when by the seaside. Inland, and bounded by urban or country horizons, I might as well be land-locked, in the middle of any vast continent—but a coastline, or even the scent or sound of one, would mean being somewhere near the edge of an island, any island. For all the lands on this whole spinning earth are islands of a sort, are islands when you come to think of it.

Then as if to make it true, as if nickname were omen too, I woke to find myself alone, alone on a faraway archipelago. Which was how it appeared that, like it or not, we do become our names.

9

Such were the thoughts I was having while, to my left, there appeared the semi-detached house of the old lady whose car we had crashed into after only a few weeks back home. Here in my country, my country after all those years away, here was the mini-roundabout, and the tricky manoeuvre of stopping on it so as to reverse into the parking space at the front of our newly purchased house. Here was where people driving up behind you would have suddenly to realize, as you hit the emergency lights, that we were intending to go backwards, towards them, in the other direction.

Given all this newness, the special adjustments to be made, the driving on the other side of the road, an accident was more or less bound to happen. But that the accident should be with someone we were going to sit down to dinner with just a couple of days later was more like fate, or chance, or luck, whether good or bad I couldn't say.

No, my dear Friday as I would compulsively call her—for fondness, and much to her annoyance—never would find it easy to settle into this Thames valley town. There was the language problem. I had, at one point, taught her the language—or had attempted to at the time we first met, then had kept on correcting her, which she always took, and this is a tribute to her tolerant and forgiving nature, in the spirit it was meant, and so wouldn't take offence.

Still, there is such a difference between learning a language to the point where you can make yourself understood in it, and the state where native speakers are not for ever having to make allowances for you; and then even more to get to a point where people wouldn't know you were not native, if they couldn't see your face, your hand gestures, or, most of all, the fact that you failed to say only and exactly the things that routine users of the native language would.

You see, my Friday was forever expressing in English the sorts of insights and experiences that were not supposed— by some at least—to be had in the terms of that language, its vocabulary and structures. For living in translation is the hardest fate of all, even if it means no one can claim to read you like a book, or for a minute credit that the words you utter are exactly what you think or feel.

And yet there is that seeming paradox about the town, the place we found ourselves in, for, as noted, it is a place of transit, not only and indeed perhaps precisely because a transport hub—for east–west communication along the course of the valley, and originally a fording place across the delta-like marshland of rivers, a fording place that formed a link between Mercia and the Saxon coast—but also because there have been immigrant populations in the town for at least the last two centuries.

Which was how we came to know that the old lady, with whose car my Friday had collided, was the surviving head of an Irish family, one with a distinct literary bent, and an interest in translation shared by at least three of her offspring, the family come here in the Fifties, just one of the many diasporas—Jamaican, Polish, Ethiopian, Nepali, South Asian, and more—that have made this town of transits what it is and will be globally all the more, despite the Canute-like efforts of the panicked and their false-allies among our politicians.

Walking on past larger houses set back from the street, threading my way along that unusually narrow pavement, I was suddenly beset by a vision of the endless iterations. For Eastern Avenue and the other streets ahead would always be leading me on in the tracks of others' footsteps, the invisible haunters of these streets, those passing through on their way to fame, notoriety, or oblivion. And it was as if, in the aftermath of that fever, I could almost glimpse them there, emerging from the polychrome brickwork of its houses, before me in the still chilly air of that early March day.

Even though the street near which our house stood was entirely deserted, it being one of our various pedestrian-emptied rat-runs at rush hour, still it was as if I could see flickering all around me, come, as I say, from its very brickwork, the century or so of others who had walked along these once peripheral avenues, in their Victorian, Edwardian, Twenties and Thirties, then their post-war, their Sixties and Seventies museum of 'ugly is the new beautiful' fashions. It was suddenly as if you were having to elbow your way through an oddly alluring crowd of old grey ghosts, the pavement too narrow and sloping into the gutter for even two abreast, just to make your way down towards the Wokingham Road.

Passing before the frontages and front gardens of the differently-styled surrounding houses—for this is a neighbourhood of mixed habitations, ranging from poor rented council maisonettes to mini-mansions—I couldn't help feeling the onset of that real-estate envy, that market-entry resentment, one shared by a great many others of us now, and especially the young. It had so beset us when first treading these streets in search of a place to live.

During our long sojourn on that faraway archipelago houses prices here had, as they say, gone through the roof, and, had I climbed onto what is called the housing ladder before my economic exile, I could have been in receipt of returns on speculations in bricks and mortar far beyond anything that Crusoe's London housewife achieved.

Mortgaging ourselves to the hilt in order to have a roof above our heads, we found we could barely find the deposit on a real estate loan big enough to secure even the smallest family accommodation. And as if in a fairy tale, the houses around here were either too poor, or too rich, or they were just right—but we could barely afford any of them, and the disheartening business of visiting estate agents and touring properties had proved another occasion for a glimpse of life as getting and spending, laying waste our powers, and a pre-visiting of the truths that the *Robinson* film-maker's researches would soon make plain upon the pulses.

Those twinges of real-estate envy would assert themselves as I walked on down the avenue, and especially about halfway along when arrested by the darkly upward-curving branches of an enormous araucaria, its silhouette high above the roofline—that monkey puzzle tree in the front garden of Burnett Cottage, number 13 Eastern Avenue, one of a semi-detached pair, the other called Luther Cottage, with the date of construction a moulded name-plate set into brickwork high up beneath the roofline: 1871.

Which meant, it would dawn on me walking by, that they would have been still new-build when, a few years later, the French Symbolist poet I was mentioning a moment ago had spent a few months here in what was most probably a language teaching job as well. Now, as my local historian informant would tell me, Eastern Avenue had begun to emerge in the 1850s, just outside the borough boundary, where the rates were less. And at the very thought of the scaffolding and bricklayers, the masons with their carts and horses, there the great Symbolist seemed to emerge, strolling along, as if in the pencil drawing with his friend, that other poet, being eyed suspiciously by a London policeman, wandering out of town towards what was probably not then called Cemetery Junction.

So I imagine him floating before me, turning right up those recent developments of what is now Eastern Avenue—from which he could make a loop back towards the Royal Berkshire Hospital, then down Eldon Road and across the King's Road to Montpelier House and the attic room, the *chambre de bonne* as it were, in which, without the slightest scrap of evidence, I would picture him spending the nights of his strange sojourn in this still semi-rural Thames valley town. For this is a location that has formed the place of both exile and return for so many before we found ourselves manifesting both detachment and displacement in that one household at the corner, half way up, on the right.

Beyond Burnett and Luther Cottages were the tumbledown lock-ups of Berkshire Bicycles and the wood-burning stove shop, whose proprietor would save the strips of plastic packing tape out of which my Friday would weave Moses baskets, fruit bowls, lamp shades, and other craft works, as a way of enduring her banishment from our island home.

Further, at the lower end of Eastern Avenue, I would be leaving behind those tumbledown lock-ups on the right used by the shops on the corner of Wokingham Road. We too had bought a couple of stoves from them to keep the winter cold away, and to save on fuel costs in the new austerity brought on by that banking failure I've touched on already—and will come back to again, including as I do its still evolving aftermaths.

On the other side of Wokingham Road, there would appear the high blank wall that divides these streets from the cemetery, with its yew trees and cypresses rising above the coping-stones, a wall keeping death at a not-so-safe distance, beyond the careering traffic all around, as it had so strangely become in the hundred and fifty years or so since the place was established.

Why this had happened in the evolution of the urban and suburban streets developed in the later nineteenth century is something of a mystery, so different is it from the village churches in the country with their crowded graveyards, through which the faithful would walk each Sunday on their way to and from worship. There are some of those graveyards here too, of course, around the parish churches of St Mary, St Laurence, and St Giles. But the graveyard at what is now Cemetery Junction was different, and, in its own small way, had become a legend too.

The churches may think they own death, but the commercial projectors who established this cemetery in 1843, and the borough authorities who took over responsibility for it in 1887, may have preferred to protect us from thoughts of it too—just as it would be the latter's responsibility to save us from the killer diseases by the construction of sewers and other enhancements to the built environment; and now here it was before me, a triangle of mortal remains, about which I could, if the mood so took me, wander, wander and brood.

10

You see I had myself left money—'O Drug!' as Robinson says aloud, 'what art thou good for'— in the hands of not one housewife, but many widows, Scottish widows. Yet the consequences, quite the opposite of what they were for Crusoe and his thousand guineas of treasure left with the housewife in London, had been disastrous. What useful memory brought back was not the providential luck that the investment had grown in all those years on his lonely island, but that ours had been one of the many signs of gullibility and idiocy when it came to the ways of the world—for the policy had been sold to us by an unregulated shark in offshore waters, whose interest was in signing up customers to 'products', as they are called in the trade, that provide a good trailing income for the advisor who signs them and the company that takes the investment, but which would require extraordinary positivity from the global stock markets for the investments to grow as promised.

Values can go down as well as up, it had of course told us in the small print. The trailing fees and management costs were such that the capital had been eaten away, and the depressed global financial world had not been able to generate anything like enough annual interest to make those investments compound. Soon after returning to these shores, the Scottish widows informed us that there was literally nothing left in the pension pot and that as a result they were terminating communications with us.

When I wrote to them suggesting that the outcome was nothing like what their glossy material had promised, or their agent explained, they simply responded by providing me with a thick envelope full of graphs showing the global performance of their 'product'—heading south.

Needless to say, the graphs were all of the ski-slope variety, until they flattened out like the readings on a hospital's cardiac monitor. So there it was, and there was nothing to be done about it: just another of the many things that we are all of us required to put down to experience— another word, as the town's most famous resident would call it, for a mistake.

But where had all this money gone? Funds earned by the sweat of our brows in that faraway isolation had been paid over to others as salary or bonuses for their failure to make the investments grow, or it had been paid out in dividends for the shareholders in that provident institution, which, provide, provide, it had—though not for me and mine.

The company directors were more beholden to their investors, and there was nothing you or anyone else could do about that either. We were simply the dupes of those advertising campaigns. No wonder I felt the need to go for my constitutionals, constitutionals that were to put an end to neoliberal capitalism, to put it out of its misery.

Public profit could be creamed off and handed on to senior employees, while private failures and losses would be passed back to the public in the form of raised taxes and reduced services. It had happened before, and it would happen again.

For no sooner had you been recruited to labour on the other side of the world in one of the apparently booming economies, than its land-price bubble had burst, saddling its banks with irrecoverable debts, and leading to more than twenty years of minimal interest rates and a flat-lined economy. Something similar had happened as soon as we were able to remove ourselves from that isolation and return to my homeland. Could it be a coincidence? Were you a Jonah into the bargain?

I would joke that what-do-you-call-him Greenback, then governor of the Fed, had requested that we inform the stock markets when and where the family planned to relocate next. It had turned into a hollow-sounding joke.

When finally able to get out of the house that spring morning, I would discover the consequences all around. Building projects had been halted mid-construction, shops and retail outlets gone out of business. The retail streets were like shadows of their former selves.

Commercial frontage in the town, along its main thoroughfares, was being offered at peppercorn rents for temporary exhibitions, charitable events, for the selling off of unwanted stock, for downsizing, for oblivion.

Never the monarch of anything I surveyed, what with the cost of housing and all, these constitutionals would involve battling with the dreadful onsets of that very real estate envy brought on as soon as I stepped out of our flaky black front door.

As the Robinson filmmaker put it, the landscape of what he calls 'literary urbanism' is made up of 'houses that are small, old and architecturally impoverished, but extraordinarily expensive.' Indeed, indeed, we had taken on such an amount of debt, and taken it on at exactly that point—a little over a year before the banking crisis and the subsequent credit crunch took its toll on nearly everyone.

But it's an ill wind, as they say, and, counting my blessings along with the money we owed, I did accept that we had got onto the so-called 'housing ladder' just in time—though without any hope of climbing it—and then, economic conditions being as poor as they were, we then benefited, being so in debt, from the minuscule overnight discount rate set, and set to stay minimally low for the best part of a decade, by the Bank of England. Now, in the aftermath of more disastrous decisions, the rate had been reduced to something in the region of one quarter of one per cent.

Our special-offer, two-year, low introductory interest rate was made to look extortionate when, going onto one that tracked the bank rate, we found ourselves having to pay substantially less per month to keep the roof—such as it is—above our burdened heads.

This series of experiences had been sobering in a number of ways—not least in making it clear that few houses in Britain, especially those that happen to be in the south of England, are actually worth—in terms of the experience of living in them—what you have to pay to be able to do so.

Yet the daily experience of those begging or sleeping in doorways made it quite clear that, on the other hand, you couldn't put a price on the benefits of being able to keep up the payments, even as you were experiencing ever widening gaps between what something cost, what the price of that cost was to you, and what the value of the thing which cost so much might be in relation to the price you would have to pay—and not only in money!

What's more—and the doggy eyes of those beggars would be enough to remind me on a daily basis—part of the price for the roof over your head was the absence of such a roof over somebody else's ...

For whatever reason, at least one local Reading house builder, especially around the time of the Wall Street Crash, seems to have favoured front doors concealed to each side of the semi-detached houses constructed during those years. And, as I say, the Eastern Avenue area is a strikingly mixed one with everything from small mansions, still in single ownership, to tiny social housing. The population, as we discovered, was mixed too and for the same sorts of reasons. There was a good side to this, which was that you could feel in the space of a very few streets that almost the whole of society, practically all of human life, was here.

I could be walking past something close to aristocratic luxury, through thoroughly established bourgeois comfort, and lower middle-class pride, to people surviving as best they could, on to students living in the bedsits of what are called 'multiple occupancy' houses, and to surviving council flats as well.

The bad side to it was that the opportunities for both envy and contempt were everywhere around. The latter didn't trouble me that much, but as far as the former is concerned I have, and would freely admit it, spent a lifetime coping with its baleful effects.

And this brought with it a host of reflections, especially for those getting on in years, about how they have missed their chances, or made misjudgments, had bad divorces, while others round about seemed more fortunate or canny.

Even the difference between those two ideas could be the cause of anguish. I might be walking down the street past one of those houses—larger and better appointed than the one we had managed to take out a mortgage on when returning to this country. Any of us could be dreaming of what it might be like to live in that one, bought at a time when houses were worth nothing like what they are now, or better, worth nothing in relation to incomes.

It was the thought that if we had moved here twenty years before, or had been able to get jobs in a certain decade, then we too could be living in one of these substantial Edwardian mansions.

Those dreadful twinges of real estate envy would come over me especially in so mixed an area as ours, bringing back yet another imaginary erratum: for 'peripatetic' read 'very pathetic'.

It was of course an error to envy others' bricks and mortar, and not only because of all of those balancing bits of folk wisdom along the lines of 'the more you have, the more you have to lose'—but also, it wasn't that hard to reflect, harbouring resentments about your fate can prove literally fatal.

This was another explanation for my poeticizing the experience of nondescript urban cityscapes and the edge-lands where suburbs and trading estates give out into residual countryside, and to counteract that envy, I had, as the cineaste of the trilogy puts it, 'made art out of our deprivation.'

'I hadn't realized it was quite that bad', he adds, and then cites another theorist whose name won't come back either: 'When one does not have what one wants, one must want what one has.'

Easier said than done! Still, in my experience, taking a non-material interest in what others appear to have, drawing from it the consolations in aesthetic benefits such as it can deliver, is one way to live in a place that is perpetually reminding us of our resentments as regards those who happened to inherit or to buy at moments when the houses were more or less worth what you would be expected to pay for them.

11

After those many weeks of fevers and frets, the worst of it beginning to subside, I was still extremely weak, and able to do nothing but rest. So once the morning's painkillers had taken effect, there would be yet another whole day to catch up on lost reading. But bodily strength and state of mind were such that concentration didn't come easily, so I had to try and find my right mind by reading through a series of comedy crime novels set around a mobile library, progressing then to the same writer's—oh no, don't ask me—novel about a small town in the provinces and a dilapidated hotel at its heart.

Then on to some spy thrillers I had never got round to before, and a private eye sequence set in various Italian towns. I even flirted with reading some of the crime mysteries by that other of my *alter egos*, plenty of which wash up among the literary flotsam and jetsam in a charity shop in Woodley's shopping precinct—the one to which my Friday would be sent off, while I was still bedridden, to scour for further reading matter.

It was only very slowly that my health improved to the point where I could conjure up the concentration that would enable the return of that inner running commentary, that parallel mental activity which goes on when I'm reading a book—one requiring our full collaboration, developing its ideas by the addition of digression, one that only very slowly gets back to its point.

It took a long time before I could cope with anything other than the simplest of sentences, anything other than a whodunit plot. And even then, the reading of those fictions was like a preparation for these adventurous constitutionals that I would be obliged to undertake.

For there was the inevitable feeling with detective and whodunit novels that, however byzantine and bad the forces pitted against the detective, and however unlikely it may seem in mid-flow, you knew the solution would be revealed, and the range of expectations, however bizarre, about human motivations would be confirmed, and illustrated in the behaviour of the half-concealed characters.

Here too would be the ambivalence, or fork, for either these revelations would reassure in the hope that the truth will out, and that some characters will be released from the nightmares of their now-revealed pasts, at the expense of others who wouldn't—except in so far as they had been killed, or because they had to live with the consequences of failing to be amongst the good.

These reassurances of an intelligible world would bring you back time after time to those series of crime mysteries, ones which helped you get through the worst of that illness and on to these walks.

As the levels of mental energy returned, eventually the moment came to branch out from crime thrillers, and, as if really to find myself again in a book, I took the opportunity of those interminable convalescent days to read through yet once more the first volume of the eventual trilogy its editor calls 'a just History of Fact'—though far from that in so many ways. Thus it was that once again I found myself relishing as never before *The Life and Surprizing Adventures of Robinson Crusoe*.

And, as that Brazilian poet—you know the one—says, calling it a 'long story with no end', what a strange and rambling book it is! For as happens when rereading, there were suddenly revealed, as if never encountered before, so many of the things that had set me thinking and then been forgotten, forgotten from all those times before. For it was this re-reading that must have been one of the subliminal prompts leading me to set out on my pretended autobiographical reflections and to pay tribute, as I am, to the effects of that book on my life.

Though it may be, or may have been, supposed 'a just History of Fact', there were its author's notorious errors and inconsistencies, for he had written the book very quickly while in hiding from debt collectors. There were, for example, the pockets in Robinson's trousers that he fills after taking them off to swim out to the wreck, the ink that magically appears when he needs to make a contract with the Spaniards.

His book had the appearance of fact, but without its substance. It circled around the need to interpret and make meaningful. It had the feeling of poetry in something prosaic, which might be why so many poets—as I also relieved my convalescent isolation by revisiting—had gone back to it time and time out of mind.

When finally able to get out of bed, and to think of doing something other than re-read that classic piece of fiction, you found yourself, as already mentioned, barely able to stand. Suddenly it was a major operation to descend or climb the stairs. So much weight had been lost, and those old bones of mine would ache from head to toe. You wouldn't know whether to laugh or cry at this sorry specimen— for recovery had left me like a castaway on the shores of whatever life remained.

I had been reduced to a skeleton by that month in bed, and my convalescence would evidently not be quick and easy. Even walking the shortest of distances would take all my breath, the muscles and bones in my legs turned to nothing but an ache. Gazing out of the front room window, there would appear people I'd forgotten existed during the worst of my illness; and there they were still, drifting by in the gloaming on their way back home from work.

Caught up in their own thoughts at the end of a long day at the office, they wouldn't dream of glancing through the window to where, behind the privet, the pine and maple, the anemones and irises, you would be sitting in that tiny living room, the TV on but with its sound down, so as not to shred your nerves.

And that was how it slowly dawned on me that fully recovering from this collapse of mine, getting health and fitness back, would be as long drawn out a process as it had been in allowing the viral effects to die down. It would be the equivalent of the time needed to effect a little epochal change.

I would have to set myself on a regime of taking exercise, of walking first short then further distances, circling around the block, and then the district, and then the different parks in the area, until finally I would be doing the kind of half circuit round the town that I'm taking you, reader, on now.

Even the thought of it did me good, and not least because I would come intimately to know so many of the nooks and crannies, the short cuts and back alleys that crisscross the districts in this provincial and riverside town of ours. I was doubtless helped by that state of mind so ably described in *The Man of the Crowd*, where the narrator has for some months been in a state of ill health.

Convalescent, he finds that 'with returning strength' he is 'in one of those happy moods which are so precisely the converse of ennui, moods of the keenest appetency, when the film from the mental vision departs' and when 'to breathe was enjoyment' and there was 'positive pleasure even from many of the legitimate sources of pain'.

Well, no, I couldn't and wouldn't quite go that far, but, like the man of the crowd, 'I felt a calm but inquisitive interest in every thing' and as one film departed another would descend, in the form of those slow camera shots, with their monotonous *engagé* voice-overs.

12

Now the next thing to do was get across the multi-directional traffic at what may have become unofficially known as Cemetery Junction in 1903 when the London Road tram branch was added to the Wokingham Road line. This is exactly the point where those two roads part, skirting the triangle of ground that, having been founded as a private project some forty years before, became, in the latter third of the nineteenth century, among the first such officially administered municipal burying grounds in the country.

It is architecturally proclaimed by a dainty-sized, creamy, classical-styled entrance—Death's triumphal arch, as some of us call it—which, like a stretch of the town around Eldon Road, and the Royal Berkshire Hospital, was built in Bath stone, most likely brought east along the Kennet and Avon canal in its brief hey-day, a hey-day coinciding with the emergence of Bath as the eighteenth-century watering place and resort that has so shaped its appearance.

Cemetery Junction, which one of my informants says is 'an unappealing name for a large oblique crossroads', is sufficiently mysterious in its conjunction of the urban mundane and the morbidly retired as to have served as inspiration for a number of contemporary poems—because, as a local poet, and please don't ask me to recall his name, had thought that 'Since early in the year now I've been meaning / To write a poem about this place', he would go on and do exactly that in his 'Near Elegy at Cemetery Junction':

> ... a busy spot, two main roads join
> Or start; a one-way scheme runs into town—
> Or (just to make the joke) through a triumphal
> Arch to this tomb-rife triangle of ground.
> Whichever way you look, it makes you hurry ...

This old poet had remained in the district, a near neighbour in one of the larger villas, after retiring from his chair up at the University. Though we never so much as exchanged a single word before his death, I would sometimes see him pushing a grandchild through the streets at twilight, a retired writer out on one of his own constitutionals, showing his offspring around the surrounding streets and grounds that had been the landscape of his homely existence.

'The surrounding area', my informant adds, 'struggles to maintain its reputation as a hotbed of Socialism and an outpost of Bohemia'. He is referring to a part of what is the parliamentary constituency of East Reading, which, as if to suggest that these struggles have not all been in vain, achieved a moment of national prominence when it swung wildly to Labour on 8 June 2017—overturning a six and a half thousand Tory majority. It includes the similarly unofficially named Newtown (euphemistically called 'East Reading' by the estate agents) towards which I am now slowly heading, and the more salubrious Redlands (the 'University Borders' in estate-agent-ese), which I'm leaving behind. So you can think, if you like, of my practically compulsory constitutionals—as they were in the aftermath of those two coincident collapses—as a miniscule part of this continuing struggle.

The junction itself is the point at which the King's Road and the London Road meet on their separate ways east from the centre of town. They join and immediately divide again into what will become the A4 heading for London and the Wokingham Road leading towards the South East, to Surrey and to Kent.

This ancient crossroads was once the place where the town gibbet stood, erected for the execution of local criminals. Arriving there, I'll obey the traffic lights and cross, with a twinge of nostalgia, from each surrounded island to the next, managing to avoiding this line of relentless cars, buses, and lorries, only to come up against a second stream of contra-flow vehicles racing one after another.

Pausing by the lights on the central of these islands, with Death's triumphal arch to my right, I'll be waiting to run for my life if there's anything like an unscheduled break in the traffic flow. Across the streams of hurtling metal, just up to the left, there stands the building which since about the year 1900 has housed a branch of the Co-op, its clock set into the height of its façade—a clock whose hands, as I write, show five-past-six for ever.

Stranded on that traffic island, as the cars, buses and lorries accelerated inches away, as like as not my thoughts would turn, don't ask me why, to imagining that, waiting there, I would be standing at precisely the point where the judicial executions had once taken place, where the highwaymen, housebreakers, and pickpockets would be hung up to rot on its gibbets—*pour*—as the famous French *philosophe* put it of that poor, unfortunate English Admiral What's-His-Name—*pour encourager les autres*.

I've heard it said that the cemetery, which gives the junction its name, began life as the out-of-town unconsecrated burial ground for those unfortunates and wretches who had fallen foul of the law and been executed so that judges and jurymen may dine. And, yes, I might well see, or at least catch a glimpse of, that great eighteenth-century poet himself, author of the memorable couplet about wretches hanging in *The Rape of the Lock*, a poem about a falling out between two Catholic families in the Thames valley. I might almost see him clip-clopping past that gibbet on the little pony carrying him from Mapledurham House up to Whiteknights Park—which is now the home of the University of Reading.

Nowadays, the cemetery is a haven of peace surrounded by the endless humming of the traffic flowing on simultaneously elsewhere in at least four directions at once.

The strange dwarf grandeur of the Bath-stone triumphal arch stands out in so many ways from the almost invisible, faded urban glory of the place's sole surviving cavernous pub (the Granby having become an ice cream parlour), its crescents of shops, its corporation swimming baths, the vast Baptist church and meeting hall, its much-repainted terrace houses—all of them having seen better days, but, just to that extent, also impregnated with the life you could almost imagine you saw emerging at the witching hour, or anytime at all.

Stranded on its central island, one evening in such a twilight, when the stopped clock on the Co-op façade might even be about to tell the right time, there with the traffic lights unchanging, the lorries, buses, and cars convergent on that calm within the cemetery walls, I'll be waiting, I'll be looking round at the boarded-up pub premises as if to catch a glimpse of that poet emerging after his beer and sandwich, striding off into—though assuming he was leaving it—literary immortality.

Opposite me there's a stressed young mother who stands pulling wind-blown hair from her face. And here's her impatient urchin son too, the rush of hurtling metal come between us. A faint drizzle's continuing to fall, and stranded on that traffic island, a Robinson Crusoe back home, surrounded by vehicles passing at speed just inches away, still looking around, like a dog at his various lampposts, it's as if the one answer to an acquaintance's 'How are you?' would have to be: 'Oh well, I can't complain!'

And with those very words I'll notice in a fit of nostalgia for a more optimistic *belle époque*, painted up there on a high gable end, half-effaced, an advert for *The Reading Dairy Company*, in its florid Edwardian lettering, and, higher, above the chimney pots, dusk's baleful, purple glow.

13

Where, though, did that nickname, 'Crusoe', come from? And what was it supposed to mean? Years after those schoolyard torments had lost their smart, the faces of their issuers long slipped from memory, though their effects by no means dissolved, I was reading *Robinson Crusoe*, the unabridged one, its first volume, for the very first time, and discovering how our other Foe, and friend, you know, Daniel, had provided an explanation. For the original Robinson Crusoe tells us at the very start of his 'autobiography' that his surname has a German origin.

This character's mother 'whose Relations were named *Robinson*' was the provider of that unusual Christian name, which must have been decided on between them so as to preserve a trace of the matrilineal side; but his father, we are told, was born 'a Foreigner of *Bremen*.' His family name being Kreutznaer, so my namesake of unwilling appropriation 'was called *Robinson Kreutznaer*'—the surname deriving from *Kreutzer*, the equivalent of 'Cruiser'.

Robinson's father had crossed what was then called the German Sea and come into this country via Kingston upon Hull. Then, 'by the usual Corruption of Words in *England*', the locals had simplified its orthography and pronunciation so as to make it take the form that would eventually become world-famous and thence, eventually, adopted by a gang of schoolboys for my denigrating nickname.

So a 'Crusoe' was a kind of warship, a cruiser, or a person who goes on cruises, and, in any case, a sailor—as doubtless were my ancestors, just as I, in a manner, would be obliged to become, and one of my descendants would, in good time, also decide to be.

Robinson's family had then passed quickly inland to York, which is where the character to whose name I would succumb had come into this world.

Although by no means a mariner of York, where, as is easily discovered, Robinson Crusoe was born in 1632, just three hundred and twenty-one years before me, I was nonetheless brought up by the seaside, brought up to be a toddling beach-comber who had stared out towards Yarmouth Roads, where my nickname-sake had got such a fright on his maiden voyage, a young fellow with rambling thoughts and wandering inclinations, and more into the bargain.

Within sight of that great and endlessly moving expanse, always careful to go there when the tide, depending on the nature of the coast, was either going out or coming in (for it wouldn't do to get cut off, or to have an exhausting hike across interminable sands), you would be led by parents, grandparents, aunts and courtesy aunts through the miles of dunes in the estuaries and havens where we were brought up, among the primary landscapes that came to feel like home.

I would valiantly step out among old rope and tar with a bucket and spade, the pale green marram grass-blades cutting at my naked feet and ankles, the sea's grey-blue horizon stretching out from the lower-angled viewpoint of that small boy, beyond the cranes and funnels of one port or another, towards an estuary, an offing, and out across the Irish, or the German, or whatever northern sea.

There you would be taken along the wharves of fish docks and quays to gaze into the stinking holds of the bigger trawlers. Haunted in dreams by the vanished drifters' rusted hulls, I had imagined a life on shipboard, in Arctic waters, icicles forming on my eyebrows, steering the boat through its mountain waves, smoke from the funnel blowing horizontally beside us in resistless gales, or fighting the living-silver nets aboard among those orange cork floats sewn onto their frayed meshes.

I too had grown up finding footprints in the sand, following them along the tideline as a cloud might cover up the sun, and the holiday afternoon begin to draw to its wistful close. Ah those post-war seaside holidays, before the likes of us could even dream of a charter flight to the scorching shores of the Mediterranean!

And it wasn't long before there fell into my hands, one after another, the innumerable children's illustrated abridgements, the simplified retellings of Robinson Crusoe's story, such as the ones that grace this large collection right behind my head here as I type.

You might even say that the development of my reading age had been accompanied by changes in the period flavour of the representations I would look at while following the retold story in its variously less and less simplified texts, starting from the beautifully illustrated Ladybird edition.

For it's another surprising thing about *Robinson Crusoe*, itself a fond shortening of the novel's original title, that in the August of the same year it was published in Pater-Noster Row, London, on the 25th of April, 1719, the book was already bootlegged, as seems only right given its 'Account how he was at last strangely deliver'd by PYRATES' on the original title page—pirated in a simplified version by some rogue publisher, who made it available at less than half price from the Amsterdam Coffee-House, London.

Now the older I get, in my reading age that is, the further back in time go the illustrations. Before even being able to decipher the words, I would gaze at those marvellous pictures: at the man in his goatskin suit, his pointed fur hat and sun umbrella, the builder of a stockade, the herdsman among his goats, or lone man talking to his parrot.

I had pitied and so learned the lesson of the craftsman hollowing out a tree-trunk to make a canoe, only to find it too heavy to move across the sand, the picture of it lying there, there on that palm-lined beach, a memorial to the folly of projecting man. That had been a lesson in foresight and planning, a lesson sadly nobody could learn once and for all.

Then, before becoming aware of having done it, I had learned to read well enough to make out the children's versions of his adventures on that desert island, of how, for instance, he had saved his man Friday from the banquet of the cannibals.

There too I had discovered that the character who would be my nickname-sake had taught his Friday how to speak a second language, a profession one day to become my own, though let's hope all those efforts in that line of work have shown better results than Robinson's in passing on our complex hybrid pidgin.

And so it was you came to imbibe the view of the world that this pseudo-autobiography implied, finding yourself thus stranded with some painfully inappropriate values whose force—like that nickname—had so stuck.

For thus you would be compelled, through being a *Crusoe* by that over-identification, to change as best you could within yourself.

Sometime in earliest teenage, too, I had watched an elegantly stylish Robinson and his Man Friday hunt for food, and dodge the pirates or the Spaniards, in a black-and-white French television series. It had nothing, I seem to remember, but an overdubbed narrative in English—though that was only after my poor parents had finally got round to buying us a boxy wood-framed set in the early 1960s.

Which is how I discovered that the French, it seemed, would call him *Crusoé*, or *Crusoë*, a name with three syllables and an accent of one kind or another on the final vowel—and discover too that there is a French obsession with Crusoe and his *Robinsonades*, which is what they most frequently call them. I've seen the word Anglicized and given as 'Robinsonads'—though that makes them sound like long national epic poems from the olden days of literature. Frenchifying the German plural *Robinsonaden*, which may be the original coinage, they had popularized the word for all those adaptations and retellings—that being one of the strongest and strangest threads in the multiple histories of his island-story commentaries and appropriations.

The name had settled especially well into the French language, for at one time at least you could take 'un Robinson', a large umbrella, with you as a protection from either the sunlight or the rain.

What's more, as it later emerged, not only is there a town in Illinois called Robinson, but it's also the name of a pleasant suburb in Paris called, strictly speaking, Le Plessis-Robinson. This unusually named place came into being as a *belle époque* playground, a day-tripper resort for Parisians, begun in 1848 when an innkeeper established a tree-house restaurant inspired by his love for the immortal character.

The restaurant was called, no, not *Le Grand Meaulnes* or *La Grande Jatte*, but *Le Grand Robinson*. The tree itself, '*le vrai arbre*', became a place of pilgrimage—though there's little more than a blackened stump remaining now of the boughs that supported the curiously suspended hostelry.

Still, the place does survive in old postcards from the period, and in surviving advertisements inviting the people of Paris to go out to Robinson and have a little *sport et divertissement*.

14

Detouring along the overgrown avenues of East Reading's old municipal cemetery, its stones at odd angles rising from the thick rain- and corpse-nourished ground, I would head off into the undergrowth along the remnant paths of its said-to-be grid pattern, head off, as is less difficult than you might think, into the place's omnipresent past.

More often than not you would find yourself entirely alone in that historical period, though a camouflage-clad photographer with tripod and zoom lens once crossed my path—as if you could go on safari here too—bringing us up short in his present. He was in search, he explained, of the legendary deer that were said to inhabit the cemetery's darkest recesses.

Although nobody could tell you how the muntjac had got here, what with the difficulty of crossing at the lights, still I did once manage to glimpse one of that endangered species. It was scurrying between the tombs and crosses, the tumbledown headstones and angels with their rain-smudged smut-mascara, disappearing as soon as glimpsed into the entangled undergrowth of their adopted home.

The cemetery's triangle of ground was formed by walling in the space between the diverging London and Woking-ham Roads at, exactly, Cemetery Junction. Its strange little triumphal arch—and our local Scottish poet may have been the first to call it that—in a classical design faced in the creamy Bath stone, constitutes the focal apex of this triangular space where the dead reside.

The structure, with rooms to left and right of the entry arch, was once used for art and other extra-mural classes, but now it only displays warnings of various kinds from the Thames Valley Police—plus advice about what to do if you have a drug problem, indicative of what the cemetery tends to be used for by some of those living around here now.

There's a row of terrace house-backs, their upper floor windows looking into this place of semi-perfect peace, which you can glimpse in the far distance along St Bartholomew's Road, and which forms the base of the mortuary triangle.

From outside, a pedestrian pausing at the lights can see the cypress and yew from the road, or look down in among the graves from the top of buses going by. Inside here you can see the top decks of these new multi-coloured buses, the colours indicating their routes, passing on their way in or out of the Newtown area.

Set up by the Reading Cemetery Company and opened in 1843, it is described on a plaque as one of the oldest 'garden' cemeteries in the country and Grade 2 listed by English Heritage. However, as yet, and not helped by the recent comedy film of that name, it has none of the pulling-power of the country's ruined castles, its battlefields, or the stately homes of England in the song.

So much is it not a place to venerate that when the local-born comedian produced his film script for a Hollywood movie, the advisory team, I can well imagine, must have taken the word 'junction' to refer to a railway line stop, as in the British neo-realist *Up the Junction*—an idiom meaning, then, though perhaps not now: 'to get pregnant outside of wedlock'.

Its being so un-venerated might also go to explain why the cemetery's asphalt paths are cracked, flaked, and subsiding, its gravestones mostly fallen into disrepair. Still, the grass is evidently mown at regular intervals, and there are municipal dustbins for your picnic rubbish, should you decide to picnic here, and in which to place the dead flowers cleared from the few graves still tended, or the cans used by truant drinkers visibly glinting in the grass around some of its tombs.

Most of the graves date from the nineteenth century, as you can tell both by the weathering of their stone, and, sometimes, from the design of the carving—your guesses always able to be confirmed by the inscriptions upon them, with the dates of birth and death, if they aren't too old, weathered, and flaked not to have any inscriptions left at all.

There you can make out, or make up, innumerable life stories from the bare inscriptions—the married couples whose birth and death dates indicate long years of widow-hood before they were finally reunited, for instance, or the infant mortalities, and children predeceasing their parents.

There was the woman who died aged 44 in 1919, perhaps from Spanish Flu, whose husband had only re-joined her in 1947. Or there was the child who 'fell asleep suddenly' aged 12 months.

It was, and has remained, intriguing and attractive to constitutionalists such as myself, as if it might be a mildly homeopathic antidote for the temptation to suicide, or better than that, because the graveyard school attitude of haunting such melancholy places is rather a stubborn form of attachment to life.

So, as like as not when passing, you would take that detour down its alleyways, or walk there with a friend discussing matters of life and death. You might occasionally haunt that graveyard casually glancing at the gravestones just to see if there happen to be tombs commemorating a Robinson or other down there. I haven't, as yet, though, found a single one.

Returning eventually to the endless traffic of the junction and managing to get across the three converging lanes, on I would drift down Cumberland Road past the famous stained-glass window shop, featured on film and television, and the Kaushal Diamonds, Jeweller's Ltd—with is 'Fog Bandit' alarm system for filling the place with smoke, the warning label on its door.

On the opposite side of the road, in an adapted non-conformist chapel, there's the SRI GURU SINGH SABHA GURDWARA Sikh Temple. In the other direction along King's Road there's the large Wycliffe Baptist church, with its good news for the area, and the dissenters for whom *Robinson Crusoe* might have been a secular Bible—they too are trying to combine an outward heroism with an inner predicament. It was for them that the book's author endured, or perhaps, rather, enjoyed, his moment in the pillory, composing that poem about it which, like the opportunist entrepreneur he was, could be sold to those who came to throw—no, not tomatoes, but flowers.

The Wycliffe Baptist church brings together, especially in the young, many of the district's different communities. I know because my daughter was for some years a regular attender there, and she too has prayed for my soul in my hour of need, those terrible winter months, prayed that I would realize God's providential care.

Perhaps because she knew that you had been a sinner and lost your way, and that if you would but kneel down and pray with her then you too could be saved—which would be to appear as religious as my life-long nickname suggests I ought to be.

So too would Crusoe expatiate upon religion in the third volume of his autobiography, writing poems on the themes of Faith and Peace. 'Let me break out here upon this glorious subject, and pardon the excursion, I entreat you.' Ah yes—pardon the excursion—as I hope you will here too.

After all, one of the things you might hold against Crusoe is the absolute congruence of his survival instincts and his value system. There is not the slightest doubt for the length of the book, at least as I recall it, that his interests are anything other than compatible with those of his maker.

It's something that for a great many reasons since 1719 might be harder now to credit. There's the challenge to the initiatives of empire building from those who were there to look back on its actions and to side with its victims.

Pardon for this excursion I do indeed need to beg myself as well, and especially in this area of imperial implosion, coming back to a microcosm of the world my namesake is described as contributing to by setting up his colony on that Caribbean island.

I would indeed need to beg pardon because I come back to a place where my fellow townspeople are made up of the old working classes, arrivals from the Gulf of Mexico, from Ireland, the Asian sub-continent, interspersed with Ethiopians and others from the African diaspora, the Eastern Europeans—people bringing with them their various religions and denominations, to which the most recent twists and turns to our island story will doubtless oblige me to return.

15

My parents were the only ones in their different families to have taken the step into tertiary education. So naturally enough, when the time came, there was the expectation—it had always been there—that I would follow in their footsteps, and set out on that course too. The aim had always been to get back to the North Sea coastlines of childhood family holidays; but those applications didn't quite reach that far, and I had to settle for the county seat—which is how of all possible places I came to reside in Robinson's birthplace—because, as it fell out, I too would pass some time in the City of York.

It was only a little too far inland, or we students were too penurious, to make it to the sea at weekends—though Whitby, Scarborough, Robin Hood's and Runswick Bay were places known from summertime visits along that shoreline. It has been called 'a coast for loners', or is it rather that the strand there makes you one? For in childhood you too had wandered among the abbey ruins, retracing the route of Dracula into this country from the East, through that site of the Synod at Whitby in 664. You too had played around the hermit's cave.

And so there it was in York that three years of life would go by, three years getting an education, there in Crusoe's birthplace. Back then most of the students, including me, looked unusually like a young Robinson with our unkempt hair and patches of straggly beard. Our clothes too, though they weren't made of goatskin, tended to look like they'd seen better days.

And it was there in York too, that perched on a fire-escape overlooking the roofs of that chocolate town, you first properly read the first volume of his book in its original English, this practically debut attempt at novelistic prose, its meandering mixture of adventure and commentary, religious tract and a period defence for the benefits of a colony.

Then, up there in that tiny garret, you would follow it with *The Storm*, then *Moll Flanders*, *Captain Jack*, *The Journal of the Plague Year* and *A Tour through the Whole Island of Great Britain* only dimly aware that this reading in the works of their author was a minuscule fraction of what that inveterate scribbler had managed to produce in a life which also found time for a great many other activities too—and not least a government spy.

It was there it first became clear how much you had haplessly taken on by embracing that 'Crusoe' nickname— the political, economic, and cultural myths and ideologies that would inevitably be incorporated as your own were you to admit having found yourself walking in his sandy footprints.

Returning to the City of York now, as I sometimes do, over the reminiscent streets, my feet unsteady on their settled flagstones, each time I'm taken aback by what's changed: those buses swarming with tourists in the Castle car park, or climbing up towards Clifford's Tower, the ruin looking almost as it had when painted by that Lancashire artist who did the matchstick men—even though the place has turned into something of a trap now, especially in summer, where it's a part of the northern loop for those swarming here from west and east, doing Britain in a single northern sweep.

I would walk on past the *King's Arms* down on its Ouse-side quay. They had a version of 'Spanish Harlem' on the jukebox there. Those evenings back then, we would sit drinking under the series of flood-level marks upon its walls.

That very same hostelry is visible in an eighteenth-century water colour of the river ... and it comes back of a sudden that it was one of my fellow students there, another—but this one prematurely-deceased—Scottish poet, who had spent some time in Paris before coming up to York, who would tease me with his memory of taking 'le train pour Robinson', that being the first time I would hear of my namesake, a suburb.

Further on along that walk, the blue wrought-iron bridge across a canal would come up on the left, just where the glassworks once had been. They had pulled it down not long after our intake graduated. Then began the long Ouse walk, with its riverside trees in their autumnal colours, just as they had been more than forty years before.

What they brought back most was the weight of culture, the struggle on foot from the station to my lodgings with a rucksack and a case of books, of eighteenth-century fiction in that second autumn, dragging them under those trees for the start of another academic year.

My father hadn't wanted to show those student 'digs' to mother in case the state of them would scare her, for she would only worry. That garret's single window, also the exit to its fire escape, was cracked from side to side. It was this same student, the Scottish poet, who found the room in that barrack-like house on Wenlock Terrace—which has since become a gentrified hotel.

There I would fret over words he had written—more taunts aimed at my nickname, as they were more or less, while the leaves came tumbling around me like the challenges friends would fling at those barely formed raw selves of ours, at a Crusoe wending his solitary way.

Still, by steps down to the Ouse, flanked with the autumn trees in trouble, now time would seem to have equalized the presence of all these later years, then unimagined, the other futures spooling out before us to these ends.

For it's a very different thing to find your way by a memory's traces and—in his words to that effect—know yourself no less at home despite those applications, hopes, know yourself as we'll have been back then, by these renovated terraces and bricked-up corner shops.

Collecting my mail from the college pigeonholes just before that nightmarish period leading up to our final exams, a period of intensive working and painful hangovers, I found a note from another fellow student, one from the year below. It contained a typed-out copy of a poem not encountered before. The verses were entitled 'Robinson at Home' by a writer then unknown to me.

My fellow student, as if to spook me in the lead up to those life-deciding tests, had underscored the following lines: 'He might wake to hear the news at ten, / Which will be shocking, moderately.' And it looked as if, to my panic-stricken eyes, he must have drawn them to my attention as a kind of put-down, as if my self-involvement and strictly limited concern for the world, or my minimal political awareness, were merely a fleeting disturbance, a temporary shock experienced after another post-prandial nap.

When that fellow student left his message with the attributed snatch of verse on it, I had taken the quotation from 'Robinson at Home' too personally, and with a recurrence of that long-developed persecutory anxiety, attempted then in the usual fashion to find out who their author might be—though not made any the wiser by the what-do-you-call-him Library and its holdings at that point. The little I would eventually find out about this American poet and his work from my desultory researches left a long list of puzzles. Finding some of them out has also helped prompt the writing of what might be called this Robinson's reply.

Panicked too by yet more about which my ignorance would seem limitless, I had hurried straight to the stacks and, not finding a copy of his poems, was once again frustrated. Eventually, after a number of surprising biblio-graphic adventures that there's no need to trouble you with here, I managed to track down his work and to discover that there are, in fact, four of these poems in all: 'Robinson', 'Robinson at Home', 'Aspects of Robinson' and 'Relating to Robinson'. They seemed to have come to their author at different points in his writing life, and were never published together as a sequence. Nor did it appear on the face of it that they were allusive of *Robinson Crusoe* either. The Kafka and Céline Robinsons have been canvassed as sources. Another prompt may have come from the poem that turns the character's mother's family name into a verb, where his 'cœur fou' can indeed 'Robinsonne à travers les romans'. 'Aspects of Robinson' ends with 'His sad and usual heart, dry as a winter leaf.' If the poet did get his 'sad ... heart' from the French for 'mad heart', he'll have been exemplifying an influence thoroughly digested.

These 'Robinson' poems have, themselves, a rising panic-like intensity—as if each vying to outdo the disturbance of the previous one, and, naturally, given all that training received in the schoolyard, I found no difficulty in identi-fying with this strangely indistinct, yet similarly mythic figure. The character's solitude, his symbolism, and their poet's education, though, all meant that the association of the two could hardly be ruled out, and I naturally added him to my anthology of specimen Robinsons in need of authentication.

So distinctive were the four poems, and so much have they too reached cult status, that they've now become the point of departure for a veritable school of imitations, all of which take this symbolic Robinson-figure with his habits, his love life, and his neurotic obsessions as the occasion to explore aspects indeed of our acculturated and anxiety-driven lives. There is now a little rash of English versified *Robinsonads*, while across the Atlantic a young author has produced an entire book, a novel in verse, called *Robinson Alone*. I've read it from cover to cover. It's as true as true can be—at least to my experience.

Thinking again, as I walked on down in the direction of the gasholders beside the Kennet canal, about that nightmarish period leading up to our exams, another haunting revenant from that past came back to mind. How strange it had been, over forty years later, to be introduced to another survivor from those three years in the town of Crusoe's birth. At a book launch, it was, and I had said out loud what his second name was sure to be, as soon as his first was spoken, for it is the same as mine.

'Then you must be ... ' I exclaimed.

'But how did you know?' his companion asked, and I found myself explaining that we had only met the once, forty years before, at a dinner organized by one of my professors, a lost-weekend-type writer whose *bildungsroman* trilogy was in the process of being adapted for the stage by this other namesake of mine.

The larger-than-life fiction writer's wife had been my personal tutor throughout the degree. For me, the memory of that night, all those forty years before, had proved yet one more haunting misery—for I had been unable to resist the plying with drink that took place, and the being lured into competitive conversations, only to have my *jejune* contributions mocked for their ignorance, presumption, and hubristic aspiration—as if yet again some unconscious attempts at parricide had rebounded guiltily upon my head.

Perhaps, though, it had been that very same youthful optimism, the feeling before any definitive decisions have been made, it might seem, that whatever you attempt will turn out right, that the world is all before you. For I know now how irritating such youthful optimism can be to those for whom such days are past forever.

But at that chance meeting almost four decades later, he didn't seem to remember any such ritual humiliation having taken place. For there it was, yet another case where my memories of the past were of events that, as far as others were concerned, didn't seem to have happened at all.

He could barely conjure a young face from the ruins of the suntanned greybeard standing before him, that survivor of shipwrecks in far other oceans, although together we could more or less reconstruct the menu and the vast amounts of alcohol consumed.

16

There was another student back in Crusoe's birthplace, perhaps doing some cruising in his own, who would pointedly refer to me as 'Hyacinth ...'

'You what?' I would say. Who's he when he's at home?'

'Hyacinth—Hyacinth Robinson', he had laughed, and explained.

Ah yes, another nickname there!

But no, I'd no idea, though of course I should have done, at that stage in my degree, what he might have meant by a name like that, or what this Robinson's fate would be—though this fellow student would make what he had in mind only too apparent, just a year or so later—while the passage of time would make me no less able, then as now, to know how to respond in a way that was not untrue and not unkind to his probing invitation.

Naturally enough, by that time I realized what that other student might have meant by calling me 'Hyacinth'—having read his novel too, and knowing what a sad end he comes to, caught between his conflicted class heritage, his involvement with the novel's eponymous aristocrat and the murderous revolutionary outrage Robinson has promised to perform, he is condemned by his author to shoot himself through the heart 'while you were fetching the milk.'

But was it our inappropriately proud poverty, my relentless cultural ambition, or innocent flirting with political radicalism that the nickname-caller had had in mind?

What you were quite unaware of, though, was that the novel's author could have derived the name Hyacinth Robinson from one—Saint Hyacinthe, it comes back by through the mists—who was the first adaptor of *Crusoe* into French. What's more, by the time you had begun at least to

82

stop worrying about what it might imply about your tastes in the same or the opposite sex, you too had been holed up alone to hide away and recuperate just off Stoke Newington Church Street.

There, another old friend was allowing that protracted sojourn in his tiny flat while away on some wanderings of his own—to Timbuctoo or Tenerife—and it has always been a life-enhancing pleasure to spend time as if trespassing in the circumstances of other people's lives.

So you would wake up in the back bedroom with, behind rooflines, a slight glow like some famous aubade for lovers who've to leave their safe house, that homely abode, since they would eventually have to move too—the light slanting its promise through the cloud like a bonus payment in kind. There the day would find you out on the pavement between that flat and the High Street, for this is where you had come to hide between Defoe and Dynevor Road, come here when back from overseas, and with your emotions in ruins, felled by a near-fatal illness from which you had practically died.

In those earlier convalescent days, it would seem like a blessing to be able to notice the remaining signs of his Friday and Robinson in the streets around, the pretty rooms, clothes lines welcoming you into this exile's retreat—while you would be cradling your wounded head again, hearing some ominous bird cry 'Nevermore', as if returning to its origins, having left that rumpled bed roughly re-pristined, having practised your fond goodbyes—for there would be no putting off an eventual return to those islands of exile.

This now lost house in Lavers Road had been one of my few safe houses, for I too had come to think of myself as cast in the role of a spy or private eye in the mazy streets of London. There, in that safe house, it was as if by another form of promiscuous identification I were able to grow in the possible light of the personhood imaginatively taken on in those surroundings. Yet this particular period of being someone else, being in the vicinity of other circumstances, was to happen in the aftermath of another almost total shipwreck, and near fatal illness, when the fragility of the person I might be had been for the first time borne in with a vengeance.

Living in the flat downstairs, as if to underline the idea of becoming someone else for a purpose, or to sustain an existence, the actor who described himself as 'resting' was in fact writing a memoir—as I would be then and now.

So when the mood took me, or a lack of provisions did, I would venture out past Defoe House, a block of rundown council flats, trying to get my health back in what might be thought a dry run for the further adventures and constitutionals I'm taking now, the gasholder on the Kennet getting larger before me with every reflective step taken further down Cumberland Road this mad March day.

On such outings, I too could be accosted on Defoe Road by the likes of your man Robinson and his Friday—for the area was much less gentrified back then. You could catch sight of them in daylight haggling with yet more pirates over the price, cash in hand, of some beaten up, rolling-junk of a pre-owned car. Both of them might be glimpsed disappearing round the corner into the graveyard late at night, or they'd be roaming around in violent mood intent on seeking out and doing to death their creator, his name hanging up there on a hostelry sign.

He had first come here, to what must then have been an outlying village, when studying at the Dissenting Academy on Newington Green, and later, about my age, came to evade his creditors and improve his precarious finances by writing an unexpected best seller, a fake autobiography, like my own, of course, to which it is so much indebted.

Stoke Newington has, of course, changed beyond all recognition. Happening to be there the other day, walking up from the Arsenal, leaving the *Robinson Crusoe* pub behind and down to our right, we would enter the precincts of Clissold Park. Here were the cut-down trunks remaining like earth sculptures, the pink marble water fountain on its cabbage-leaf-surrounded hillock. Here were the growing communities' wired off allotment plots, the chatter of birds in the mini-zoo, and all around the joggers and buggies taking air and exercise.

The old church that gives the street its name was inviting passers-by in to hear a wind-harp playing, so that what with the Tapas bars and eateries, the high-end butchers' shops and bistro menus chalked on pavement boards, the place's uneven gentrification appeared to be in full swing.

It was there we sat one Saturday afternoon, in a Turkish place right on the corner of Defoe Road, with what I'm sure used to be called the *Daniel Defoe* pub directly opposite. But now, you could hardly believe it, how could they have done such a thing? The pub has been repurposed—has been chi-chi-fied out of existence, and its name changed into the bargain. Now it's called the *Stoke Newington Tearoom*! Oh no, I thought, they've gone and decided the old author's name is just too politically incorrect to be remembered.

So there we were, lazily watching the celebrants of an early summer weekend traipsing past its windows in the fading afternoon, my Friday and I, and there was the world going by, the two of us reflecting on how the place had changed since first I came here during that earlier convalescence.

We were as good as discussing that curious sensation you get in public in London, in bars and cafés, often crowded to the doors. You know the way people can form intimate groups, groups that are entirely exclusive of others, and hermetically so, even when they're surrounded by people doing exactly the same thing. What's more, in the capital there are so many more people crowded together who are each behaving in exactly the same ways to preserve a little bit of personal space and privacy when required to live so much of the time in a sort of inescapable public arena.

Not that they don't do similar things in other towns too, but it's the practised extremity of the ability to ignore the existence of others or anything else in their surroundings that is so striking in the capital, and had so struck us that day on Stoke Newington Church Street.

It's almost the opposite of the man of the crowd in his café corner watching the world go by, the opposite of being a *flâneur* or poetical drifter—whose very existence is animated by all that anonymity around. Now the way to survive sociably in cities appeared to be strictly to limit the scope of your social group and then studiously ignore the existence of anything and anyone else.

Those months of my first convalescence were back in the days when you could still buy mansions round here for a relatively modest sum, which was something else we couldn't help reflecting on, yet again, as we sat sipping our tea: how the cost of everything was silly now, and the price being paid—so much so that you couldn't help wondering, as the bill arrived, whether life itself was worth it, or indeed whether 'worth it' could even be measured in numbers any more. It was a theme close enough to Crusoe's mad or saddened heart—and that of his debt-ridden author, no doubt.

Back then another old writer friend would take me walking round those familiar back streets of his London village home. He'd be pointing out the landmarks, ones practically invisible to the eyes of a non-native pedestrian. He was talking about who's in and who's out, trying to keep me abreast of the times—times changing so quickly you could never hope to keep up anyway.

There, for instance, was the churchyard and cemetery in the direction of dear old Clissold Park, its island-like menagerie and zoo, and all the way down to that far end with the pub that bore my nickname's source on its opposite corner, where the daytime drinkers would ornament its door.

Later, it became even more familiar, after those weeks of my more drastic convalescence, when I had been lent that little first-floor flat down one of the side roads not far from Defoe Road, a road parallel to the one where another sailor home from the sea would lodge between commands.

For the author of *Heart of Darkness* too, though before he was known by his English name, or had called upon the help of a Huntley & Palmers biscuit tin, had regularly lodged here at 6 Dynevor Road—where between voyages from 1881 to 1886 he rented a room.

'Dynevor Road', this sailor novelist's biographer reported in 1983—and he leaves it unrevised in its recent reissue: 'is a grey, plain-looking street far from the city's center, in a cheap, unattractive northern district of Stoke Newington. Number 6 still exists. It is a two-level Victorian house like thousands of others along endless miles of streets.'

Well, it's not like that anymore, you can take it from me, for on the 27th of September 2013—as it proudly boasts on the estate agent's website—6 Dynevor Road, by now well known as the address most immediately associated with the great novelist, sold for one million pounds!

The sailor and future novelist will also have walked these little streets, and he would write from Singapore on the 13th of October 1885 that 'When speaking, writing or thinking in English the word Home always means for me the hospitable shores of Great Britain'—as had I in that year of my illness, painful surgery, and long-term convalescence.

What's more, having managed a much longed-for return from our own desert island story, we would in no time at all grow nostalgic for those years of being thrown together on an archipelago far from anything either of us had ever known before.

A fellow-sufferer from such returnee longings asked us just the other day whether we felt any nostalgia for those years lived far from anywhere.

'Yes, we have,' said Friday, 'and yet it's so sealed off from everything. Hardly anyone around here seems to have experienced anything like that—and there's so little use for the things we learned, things like how to survive the solitude, to make a shed from drifted waste, or a basket from packaging strip—'

'Which is why you can never talk about any of it to anyone,' I would interrupt, 'and when, occasionally, you do, the people you're talking to, they've no idea what to say.'

'Because they don't ever expect to be in those kinds of situations,' she'd come back, 'the ones we grew used to, and learned so much from. That's why they leave whatever it is you might have said still hanging in the air. They change the subject, or go back directly to what you were trying to comment on with a "be that as it may" or a "whatever".'

'I know exactly what you mean,' our fellow-sufferer said, and sighed. 'It's like being exiled from your exile, isolated from your isolation ...'

With no one to speak about it to, how the once relevant words would wither unnoticed inside. Like so many graveyard mausoleums, those language dictionaries stood unopened on our shelves. Only at odd moments, a useless phrase might force itself into your consciousness, prick up its ears as if from a long hibernation, and speak again from who knows where.

'*Tasukete kudasai*,' it might call out, a far cry for help still trying to escape.

17

Back then, on that faraway island, I found myself not so much cast away, as cast in the role of a *homo economicus*—the emblematically singular devouring subject, the quintessential small entrepreneur, the solitary producer and consumer, whose presumed devices and desires provided the grounds for so many of the world's most famous economists to make their endlessly varying calculations—and provide the reason why even in our rampant heritage culture that pub in Stoke Newington would feel the need to change its name.

But there was yet another irony in the life that schoolyard nickname had prepared me for—as if as a providence, chance, or fate. By taking on the identity of *Crusoe*, you too would have to symbolize that singular accountancy unit, the solitary economic man in all those state-of-nature justifications for our rapaciousness, our being red in tooth and claw.

Such a figure the classical economists had developed as an ideal model of selfhood—me, myself, alone—and made it the entity whose providential competitiveness was the one and only route not just to individual self-esteem, but also to global economic success, and the quantification, the monetization of everything and all happiness into the bargain.

So it followed that if my desiring had changed the climate and threatened the very future of the planet, then, yes, I was personally and singularly to blame. Again the fault was mine—or so you couldn't help thinking as you reached out towards the shelf in a book or record store, or picked out some more wet fish from the metal market slabs.

And so it was the solitude of those years would appear a punishment for being that singular consumer, that model of the individual who the theorists of revolution would deconstruct with their disjunctive syntax—or with any-mad-version they could throw at it. But perhaps it was those very radicals in their unholy and unforeseen league with the theorists of anarchic economic freedom who had done it? For this was, doubtless, another case of the cure being a symptom of the disease from which it sought to save us.

And why would they want to deconstruct something so precarious—you would try to ask yourself—something defended by habits too deep for tears, and visible in all those marks of weakness, marks of woe.

'Because they need their enemies,' I would reflect, 'just like those schoolyard bullies who had called me "Crusoe" in the first place: now they have to cast me as the villain of the piece, the kind of person who has to be extinct if the world is to become a better place.'

Oh *homo economicus*, oh economic man, why then aren't you ashamed of yourself? For if you can't cope with lone-liness, don't think of getting married, let alone having progeny. And why exactly was it that the individual consumer, engaging with the market, as it's called, had come to manifest the essential condition for the proper working of that market, with its self-righting dynamics and its mathematical equations for interdependent adjust-ments?

After all, those very individuals had to be produced by collaborative parents, until recently in large, extended, or feudal families, by people teaming up for self-preservation, and doing so amid attempts on all sides not to operate in such an ideal or natural market, whether it be through client cliques, cartels, unions or boycotts—all means for fixing them in fractionally communal interests.

Theirs was the natural behaviour, theirs the market in a state of nature. For market economics had established by abstract calculation and hands-off intervention that the purity of the supposedly deregulated system had nevertheless to be regulated into sustaining rule-less-ness. That's, after all, what a monopolies regulator was for.

Yet there was I, a Robinson Crusoe in myself; and, as now you knew, he had himself been set forth as a model for the emergence of this market's essential presumption, this unitary item of accounting, my desires alone, which, as I looked out from our tearoom on that Saturday afternoon, were being broken into innumerable reflections, into a flickering chimera on the flow of passers-by, on that watery substance of our lives.

'*Robin, Robin Crusoe*, poor *Robin Crusoe*,' again that voice came taunting me, my fatal nickname played back, as in a pronunciation class, its intonation tunes an echo of my own.

'*Where are you? Where have you been? How came you here?*' as Robinson's author writes, along with other 'such things as you would think I taught him'.

Yet to 'a teacher of languages', as the other sailor novelist put it, 'there comes a time when the world is but a place of many words and man appears a mere talking animal not much more wonderful than a parrot.'

No, I never consciously taught them, my green parrots in their habitats, how to speak those words in such bemoaning language, words I could hardly have said out loud. But it was as if that parrot had read my mind.

Sometimes their sudden crying would wake me in the night, wake me again to the thoughts of my misfortunes, every last one of them codified through the subsequent sleeplessness. Yet it was also as if, like a small miracle, when the parrots died, died of boredom, as it seemed, sick to death of repeating their lessons from the chalk-face in that cage— so, with it, died my own self-pity. No, I have no parrot now.

But the days before Friday, my dear Friday, with only those nightmare parrots speaking to me, they were filled with relentless work and dreams of home. Why hoard the useless money? Why be wondering what happened to the others? Why even complain?

The days before Friday, compulsively till late, I would write my journal entries: each setback, inspiration! Each success—one more lost reason to keep on keeping on!

Each footprint in the sand would make me dream once more of my distant lost loves. Like an apparition it was overwhelming, like a cloud of unknowing. I could not imagine any other.

Before Friday, my language had frozen up inside me, had seemed to evolve of its own devices, inventing words for experiences that no one else would ever have, though it was only years later I discovered that the philosophers were more than divided about whether Robinson could even do that— whether there could even be words if I'd invented them only for my idiolect of one, only to name all that I could neither be lord of, nor survey.

18

Thank heaven at least for Friday, Friday who would rescue me from myself. For among the many uses to which Robinson has been put, perhaps the strangest is his contribution to the debate over whether it is, or is not, possible for a new language to be invented by an individual who uses it to refer to his or her own sensations.

Where the economists had called me to account, to be the accounting unit for their systems of supply and demand, the philosophers had used my nick-namesake to debate the existence of a private language.

The competing arguers would consider the case of Crusoe on his island, another state-of-nature case, assuming from their different positions that the so-called 'private language argument' excluded Robinson from language.

For some of them the argument must be wrong, because we can logically imagine Robinson making up a language; for the other the argument is correct (there can be no private language) because he can't invent one, and what he uses—in, for example, his journal—isn't private at all.

And so it was that I found myself entering the strangely airless world of philosophical examples, one in which we are to imagine 'a Robinson Crusoe left alone on his island while still an infant, having not yet learned to speak', and to accept that 'it is not self-contradictory to suppose that someone, uninstructed in the use of an existing language, makes up a language for himself.'

But not only is this infant Crusoe not the one of Daniel's proto-novel, but the place we are to imagine him is one where irritatingly incoherent or apparently irrelevant details of the case (such as his ability to survive, like a Spartan infant, should there happen not to be any empire-building wolves on hand to suckle him) are conveniently allowed to drop out of the picture.

The philosopher with his counter-factual examples needs a Robinson whose being on his island resembles more the early life of that mysterious German child, a figure said to have been isolated at birth from contact with any language—which he then invents as his only way to externalize his sensations. Yet this Kaspar—if I remember his name rightly—was able to say a few words when he first presented himself in Nuremberg, and these were not sounds he had invented himself that together formed a language, with all the relevant grammatical and semantic elements in place. No, they were German words like *Ritter*, perhaps. And, indeed, the question is rather begged why he would feel the need to communicate them when, in so far as he could know them without naming them, they would be him, not something other, and him alone.

If an infant had no interactions with any other persons, if it were, in this sense, isolated from birth on the island of itself, it is quite difficult to imagine how the idea of communication with another being would emerge at all. The organ of speech might make noises, but it is hard to imagine that these noises could be produced as intended acts of communication—communication with what or whom, I ask you?

Crying babies—I'm told—give up crying if their desperate noises fail to attract attention. Medical professionals at scenes of widespread distress are most concerned for those who are wounded and alive, but making no sound.

And it is in the light of thoughts like these that I was caught up in the so-called private language argument—because it had been based upon imagining my nickname and alter ego in freshly unusual situations, alone from birth on a desert island, the desert island of the individual self, such as I had already imagined, getting out of the shower, for instance.

So then, this impossibility imagined, for this creature would have surely died a Spartan weakling's death, then these philosophers would ask what it would be like for this solitary to make up a language to express perceptions of a world, a paradise of one, as someone else had envisaged it, with which no one but that solitary had or could have relations.

Yet no sooner had you begun to think about such matters when, as if to add insult to injury, no sooner had you found yourself alone, than another schoolyard taunt, one as if from a message in a bottle, accused you to your face of solipsism. It was a debilitating blow, aggravating actual isolation with the charge of being psychologically incapable of imagining anyone other beyond—not just alone, but selfishly alone into the bargain.

Nor is it by any means easy to rebut such accusations. But if you were such a solipsist, perhaps you wouldn't feel the need to rebut them either, their having no other existence than in your thoughts themselves. You wouldn't need to rebut them because you could simply dismiss them.

But the problem of rebutting them is that the more you try to effect a convincing argument against them the more it seems you *are* one, protesting too much, others seeming so unswayable by anything you might find to say.

Then you might think that the only way out of this accusation of solipsism is to be rescued from it by someone else who confirms your existence—though that might only turn out to be the constitution of a *solipsisme-à-deux*.

Nevertheless, and however hard you try, the fact of isolation will make you wonder to yourself if your accuser isn't right, and, stung by those words, I had spent years on that imaginary desert island trying to find an antidote, trying to work out why what he had said just could not be the case.

Not, you understand, by reflecting on the kinds of care for the existence of others that I willy-nilly showed in my day-to-day existence, in the recognitions that were needed merely to go into a shop and buy some groceries, even in this age when almost everything is done by machine.

No, I tried to do it by understanding from the way we speak and use pronouns, the way we say 'my life' for instance, that this can't be a sealed off entity, because the use of the 'my' requires the existence of other lives that are not 'mine' to make the little word signify at all.

So if any language use required these pronominal and other contrasts to be meaningful, then to speak a language was, by definition, not to be a solipsist. And this would be the case even when no intonation force is being added to words to underline such contrasts, as when we add stress to a first-person pronoun to imply that it is the speaker who is being intended, and expressly not 'you' or 'him' or 'her' or 'it' or 'them'.

So I didn't want to show that I wasn't a solipsist because I was not alone in my life—how could *I* do that?—but by showing that even the fact of calling me one would have to mean that I wasn't and couldn't be. It was a triumph of sorts, but Pyrrhic really. For what else could the desire to prove this accusation wrong show but that I was even more wrapped up in myself than my accuser had dared to suggest.

I had in effect demonstrated my self-absorption by proving that the accusation of solipsism could not be levelled at me, or at anyone else, at all, for to level it was to disprove it. But then, my dear Friday—as I can't help but call her—how she had come along to substitute that problem with others, others of a far more preferable kind!

Yes, Friday was nice, too, and a woman—and we were friends as well. And thank Heaven she would eventually make those arguments defending me against the charge of solipsism quite unnecessary—her presence there on that island after those first lonely years having so relieved my isolation.

My Friday being a woman, the anguish expressed in some Crusoe-back-home writing about their not being able to engender offspring didn't, as it happened, apply to us either. It was as if she could get pregnant—though this wasn't how we did it—should we so much as take a sip from the same glass of water.

My dear Friday, she too had been stranded by yet another economic downturn, and by a crisis that was none of her making either.

'I just couldn't go on. My eyes were so full of tears,' she told me. 'I had to stop the car on the hard shoulder. I felt so helpless in that dog-eat-dog existence.'

She had shed tears of grief and anger at the desperate state of things, of how the commission on her independent sales initiatives was drying up as a direct result of the evident lack of spending power that had suddenly made itself felt once more—their economy too in one of its cyclical downturns.

You had rescued your dear Friday from her humiliation, only to set the challenge of making a life together on that other side of the world, as if a pair of mutineers from some imaginary *Bounty*.

We were no longer young and, being naturally bolshie in our different ways, couldn't bear the taunts of any

Captain so-and-so or other representative of how economic prudence would demand that we lived our lives—a further reason why my identification with *homo economicus* had come at the price of anxiety and fear.

Which was also why I could never quite rid myself of the fear that my Friday might think of me as the aphorist who had written of an inhabitant from what is now the Dominican Republic: 'The American who first discovered Columbus made a bad discovery.'

Oh but thank goodness, thank goodness—and thank goodness that not so long after being washed ashore I found my dearest, my only Friday, and I can't help but think of her by that name, even though, of course, she doesn't like it. Ah but, then again, you might as well say she found me!

We too would pick our way through the wrack of its deserted beaches, past the heaps of clamshells where she would collect seaweed, old rope and packaging, things to adapt for health-giving food, or employ to weave baskets for further hunter-gathering activities.

She was a dab hand at making our furniture out of driftwood, our plates out of seashells, plastic packaging strips, or glasses from the worn-smooth bottles with no messages that washed up, from time to time, there along the shore.

She would go foraging for food among the shoots and leaves in the overgrown forests around our alien enclave.

If I were the provider of spiritual resilience in all our years on those shores, it was she who did most to ease our material predicament.

Oh Friday, O Friday, how could I ever have survived without you?

19

'Makes you realize just how difficult it must have been coming back to England for Crusoe and Friday,' that same fellow sufferer in Stoke Newington continued. 'Did you know that the pair of them waylaid and mugged their author somewhere round here?'

Yes, I did; and I knew that this piece of disorderly behaviour was supposed to have taken place in a great field somewhere between Newington Green and Stoke Newington, perhaps down there along what is now the Albion Road, the route of the 73 Bus, at one o'clock in the small hours of a moonlit morning. And though the dunned writer was carrying a brace of pistols to protect himself, Son Crusoe and Friday, like Sin and Death in *Paradise Lost*, had easily got the better of him.

It was there his creations appeared before their author, armed to the teeth, like the highwaymen and housebreakers with whom their author compares the bootleggers of his book, threatening to bring them to the same punishment—depended from a gibbet—for the then non-existent crime of breaking a copyright (it was the publisher of *Robinson Crusoe* that made the killing, not its author, who sold the work outright and then, to preserve his continuance, set to work on *Moll Flanders, Captain Jack, Roxana*, and the rest).

'No shoot, Master,' says Friday, 'no shoot: me show you how we use Scribblers in my Country.'

'Why, ye airy Fantoms, are you not my Creatures?' asks their creator, in fear of his life, and adds: 'mayn't I make of you what I please?'

Thus, on that far-off moonlit night, did the author of what was once believed to be the work that began the rise of the novel in English use a line of argument, the line that has toy-box puppetry metaphors subordinating characters to authorial whim—while those two airy, but larger than life, phantoms were staking the claim of 'rounded characters' to live an independent life, with the author's hand taken out of one pan or the other on the scales of justice, staking so firm a claim to establish their autonomy once and for all by threatening to turn upon their own creator, and to do that debt-burdened fellow to death.

Crusoe's reply to the writer concedes that he is indeed the plaything of his creator, but that having made such a bad job of producing himself and Man Friday, they will return to him in the forum of his conscience, forever haunting him with the hasty and slap-dash performance that would nevertheless form his primary passport to eternity.

Thus would the writer's inventions, even if the ghostly figures of his brain, claim for themselves independence not only in the form of reconfigured characters in others' fictions, but also as they would come to live through the returning repressed in the subconscious of innumerable others—including the present bearer of that ineradicable nickname.

'Yes, I did,' I eventually managed to put in, having read how *Robinson Crusoe*'s author was the target of censure in 1719, almost as soon as the first two parts of his book had appeared. He was criticized for the way he had treated Man Friday's language learning, describing how Robinson had taught him to speak quite quickly, but that Friday always resented his being portrayed as speaking an inept grammatical muddle, unable to do more than utter such a smattering even at the time of his death in the *Farther Adventures*.

In the second volume poor Friday's fate is sealed when he agrees to go out and parlay with another tribe of restless locals—suggesting that all such tribes spoke the same savage language. This was something that the writer is also accused of—knowing they didn't, but ignoring in his haste to rush out a follow-up to his hit of that April 1719.

Thus wrote one wag, who as well as *Robinson Crusoe*'s first great critic is the *de facto* inventor of the first of the Robinsonades—the first of those works in which these creations take on a life of their own, and start to spawn fresh inventions.

In his satire also rushed out that very year, the fictional characters confront their creator at the start of old Stoke Newington, on Church Street, by the graveyard gate, a little way beyond the interwar classical town hall, for this is exactly where I can't help thinking the encounter took place.

'Have injure me, to make me such Blockhead,' says Friday, 'so much contradiction, as to be able to speak *English tolerably well* in a month or two, and not to speak it better in twelve Years after; to make me go out to be kill'd by the Savages, only to be a Spokesman to them, tho' I did not know, whether they understood one Word of my language; for you must know, Father *D...n*, that almost ev'ry Nation of us *Indians* speak a different Language.'

Having said which, Friday is about to shoot his creator, in what would have been a further act of parricide prompted by the fiction. Yet the satirist is even-handed enough to provide our author with a speech of exculpation by means of identification with his most famous character, and so is also the first to see the form of Crusoe's narrative as a transposition of his author's own vicissitudes into the wanderings of his creations.

'Then know, my dear Child,' says the waylaid writer, 'that you are a greater Favourite with me than you imagine; you are the true Allegorik Image of thy tender Father *D——l*; I drew thee from the consideration of my own Mind; I have been all my Life that Rambling, Inconsistent Creature, which I have made thee.' Yes, you too had looked up *The Life and Strange Surprizing Adventures of Mr. D—— De F——* as soon as you got back, just as you looked up the works of such others bringing Robinson Crusoe and his Friday back home, works like *Images à Crusoé*, *The Notebook of Robinson Crusoe*, *The Crusoe Factor*, and 'Crusoe in England'.

There's no end to them, it seems, for the latest I've come across and added to my collection is called *Robinson* by Jack Robinson, a *nom de plume* if ever there was one, in which he as good as accuses Robinson's and Friday's creator of contributing to the maelstrom of little Englander anxiety and fear into which we have so precipitously descended. He exposes the *vrai arbre*—which, as already mentioned, helped with the development of that Parisian suburb with our name—to some close-up diagnostic deconstruction, though clearly it wasn't only Little Englanders who took up the cult of my nickname-sake. What's more, he takes as his epigraph some lines from 'Robinson in the City' by a contemporary German poet of the *Robinsonaden*, who exclaims: 'Stranded somewhere in the interior, / The suburban roofs are the horizon that he scans. What for?'

'For a memory of health', I couldn't help replying, 'a memory of health—that's what.'

Ah yes, and could you ever forget how you too would be criticized for your ability to teach the English language? It was how I got that first glimpse of my future Friday, and some lines of her tiny hand. I had attempted to improve her speech and writing, had corrected her out loud in company, just as she would teach me to fumble my way with her own native tongue.

'Well,' she'd say, 'now you have done it'—until I encouraged her to produce the contraction, for without that tiny change the expression just doesn't seem to work at all.

I had taught pronunciation by encouraging students to parrot imitations of my native intonation tunes, my pitch contours for different kinds of questions, and had encouraged them by exaggerated example to imitate my dropping notes at the ends of sentences—sentences such as this one ...

'I did, yes, and can't say I know which I blame the most,' I said. 'After all, the poor fellow was in hiding here at Stoke Newington, trying to clear his debts and keep himself out of jail. As you know he was more than once jailed for debt, and would die pursued by creditors.'

'All a lot of gross misrepresentation,' is what my fellow sufferer concluded, and I couldn't help identifying with those words too.

Nor had managing to get back home put an end to my hankering for a horizon to stare off towards, for a beach and shoreline to mooch around nostalgically. So much so that the reflections of our shower curtain, with its greenish-blues and yellow patterns, on a shiny waste bin lid, had suggested to my tired eyes a seafront in bright sunshine, or at least that's what it had been mistaken for one sleepy morning in a late summer soon after returning.

And as if in a waking dream, there appeared within the morning mist my Friday beachcombing once again through bladder wrack, past the broken staithes and boarded up boathouses. Momentarily, we were repaired from the picked-up sea wind blowing in our element, and it was not as if I didn't know she cared, that she had agreed to leave that archipelago on the far side of the world and come back to England, to make what she could of a life washed up here, of what life washed up here for her.

Just so, we were resuming our reiterative conversation, our reassuring each other of our continuing devotion. Again we would be running over the accidental circumstances that had brought us together in our loneliness, rehearsing to each other our own love story, the one that only she and I could know.

And, as I would discover, there is such a difference between ordinary, existential loneliness—that feeling when getting out of the shower, for instance, as if re-enacting your own birth yet again—and the radical kind when, thanks to your profession, or lack of progress in one, you have loneliness thrust upon you.

On clear nights like those, transfigured as they might be, there would be nothing else for it. After my Friday had retired to bed, exhausted, I would stand out on our patio, staring up at the deep blue sky, at all its interstellar spaces. Alone here on this tiny piece of rock, alone in an endless ocean of space, and from my own known desert places, I too would float a message to the stars.

20

Thinking these thoughts, getting lost in their tangles of past reflection and possible conclusion, I had walked on all but unawares until, up ahead now, at the far end of the perspective-diminished terrace-lined Cumberland Road, there came into focus, as large as life, right before me, the old late-nineteenth-century-style gasholder—another sign of this town's *belle époque*.

Eiffel, designer of the famous tower, had also been a builder of gasometers—such as those painted by one of the tiny-dot painters in the outskirts of Paris, built about the same time that this county town was in its greatest period of expansion, the one that would produce these networks of industrial terraces to house the Huntley & Palmers work-force. Up ahead, as I say, loomed the great gasometer on the far side of the Kennet canal, its grey structure picked out in broad daylight by an etched fringe of rust. It was one of the things that helped make the place seem like a possible berth for yet one more sailor home from the sea—because the gasometer would bring back my Northern childhood, bring back one more Robinson at home—that extensive sub-genre of the Crusoe story.

So on I would step, putting one foot in front of the other, along the narrow pavement, way beyond the Sikh temple and the Indian jewellers, the frame of the empty gasholder before me up above chimney level, clouds passing in and out of its geometrical frame. Then, going by the old brick-walled playground of the local Infant and Junior School, I would drop down below the level of the pedestrian bridge, and find myself beneath the gasometer's structure, walking along the riverbank eastward towards the conflux of the Kennet and the Thames—meeting the groups of people out for a stroll, or feeding the waterfowl, especially at weekends, and catching snatches of their conversation.

This in itself had been a curious experience—to come back after so many years away, because the language had naturally evolved in my absence.

'So awkward,' a teenage girl would say, or her friend reply, 'so vexing.'

I would start at the sound of their words, would marvel at the way newfangled usages had been unearthed, phrases found newly repurposed—like old bottles dug up in a back-garden plot.

But the part of the *Robinsonades* that such experiences most seemed to reproduce was the operetta, the operetta with its extended *dramatis personae* needed for the purposes of a musical drama with romantic plot and choruses, an extended cast for which I have my equivalents, even if they only have occasional walk-on parts in the constitutionals I'm compelled for my health, and not only mine, I hope, to be undertaking here.

'We'd rather be homesick,' as the operetta characters sing, 'than sick of home.'

For the truth is that when you have suffered from such failures, as if the diseases were a judgment on you personally, when their consequences have been made all too real to you, then it is as if you have lost confidence in yourself forever. You can never be sure it won't happen again, an end to boom and bust notwithstanding—since the collapse had come on so unexpectedly, even if anyone with any sense might have told you that your system could only stand so much of that mismanagement.

It had brought on the fear that you would not be able to support those nearest and dearest, the *dramatis personae* in my own little domestic operetta, the inspiration I can't stop myself calling Friday, and Crusoe's daughter, no, not an elective affinity, my own flesh and blood, my human necessaries—like the additional characters herded together, as I say, in *Robinson Crusoé: Opéra Comique en Trois Acts et Cinq Tableaux*—only very loosely based on the original fiction.

I had known of the operetta's existence for years, but never come across a copy, until a boxed set of 3 CDs on the mysterious *Opera Rara* label washed up in the charity shop where Friday could now accompany me—no longer needing to send her—during that slow recuperation from what, you'll recall, had laid me low through much of a late winter and spring.

This was how I found out that, unsurprisingly for an operetta, the main interest is in Robinson and his family, Robinson and his girlfriend, Robinson and his desire to find out what lies beyond the far horizon. Needless to say, the love interest in the form of his cousin doesn't want him to depart, but of course he does go anyway—and, the thought crossed my mind, they would have had to invent something, for the original's author, though a married man, gives his hero almost as little interest in the opposite sex as the Bible manages to imply for the Saviour—who does at least have a prostitute to wash his feet. There is that one brief passage mentioning him marrying and moving to Bedford, their producing two sons and a daughter, then his wife suddenly dying—which sends him off on his wanderings again, that one touching passage in the whole of the trilogy.

The librettists had been obliged to create a whole cast of additional characters: Robinson's cousin Edwige, Sir William Crusoe, Lady Deborah Crusoe, Suzanne, their maid, Toby, her sweetheart, Jim Cocks, Will Atkins, a pirate captain who, in this version of the story, had been the cause of their being found upon this island stage together, plus a chorus of sailors, cannibals, and pirates.

Robinson and Vendredi are there, of course, Vendredi, whose mother, they joke, had been frightened by a calendar—but also 'Good Friday', as Suzanne religiously calls him, and kisses him into the bargain, something for which she is criticized in the libretto and defends herself in a further aria.

'Your Bible, your parasol, your parrot, and other souvenirs...', I would hear in a recitative, having bought and taken home that second-hand boxed set one of those afternoons when driven over to Woodley's 1970s precinct to shop for the week's groceries.

The locals, that windy day, were dotted around the open cement-flagged piazza like figures in an architect's drawing—though chubbier than ever imagined inhabiting the sleek designs that spring from those foreheads in city planning practices.

That place had developed, or so it seemed, from remnants of farmsteads and rural constructions into a 1930s suburb approached by a particularly fine example of a setsquare-straight, bungalow-lined avenue. But the shopping precinct itself must have been conjured out of nothing back in the 1970s, and, so unlike the streets of shops built in the Edwardian period and earlier, the constructions on the edges of this bare and oddly tree-less space didn't appear to have inhabited flats and apartments above the shop. They didn't seem to cater for more than a transient population of purchasers and chain-employed retail-industry staff.

So this didn't appear a place where people lived, but only where they shopped and passed the time in cafés and restaurants, or on the one or two benches that had been provided for the older ones to rest their weary legs.

And there was nothing about this development in the modernistic style of urban renewal that could have suggested how not far from here was the aerodrome where the future fighter ace had crashed while attempting that acrobatic feat in his Bristol Bulldog biplane.

This Berkshire town had been commandeered during the Great War as a training area for the fledgling Royal Flying Corps, with a building from what would eventually become, in 1926, part of the University, used to house the trainee pilots. The author of the *Biggles* books—another literary source for my shifting and makeshift identity—had been trained to fly in this very place.

That real-life Biggles had crashed his interwar fighter on 14 December 1931, and consequently had his legs amputated in the Royal Berkshire Hospital just down the road from the house out of which I had emerged on these constitutionals of mine.

His autobiography I had read as a boy, but didn't remember that those crucial events for his subsequent career had happened in the vicinity of where we now lived, I worked, and currently convalesced. Come to think of it, back then when a local library copy of *Reach for the Sky* had been devoured, I had never been 'down South', and never heard the name of the town that had become our family home.

Some ten years later, this same real-life Biggles had bailed out of his stricken Hurricane, leaving his metal legs behind, been taken prisoner, and, in a collaboration strangely reminiscent of that game of football at Christmas 1914, had replacement legs provided for him by air-drop through the intervention of his fellow pilots in the German Luftwaffe.

So here he was, another of my childhood heroes—but one, unlike Crusoe, that would have to be grown out of... or at least, that is, until I found myself needing to get out of my bed of pain and learn to walk again, taking the constitutionals around this place's back streets and alleys, its avenues and squares, its canal bank walks to which I was now drawing near.

21

Yet once more, descending steeply past that playground and school outbuildings to what was once the towpath, now an asphalted promenade, I would then turn right underneath that lovely old, rusty old gasometer and head a little way east towards the Kennet mouth, to where, approaching now, it enters the Thames. There, it being springtime, you might see a swan sitting in reeds on the opposite bank, the male patrolling the waters around her, driving off any other swans that happen to venture near, protecting his life-long mate, and that year's paddling brood.

So then I would find myself stepping on towards Brunel's bridge, past the more recent gasholders on the right, with their faintly gassy odour, and the remnants of terrace houses that once lined the entire canal front, the families feeding the swans, and the other water birds fighting it out for a crust of bread. The sunlight on such days is reflected in a delightful dappling off the waves and onto the salt-encrusted brick curve of the bridge.

Reaching the conflux of the two rivers, I'm then presented with a dilemma about which way to go—downstream towards Sonning lock, its village, and eventually, if you can keep going, the great capital itself, or upstream towards the middle of town. But Sonning is a step too far for these constitutionals of mine. It's a very different prospect, where the lead guitarist who helped invent heavy metal and a Hollywood actor both own mansions. It's also where the present prime minister, as I write, and her husband have their constituency home.

There are signs of local resistance here: literally signs on the wall, a local fight seemingly won some twenty years before, a conflict fought on a long-standing battle ground, when there were plans to put in a link from the London

Road to the IDR, the Inner Distribution Road, that would bypass the main bottle neck of the King's Road heading west.

But the plan had been to take the road in a flyover right across the conflux of the Kennet and the Thames—a point that had already been crossed by two railway bridges, indicating, if there were need, what a strategic point it is. In the light of the threat to the local environment, a protest group started up by, among others, writers and artists living in this socialistic and bohemian enclave, who didn't want a flyover crossing above this historical conflux, had set about overturning the plans.

They had even established a publishing collective or cooperative, one called Two Rivers Press, which was named after this point of intersection—and after a great deal of lobbying and publishing of protest pamphlets they had actually won! Grass roots activism had, for once, succeeded, leaving the traffic flow around Cemetery Junction as bad as it had ever been, and getting worse, but saving this historically compromised—but still surviving—beauty spot.

So the road had not been built, and you have to go all the way down to that same village of Sonning some miles nearer London if you want a road bridge over the Thames other than those in the very middle of the county town's heart— and that one in the prime minister's village is a narrow brick bridge which only allows traffic in one direction at a time, the area also blighted by cars, especially at weekends, their engines running at the lights that manage their flow.

For, sadly, the blight was everywhere to be seen, the last stands of local people wanting to save their environments only seeming to make matters worse as the ever-increasing traffic attempted to funnel through ever-greater bottle necks. And now they want to asphalt over some more of these green spaces by setting up a sticking plaster Park-and-Ride scheme.

The state of the houses and their front gardens could also be put down directly to the tyranny of the internal combustion engine, or our addiction to its power. The problem of the traffic flow had not been solved, and the endless roar of accelerating engines had, of course, blighted whole stretches of the urban scene in this area of town— especially along the once grandly flanked King's Road.

Down there towards Sonning you can still enjoy the great broad fields, the sailing club, and places where people will fly their kites and model planes, where families take their own Sunday constitutionals, across which they often keep going all the way to the village, perhaps to have lunch at the Great House on the Berkshire side, or the French Horn in Oxfordshire, before heading back here again. Yet with my weakened health, I would not be going downstream on these occasions, and would merely gaze a moment from the Horseshoe Bridge towards those further distances, those other responsibilities, roads not taken, at least in this series of divagations.

In just a few months' time, the summer at its height, here too you could be passed by the converted narrow boats, or the great white cruisers like floating flat irons, only to catch them up where they were waiting at the lock, with more memories of the *belle époque*—which I'll get to on this walk of mine.

But that day, as chance would have it, walking along in the direction of Brunel's bridge, thinking to take my usual loop round by way of the town, up from behind me, like a figure sprung from my convalescent imagination, there came a designer and typographer friend and colleague, a young woman from the south of Germany—another exilic wretched stranger, a woman in her early thirties, whose English was quite perfect in its grammar and vocabulary, but remarkably expressionist in its dynamics and pitch, revealing her immediately as not quite a native speaker. And you won't believe it if I tell you—given the aphasia I've already mentioned—how it comes back to me now, if I'm not mistaken, that her name is actually *Nadja*.

Dressed in sports kit, out for a run, she asked me where I was going and what I was doing, practically how it was I lived, and we agreed that we might accompany each other along the same route a while—because she didn't mind dropping down to my walking pace, and was anyway aiming to go and get in some provisions from the Tesco hidden in the undergrowth down this way. Then she would jog back to the room she was renting in Kendrick Road.

Because she was wearing her running kit, I couldn't help noticing the various tattoos she sported—and, she being a typographer, they consisted more of crafted writing than images, for she has inscribed a number of mottos upon herself.

While we were crossing the pedestrian bridge over the canal at Kennet mouth, she pointed out there on the left-hand parapet a piece of oddly spiritual, cursive-script graffiti, the words *To Dare to Dream* painted in large white letters.

'I stole that one,' she told me, and proceeded to reveal a patch of sun-tanned skin on her left shoulder where, indeed, the very same words are inked, in beautifully designed lettering, haiku or aphorism, into her brown epidermis.

'Lovely,' I said. 'Inspiring too.'

'Thank you,' she said, and despite the wildly distracted

speculation that those tattoos would stimulate (for I can dare to dream, can't I?), such distractions being doubtless another symptom of my convalescent state, it turned out there was nothing at all funny about the slogan on her shoulder—for that piece of graffiti had helped her through some serious heartache of her own.

This is what she was recounting as we passed the very end of that spit of land forming the separation between the Kennet and the Thames, a place she liked to call 'Swan Island', even though, as she also said, it wasn't really an island. Yes, she was telling me how this stretch of the Thames Path had been her regular haunt as a long-term relationship had come to its even longer-drawn-out end.

'I've wept buckets down here,' she said. 'This is where I used to come and cry my heart out all those years.'

22

'Her cuom se here to Readingum on Westseaxe'—and there it is, the first mention of this county town, described as a village in Wessex, as it appears in *The Anglo-Saxon Chronicle*. It's a reference to the location of a confusing series of skirmishes and battles against the Danes. So in the year 871 the Saxon army was on the move, and you can read of how two Danish leaders, who are called earls, meet a Saxon leader who is called an alderman—titles that in modern English still suggest a contrast between possessors of great swathes of land and the administrators of moderate-sized settlements.

Only on this occasion, at Englafelda, a place still present on roadmaps of the area as Englefield, Alderman Ethelwulf fought and defeated the two Danish earls, slaying one 'whose name was Sidrac'—which sounds like it's an earlier version of the still-used forename Cedric.

Some four nights later, King Ethelred and Alfred, his brother, marched the main army up in this direction, where it is stated that 'they fought with the enemy' in what sounds like an indecisive encounter. As it says, 'there was much slaughter on either hand'—among the slain being the recent victor at Englefield, that same Alderman Ethelwulf. However, despite their own losses, the Danes are said to have maintained their positions.

The campaigning continued with numerous battles, the Danes being victorious amongst what are now the interminable roundabouts of Basingstoke, and again at a place called Marden.

Then the *Chronicle*, a word preserved in the name of the town's local newspaper, reports that there came 'a vast army in the summer to Reading', which appears to mean a large force of Danes.

I can see them now, encamped in the naturally moated, easily defended area formed by the spit of land that runs westward from the conflux of the Kennet and the Thames, a place of low bushes and scrubland, marshy and dividing into a form of local delta at that time, with, at its highest point, a Tesco supermarket—itself strangely marooned there thanks to the outcome of a later battle, the one I'll briefly chronicle for you now.

As the battle of Englefelda, contemporary Englefield, suggests, this area at the time was another indeterminate, disputed terrain, and an *ad hoc* border between the north and south, a place which does, thanks to its various, and yet still not fully repurposed, post-industrial remnants, have the air of a pocket of northern grittiness sitting pretty in the luscious and prosperous Thames valley. Here it is— homely in its canal banks, its factories (now demolished), its workers' brick terrace houses, and its old gasholder to keep me dreaming—as I say—of my northern roots.

The first battle of Reading took place about eleven centuries before the battle of the Kennet mouth which, as I mentioned, incidentally helped found the Two Rivers Press, and was won by the forces of local protesters against the Tory Berkshire County Council's plan, one also opposed by the Labour Reading Borough Council—and it's perhaps less of a coincidence than you might at first think that the two battles had been fought over almost exactly the same terrain.

Then, with Nadja, the inscribed designer and typographer still at my side, we would reach the supermarket where she bid me farewell to purchase her provisions, this branch of Tesco hidden in the undergrowth, signalled by the shopping trolleys rusting under the surface in these Thames-side shallows.

Though you can't buy Reading Sauce there any more, for the firm that used to make this widely known product—it appears in *Around the World in Eighty Days*—was bought up by Lea and Perrins Worcestershire Sauce, and the brand and taste subsumed into that recipe. Still, you can, if you want, buy Huntley & Palmers biscuits in tins such as the one used to mend the hull of the boat that will take Marlow on his journey—no, not round to Marlow—but up the Congo in search of Mr Kurtz. They're not made in Reading any more, for some conglomerate bought that trade name too.

'But what's this supermarket doing in the undergrowth?' I had asked my typographical friend, for it can't have been put here merely to provision the canal barges, some of them year-round habitations, but the majority seasonal holiday craft that do, especially in the summer months, tie up alongside it all along the towpath.

'What I've been told,' she said, 'and I've got it from the locals, is that the Tesco chain was granted the right to build here on the understanding that there would be a bypass with slip-roads running right past it, and there would be a turn off into the supermarket car park. But then the link road didn't get built, though a new pedestrian bridge was, as you know, the one under the shadow of that old gasometer back there, which does at least allow the Newtown population to trudge back and forth with their bags of shopping.'

This is what she'd picked up, like an urban myth, from odd bits of conversation with the transients—for we are all that in the end—of much greater longevity. Though the supermarket chain had built its outlet here on that understanding, the town had also granted planning permission for a series of modernistic blocks of flats to be built in the flood plain that's called King's Meadow, so that this Tesco does have a neighbourhood for which it can be the corner shop. The majority of its customers, though, despite the pedestrian bridge from Newtown, do have to drive to the set of roundabouts that take you under Brunel's railway embankment, which also functions as part of the town's flood defences, and then come back down the other side past the developments of flats and sports fields, to reach the supermarket's car park.

Here then was another instance—like the relief road that despite its various crossing points still spiritually cuts the town in two, isolating its West Berkshire side from its eastern stretches—of how the town's being at a strategic point of transport and crossing, east to west along the Thames valley, and north–south fording the delta of marshy rivers at this point, how the town's being a transport hub had divided it from itself, oddly twisting and deflecting the paths that its people would take to do their shopping or to visit the other parts of town.

Down here on the path beside the undergrowth in which the supermarket was mostly concealed, this is where in summer you would see the canal barges moored along the tow path, shopping trolleys parked beside them, for now the supermarket was the victualling station for those waterborne migrants on their leisurely holidays, and I would drift down past them too.

So there it remains, tribute to a compromise between the entrepreneurs, developers, town planners, and local people, half-hidden among the riverside undergrowth where once the Danes and Anglo-Saxons battled it out for control of the Thames valley and its hinterlands. Tesco had, nonetheless, managed to secure a sufficient catchment area of

customers not to go under, customers including my friend
the typographer—and, you won't believe it, but I hear her
heart's been mended by a Robinson! There she goes, turning
her head and bidding me adieu, heading off in the direction
of those parking spaces, bins, recycle stations, bollards, and
the ranks of shopping trolleys.

24

Continuing on along this path would inevitably remind me of my favourite film, Jean Vigo's *Atalante*—remotely recognizable in the barges converted to houseboats, some of them like gypsy encampments, moored down the far bank almost to the boatyard, before you get to the open, tree-edged green spaces of King's Meadow—which gained its name after the dissolution of the monasteries. Before that, my informant tells me, it was called Abbey Mead, the mead which is now a space of playing fields whose later name also recalls the fact that the royal court used to escape here from London when the recurrence of the plague would send them seeking more salubrious air.

On the other side of the Thames from here, permanently moored on the Caversham side, there's an old hulk that appears to have been converted into a pirate commune, smoke drifting from its metal chimneys, higgledy-piggledy portholes and windows, with canoes moored alongside it—and a little further along you find another old boat with STOP POLLUTION painted on its hull, and there's a workman to be seen, even on a Sunday, in a green hard hat struggling as he is now with a massive sheet of plastic in the water.

Then moored along the planking jetty beside the entrance to the supermarket's higher ground, there you would always see, even in winter and early spring, a few more barges and narrow boats moored, boats with their charmingly inventive names, such as the *Serendipity* and the *Aimless Drifting*—inspiring in their way, and prompts to what I'm doing now.

They would always be enough to start thoughts of selling up and casting off, thoughts that however un-acted upon are the kinds of yearnings that you can pass on to your offspring without even intending to do so.

Still, it would be part of that aimless drifting, that hopeless yearning, to make a note of all the sorts of converted boats that would moor here—including a sealed orange one with no windows that turned out to be a decommissioned life boat from a tanker or liner, the maximum number of passengers in this tiny pod being fifty—and it seemed the thing was fitted with an automatic launching system so that as soon as it was fully loaded it could be shot down from the listing ship's side into the boiling sea.

One of the symptoms of that illness—and, forgive me, but it has to be confessed to explain some features of my carefully chosen itineraries—was the dreadful embarrassment of forever being caught short. So the supermarket was, in these terms, a key point on my map of such facilities as I would both carry around in my head, and use as the inescapable staging posts on these constitutionals of mine.

It's the kind of thing that could once have given you a bad reputation, and may still do for all I know, this intimate knowledge of where the publicly available toilets are, but only wanted, I promise you, for the most necessitous of reasons. So I was grateful for the history that had put this supermarket hidden amongst scrubland between Brunel's railway embankment and the river Thames. And I too would sometimes come out of the scrubland undergrowth to relieve myself in the Tesco supermarket toilets—no distance, as it were, from the rampart defence built by those ancestors of mine between the Kennet and the Thames to hold off yet one more counterattack from those stubborn West Saxon cohorts—for, as I've already mentioned, I'm from the Danelaw myself.

On the western side of the town, though way off the route of any constitutional I could then manage, you find

Battle Hospital and the Battle electoral ward. Naturally you might wonder if there had been another skirmish between the Saxons and the Danes on that side of town, a skirmish that gave the area its name—and I took the occasion one evening to ask my informant for an explanation of this curious bit of topographical nomenclature.

'No,' he said. 'It comes from land that was granted to an order of monks whose main abbey was on the site of the Battle of Hastings in Kent, a religious foundation built by William after his victory there. The farmland granted to the monks of Battle Abbey took its name from them.'

It was a victory that had, of course, spelt the final end of the Danelaw too, for poor old Harold had managed to march his army way up to York and won the Battle of Stamford Bridge, only then to have to tramp all the way down to the east Kent coast and suffer his famous fate.

What's more, Reading's indirect relations to that fatal end, to the Norman Conquest and the Battle of Hastings, are preserved now in the Town Hall Museum, where a copy of the Bayeux Tapestry, made in the 1880s I understand, is part of their permanent display.

25

Continuing this rambling inclination on round the curve of King's Meadow, past the boat yards on the northern bank, the riverside houses beyond them, and, on the town side, the curving approach to Caversham Lock, I would be as interested as ever in seeing what had become of the Edwardian ladies' outdoor swimming pool.

Now, finally, after much speculation and debate as to its fate, the council had sold the building to a firm of private developers. Half concealed behind a screen of trees, the once open-air construction sported a temporary—or so I would hope—roofing of what looked like corrugated aluminium.

Its old brick walls had been concealed behind another form of temporary covering—one that might have been industrialized wattle and daub. Around by the entrance, on the opposite side from the river, facing towards the green expanse of King's Meadow, whose limit was Brunel's railway embankment, there was, on the most recent day I passed by, a contractor's white van and a portaloo, but locked and only for the workforce.

They had already improved the brickwork, the roof and window frames of its elegant entrance. Yes, the old 1902 Ladies Open Air Bath, left to fall into decay since 1974, was to be turned into a health spa, swimming pool, and restaurant.

When I first set out on my constitutionals in those earliest March days, it was still in need of saving, and there was a local pressure group called the King's Meadow Campaign occupying its derelict outer area—a rear storage space, as it had probably once been.

They had their posters and petitions, an amateur art exhibition, and some stalls of second-hand books at minimal prices. There was news about the latest discussions of the open-air baths issue at town council meetings, and how the cost of saving the building was said to be prohibitive; but the preservation society were raising funds—and they asked me would I donate—to do precisely that, and save it from destruction by neglect.

There too, if the area were open, you would find the volunteers for this seemingly thankless task. Some days they would be selling their homemade cakes, and you would naturally buy one to have with a cup of tea, though mainly out of solidarity for the cause, since a cup of tea in my state of health might bring on another emergency, an urgency, or a constitutional crisis of my own—and in no time at all.

But as I sipped, those members of the preservation society would bring me up to date with their attempts to persuade the council to invest in saving this piece of the town's civic heritage. Only the ladies' pool survived, the gentlemen's having been allowed, un-honoured, to disappear many years before.

'Would you be willing to make a donation to our cause?' they would ask, pointing to the sign which says how much more they needed to raise, and I would drop a few coins in the box, improvising on my theme of what would be required by way of a change of heart, or how, for that, the world would have to change.

'Is it possible to see the pool?' I found myself asking.

'Of course,' one of those volunteers would say, and then show me the way through the back to what survived of this antique amenity.

Going through the padlocked backdoor, I would be standing in the old open-air swimming pool itself. There was no longer any water in it, so you could see the sloping tiled floor of the bath with its markings for depth, and the great big sign that indicated the one farther from where you were then looking around was the SHALLOW END.

There stood the remnants of the changing cubicles along both sides of the pool—some with their doors mysteriously missing, though still recognizably like those in which we used to change, ones with a mushrooming of damp-mould growing across the ceiling, back when 'Crusoe' would frequent the baths with friends from the local schools.

Those cubicles were similarly raw, with fungi thriving on the cubicle roofs, and an awful lot of chlorine in the water so that we wouldn't be passing on our various skin and other infections—or at least that's what I assumed was the explanation for the addition of those eye-stinging chemicals.

There was a very good reason for going swimming then: a group of girls would accompany us some evenings after class. Those romances didn't go anywhere, of course, but, being among the first, they did retain a piercing vividness, wrapped up as they were with the stinging of the chlorine and that treading water to talk with those lovely girls, shivering, as they often were, in the shallow end. It was as if those municipal baths were the council's way of letting us get back into our amniotic fluid, into the pool of life, in our own hometown, as if we would never be so close to each other, any of us ever in our lives again.

Yes, the pool of life, the swimming baths, 'the naked democracy of the swimming pools', as the author of *Animal Farm* would put it—and our visits to them in early teenage, they were like a rite of passage, my tentative attempts to get near to the opposite sex.

For you had to admit that in this respect, at least, you hardly appeared to resemble the figure from whom you had taken your nickname. That Robinson, despite his paragraph of eulogy upon his wife's sudden death in *Farther Adventures*—and how he regrets that unexpected blow from Providence—his creator doesn't allow him to writhe from the anguish of unsatisfied desires all the years of his being stranded on that island in the *Life and Surprizing Adventures*.

No, rather, in the swimming baths back then I had been a satyr-like 'Crusoe' among those sporting teenage nymphs— that nickname being the one that inevitably those girls too would call out as we splashed about in the pool of life.

Then one day, when my health had improved, I didn't turn back at the bridge beyond the Ladies Baths, but went on upstream along what's called the Thames Promenade. I was looking into the crowd, not seeing myself among them, which even by that token, I knew to be a failure, a failure of perspective, or of perspective's failure.

Crusoe's curiously romance-free survival, which had obligated the operetta's librettists to their invention, was so unlike my own lovesick existence. Nothing had changed, it would seem, since that teenage boy had splashed about in the populated swimming pool. Stood there on some uneven pavement, I would be wondering what a voice from years back could possibly have meant, wondering among those Sunday crowds, stood still a moment, as they came swarming round me, stunned and left alone among them.

No, there couldn't be any other explanation for the suddenly vivid cloud cover, the house-brick contrasts, and the haze about those fresh green branches, or that still equivocal spring weather. Like an extenuating angel, what that voice had seemed to say, like a bolt out of the blue, was underscored by the late spring morning, and by the precarious state of my recovering health, for a lifetime's self-misunderstanding had been so shaken by her words, her words that so discombobulated me—for she had declared this Crusoe in his patches of clothing and beard to be *strikingly handsome*. Dumbstruck, I couldn't but carry that thought back home.

Edwardian entertainments, rowing parties and picnics—that was the ghostly presence still haunting those boathouses. But was I trying to exorcise it, or to call that spirit back to life? Because you never can be quite sure if you're trying to establish a habit, or trying to break one, or are for ever doing both at the very same time. So there you would be pondering those words, stood still in the living stream and pool of life, trying to break the habits of a lifetime, and yet to recover yourself—for, put in the language of a religious life, like a bad constitution in the soul, if I'm trying to get my health back, I must of course first lose it.

Beyond the Edwardian lido awaiting its refurbishments and arched windows with their biscuit-brick unevenness surviving down the years, here would come this swarming birdlife, birds in defensive mode hissing at us all near their river on the Thames path's promenade: they had mottled it in droppings where wake-ruffled water is maculate with sky and pleasure boats are surging by on this swan's way, on a warmer spring day, when you might turn to face the current flowing through your Sunday reverie.

No painters or naturalist fiction writers, but oddly reminiscent of them and their works, there would come crowds in their motley holiday array, swarming like the English language—the language stippling us with sun splotches, shadows daubed in the air's ephemera of scolded kids and kisses, the idle drift, or ripples from the cygnets' down, and, pausing, out of breath, I would have to let them flow by like a pebble in that stream.

This atmosphere of a Sunday outing in an impressionist painting was oddly countersigned by the discovery that one of those French painters escaping the Franco-Prussian War and the Paris Commune of 1870–71 may have come this very way on his journey to visit a friend of his—that suave American painter of titled society ladies' silks and satins.

26

Crusoe's author, too, had visited this Thames valley town, and characteristically obsessed with its commercial value and prosperity has this to say of the place in *A Tour through the Whole Island of Great Britain*. His book's existence was one of the selling points for the fund-raising that would allow the film *Robinson in Space* to be made—for the intention was, in some sense, to re-enact his earlier survey of the country. Our author, in his originating example of this now classic genre, the travel book back home, describes the 'next town of note', as 'a very large and wealthy town, handsomely built, the inhabitants rich, and driving a very great trade.'

He then adds that the 'town lies on the River Kennet, but so near the Thames, that the largest barges which they use, may come up to the town bridge, and there they have wharves to load, and unload them.' Unsurprisingly for this author, his main concern is with reporting on the wealth, or potential wealth, of the area: 'Their chief trade is by this water-navigation to and from London, though they have necessarily a great trade with the country, for the consumption of the goods which they bring by their barges from London, and particularly coals, salt, grocery wares, tobacco, oils, and all heavy goods'—in the cumulative listing style that he uses so effectively in his classic fiction.

You also get the sense from his report of how important the waterways were for the prosperity of the Thames valley back then:

They sent from thence to London by these barges, very great quantities of malt, and meal, and these are the two principal articles of their loadings, of which, so large are those barges, that some of them, as I was told, bring a

thousand, or twelve hundred quarters of malt at a time,
which, according to the ordinary computation of tonnage
in the freight of other vessels, is from a hundred, to a
hundred and twenty ton, dead weight.

Our author further adds that they 'also send great quantities
of timber' for 'Berkshire being a very-well wooded county,
and the River Thames a convenient conveyance of the
timber, to London, which is generally bought by the
shipwrights in the river, for the building merchant ships; as
also, the like trade of timber is at Henley, another town on
the Thames, and at Maidenhead ...'

Here, in his tour through the isles of Britain, this writer's
characteristics are plain to see, and the state of trade in the
economy is as important to him as the means for looking
after the poor. For in his account of the town he lists yet
more trades and refers to a Mr Kendrick, whose beneficence
(£7500) is still recorded in the names of a road here, and a
girls' grammar school—the same name, in turn, alluded to
via the surname of the hero's middle-class girlfriend in the
Hollywood comedy *Cemetery Junction*, the comedian who
wrote it being an escapee from the much less salubrious and
unfortunately notorious suburb of Whitley Wood.

Watching the canal barges on that spring day, now no
longer commercial but only pleasure craft, how I loved to
see them rise and fall in the narrow Blake's Lock on the
Kennet or at Caversham Lock on the Thames, being held
off from the sides by their weekend sailors, then slipping
out into the basins, usually lined at this time of year with
queues of moored barges and other vessels waiting to travel
up or else down stream—and they'll be accompanied by the

flat-iron cruisers and the narrow boats, the kids in canoes, and parties on their hired pleasure craft all waiting there for more messing about on the river, as is recorded in another work that evokes the town, the *Three Men in a Boat* by one of those three-part memorable names where the first and last ones are the same, though, forgive me, I'm unfortunately unable to bring it back to mind right now.

Some of the locks around the town still have their lock-keepers' cottages and adjacent gardens carefully tended with marigolds and geraniums in boxes, but Caversham Lock is unmanned, its garden unmaintained. A few of the locks have pedestrian walkways across them, and from one near the middle of town you can pass over into a mysterious backwater—for let me admit that this other side of the river is a near no-go area, an elsewhere that will make me wonder how such private psychological states of restricted territoriality come to be assigned. I've only been amongst its confusion of water meadows with their houses built precariously down in the floodplain on one or two occasions.

The other side of the river, that mysterious area of wide parkland, it's the place where the travelling circuses pitch their tents and the funfairs assemble their rides. Those mysterious spaces of water and flood-threatened habitation must be remnants of the lie of the place's riverine, delta-like land back before its canalization.

Naturally, I don't count among those adventures our passing through here by car. The first time I ever set eyes on this town was when driven over the Chilterns from Watlington, heading for Southampton Water, and, having descended through the avenues of well-heeled Caversham, we found ourselves in that little green Renault surrounded by the concrete-sided cutting of the IDR, the Reading Relief Road, which would deposit those in transit firmly on the route off down into Hampshire.

By contrast with the largely well-heeled suburban roads on the northern escarpment above the Thames, once a separate village in its leafy glory, the town itself, seen from the grey concrete sides of the IDR in that fashion, was all but invisible and could have been anywhere.

Yes, my only time in the vicinity of this place prior to our isolation on those far-off islands had been that drive over the Chilterns and down off Caversham Heights into the town, across the river bridge and onto the IDR—the Inner Distribution Road that I still think spiritually cuts the town in half—and then on out into Hampshire and the Solent coast.

The concrete cutting of the relief road, as it slices through the town, dividing the bohemian East from the variously more nondescript, urban and suburban West, with its poor streets and its more salubrious expanses, had given me a quite false impression of the town's architecture, its polychrome brickwork and leafy avenues, the neo-classical façade of the Royal Berkshire Hospital less than a stone's throw from the Waterhouse brick-gothic pinnacles and lanterns of the Reading School for Boys.

There's such a dramatic and misleading impression as you descend through the affluent leafy suburb of Caversham, once in Oxfordshire, for the old country boundary used to be the Thames, because you're suddenly surrounded by flat grey concrete slab walls, bringing you down as if under the level of the town, and funnelling you out on its other side—which when I was driven through it would have been undergoing the terminal stages of its rapid de-industrialization.

Coming over the brow of Caversham Heights, you would have, in effect, been picturing the view of the town from the artillery positions commanded by Prince—Prince Rupert, it comes back, who had marched down the road from Oxford, during the town's protracted sieges during the English Civil War; though, history appears to record, unlike the Serbian and Montenegrin artillery above Dubrovnik in 1991, they hadn't set about demolishing the town, but rather encamping until they could take possession of it peaceably for the crown.

But here, standing still and catching my breath another moment on the edges of King's Meadow, looking towards the rising land where the Abbey would have been, I couldn't help reflecting on the relation of the town to kings—and on that siege over the winter of 1642–43 when King Charles I's garrison eventually surrendered to the Parliamentary forces of the third Earl of Essex, whose name, lo and behold, was the same as Elisabeth I's ill-fated favourite.

That as good-as-anonymous first encounter with this place is among the reasons why when we came, my Friday and our daughter, eventually and entirely unexpectedly to live here—it really felt as if I'd never seen it before. Quite unknown to me beyond the grey concrete walls of the IDR there were the remnants of an architecturally various, a not overcrowded, and, despite the noted effects of the global financial crisis now, a still relatively prosperous county town. Not a part of that sense would have been lost had I visited, or passed through more consciously, because the place in the meantime would have changed so much— by the construction of further roads and towers—that its differences would have been overwhelming anyway.

The photographs of our old industrial blot in the middle of the delightful Thames valley, most of them in black and white, give a good sense of how transformed it has been, for better and worse—though talking to acquaintances who grew up in Reading before the end of the 1970s was enough to suggest that the changes had been mainly for the better. That period had not only included the cutting through of the IDR but also the construction, just to the south of the town, of a new motorway—placing it squarely in what is now known as the M4 corridor.

Its pre-1980s self, just like its mediaeval one around the edges of the Abbey, has to be picked out in surviving patches between the bulk and dazzle of the financial and commercial office buildings that have, along with the blocks of inner-city living, mostly taken their place.

Surviving drawings and paintings of the Abbey suggest that the greatest damage done to the prestige of the town was not effected by the planning blight of the 1960s and 1970s attempts to apply the white heat of technology in the piecemeal style of America-imitation and cheapskate international modernism, but rather through the dissolution of the monasteries.

The size of Reading Abbey and its nearness to London meant that it was a prime target for the sacking of Catholic England undertaken at his majesty's behest by the other—the first—historical iconoclast with the name of Cromwell. Its last abbot, whose name, I think, will have been Hugh, was one of those martyred for refusing to accept Henry the Eighth as head of his church—during that earlier assertion of our island sovereignty and separation from the powers-that-be in Europe.

Had the Abbey survived and not been pillaged of its stone by locals for their own secular building purposes, its impressive structure would have given the middle of town a focus not unlike that enjoyed by Canterbury, a focus that contemporary financial structures and glassy office blocks such as the Blade and the Oracle fail to provide—though the Gaol, to the east, included in what has now been named the Abbey Quarter, as part of its long overdue refurbishment, is quite the opposite of such a place-defining focus, seeming more an oubliette right at the old borough's heart.

27

It was by way of such reflections on time and its wounding ways that I found myself approaching the new railway station, the most prominent symbol of this transport network of coaching roads, rivers, canalized waterways, railways, and even, once, an airfield where, I will have already mentioned, that famous air accident took place—at Woodley aerodrome—when the future fighter ace lost his legs.

The railway through Reading will always be famous for the case of the man who was killed by a rush of wind. There are plaques to his memory in St Laurence's churchyard and on Platform 7. It is also well known for the permanent mislaying of the manuscript of *Seven Pillars of Wisdom*, the book about the wartime adventures written by that other writer with two different initials and a name like the parish church's here, a loss which required him to rewrite the whole vast manuscript.

But it is I.K. Brunel who is the presiding genius in this part of town, for it was he who created an enormous embankment between the gentler slope of the Forbury Hill and the low flood plain of the Thames—the Hill itself an earthwork and piece of human landscaping probably produced as part of the Civil War defences (core soil samples, I'm reliably told, are being taken now) and not, as assumed, by the Abbey masons to secure their construction from flooding by the surrounding rivers and rivulets. Yet it had evidently been built on secured higher ground between the channel of the Kennet where the Holy Brook flows into it, which was once the Abbey's provisioning wharf, and the more distant Thames, which would have not, back then, been shielded from view by Brunel's railway embankment.

Walking along beside that prodigious navvy-work and up towards the station, seeing all around its part of the town's more recent financial and business district, the latest glass-fronted buildings, the new office floor-areas adding to the un-let office space—while the recent inner-city flats are all well-and-truly filled and over-subscribed. And there they were before me, suddenly expressing themselves, that clutch of dwarf palms, their leaves cracked, brown-edged and drooping, as good as shivering in the breeze, with around them the cream-coloured gravel and upright standing stones. Were they attempting a Japanese stone garden here in front of some company's headquarters? It was as if those symbols of southern or of eastern climes had been accidently deposited here, as mementos of other far-distant journeys. And yet how was such exoticism outside reflective offices, I wondered, supposed to invite me to travel or compensate for resisting that very temptation?

The entire area of the railway station, and there are now three such structures side by side on the site (not including the first that no longer exists), was also created on an artificial mound lifting the town up here to the level of the embankment crossing its river valley floor—and as a result this area is still referred to as Station Hill. Brunel's own is the one that's long gone, with buildings on both sides of a single-track line, while the second, the one that has a later Victorian air, was built in 1867 and is now *The Three Guineas* tavern, with a short clock tower in the middle of its roof, a pub serving its customers located between the later twentieth-century station, and the new structure opened by Her Majesty Queen Elizabeth a year or so before her ninetieth birthday.

It is with this raked bluish structure that the modernizing one from 1985 has been replaced, providing the town with one more platform than it had in 1901, though with more efficient two-way tracks and a much wider covered footbridge, called the 'transfer deck', producing a station that—see for yourself—looks much more like an airport terminal. The appearance of the place might even have been intended as a hint, for, despite much lobbying from the town's chamber of commerce, there are still no concrete plans to build a railway spur through from the town to Heathrow Airport—and, as you can imagine, the pressure group and local business interests think such a development would do wonders for the economic prospects of the town.

Speaking of which, that global air-transport hub, threatening its neighbours with the construction of a new runway is, in effect, our local airport, the nearest to us, apart, that is, from White Waltham or the fading memories of Woodley aerodrome, long since gone—Heathrow being, of course, one of the world's largest, with one of its flight-paths taking intercontinental aircraft over the eastern part of the town and the very roof-slates from which I started on these constitutionals of mine.

But where, at the western end of Station Hill, the terrain now falls away below our latest station, newly inserted steps descend, vertiginously, taking passengers in search of a replacement bus service, along the hidden underpass, white-tiled, a sterile corridor without its complement of poor transients, their fugitive traces, and which takes you under the entire width of this new fifteen-platform station.

It's one of those God-forsaken, signposted, 24-hour omniscient surveillance spaces leading into new non-places beyond the nightly deserted platforms. And it leads out to

stands with disorientating timetables for the migrants here
from Italy or Spain, left to their own devices, here in our
gathering darkness yet once more.

28

'I did not think that Robinson's move to Reading was a good one', the anonymous narrator in the second of that trilogy of films by Patrick What's-His-Name remarks—and I've had the chance to test that too. For, as if to get the opinion into focus, a little while after my near-fatal collapse, with two young fellow-researchers, I paid a visit to the so-called Robinson Institute.

Its putative founder explains that during 'the interval between the completion of *Robinson in Space* and the commencement of *Robinson in Ruins*'—that's to say about a decade—'I sometimes mentioned or alluded to a semi-fictional body, the Robinson Institute, most explicitly in an essay of that name, in which I suggested I might be one of its employees.'

'This Robinson Institute', he continues, noting in passing that there are at least two others of that name, 'was conceived in July 1999 with the aim of continuing the work of the protagonist of *London* and *Robinson in Space*, there being then, it seemed, no possibility to make another film in which he might continue the work himself.' This fiction, if fiction it is, appears to have been another of the cineaste's devices for attracting funding, and is also an instance of what I'm told writers hope to do—namely bring something into existence merely by naming its existing.

But now this latest manifestation of the Robinson Institute, real enough in every sense, turned out to be a curatorial installation set up at the old sugar-baron's Tate Gallery, now called Tate Britain after the development, also in my absence, of an enormous power station, one that did its damnedest to dwarf into insignificance many of the classic early modernist artworks it contained, which was now called Tate Modern.

The filmmaker himself had organized the exhibits and announced in the exhibition's catalogue: 'The Robinson Institute aims to promote political and economic change by developing the transformative potential of images of landscape.' This was the sort of project you would almost like to think you could get behind yourself.

Another irony there, though—I reflected as I climbed the steps towards its classical façade—having an exhibition dedicated to the Caribbean shipwreck victim and hero in an artistic tabernacle whose benefactor had made his fortune in sugar plantations. It is an irony that the cineaste himself was only too aware of, noting, as he does, that 'it is not difficult to see a propensity for colonization in "the commodification of all social goods", as Robinson Crusoe and his contemporaries in the sugar growing business amply demonstrated.' Still, perhaps the irony was a sweet one, in that he had been able to insinuate his Institute into such a symbol of the country's glorious-inglorious history, into very much the sort of environment he and his allies would need, somehow, to repurpose.

The cineaste's Robinson—it had become only too clear—has to be a post-modernized version of the author's original hero, for, when they reach Bristol in *Robinson in Space* they visit the *Llandoger Trow*, a seventeenth-century half-timbered pub in the old part of town. There 'Defoe is supposed to have met Alexander Selkirk, the real Robinson Crusoe' and they explain—as was pointed out to me on one of my own namesake-pursuing-pilgrimages which took in the landscape of Sedgemoor, the Bloody Assizes and this very same building, that a 'Llandoger Trow was a boat which carried coal to Bristol from South Wales.'

Yet, let's face it, such ironies as the Robinson Institute's exhibition in Tate Britain are two-a-penny in so deeply ensanguined a post-imperial country as ours, and that's why for the likes of me, with my name combining both the experience of being enslaved and of slave owning, every act of any kind amounts to being—or should do, like it or not—a form of reparation, a matter of making amends, a settling of accounts with the past in the present so as to be able to look forward to a more equitable future. For it isn't true that you can't change the past, though you won't do it by haplessly or actively forgetting, or effacing, that's for sure. You can change it by altering the way it is remembered and thus changing the future to which it is differently attached from that to which it had been—had, that is, nothing been done to make precisely those amends.

Now when the three of us, those two more junior researchers and me, had met up on the steps outside the Tate and entered, we found the Robinson Institute to be a mixed media themed exhibition of *Robinsoniana* staged in the high-ceilinged main entrance hall to that enormous neoclassical palace of art.

Similarly dwarfed, though by no means on the same scale as at Tate Modern, there beneath the vaulted ceiling of the north Duveen gallery, were the paintings and photographs, video screens and exhibition cases of a carefully curated exploration into the associations of that still mysteriously absent Robinson's name, with books and pictures connecting him to the many byways of the *Robinsonaden* and their themes.

The installation's mission statement was to show—as like as not a homage to the great British painter, who in 1840 had exhibited a slaver abandoning its cargo with a typhoon coming on—the politically transformative power in a reconsideration of landscape, an idea less modishly radical than it sounds if you think that the countryside has been consciously transformed in representation and in fact throughout human history as a way of first establishing, then altering or reinforcing, the lineaments of our sub-jection to the power of wealth or idea.

The Robinson Institute exhibition was divided into seven stages, like chapters in a book, or stations of the cross, or way-posts on a journey, the first introducing us to what it calls 'Robinsonism', the second to 1795, its political and artistic ramifications, then to Newbury and Greenham Common, then the non-human, then agriculture, then the road, and then, finally, the destination—ending up in a disused cement quarry 'which is perhaps where the Robinson Institute is based.'

My two young friends were of distinctly contrasting temperaments and playing their parts in character. The younger was 'not getting it'. He couldn't see either the art or the joke, and was puzzling out loud for my benefit, or so it seemed, in front of every exhibit.

The slightly older woman, a born *bricoleur*, was making a meal of her knowing amusement, her 'getting' the pathos and comedy of Robinson's defeated but indefatigable idealism. What she understood was the use in contemporary art of status mystique, how a little obscure knowledge could get you a very long way.

This is something search engines have now upped the ante on, for since practically everything known awaits the right question being asked of these machines, so the stakes for being exclusively in-the-know are that much higher, and they tend now not merely to involve information or facts, but a hyper-sophisticated, occulted attitude towards the mere knowledge that is so much easier to access than it was. And this is doubtless why in the current dispensations we appear to value 'correctness' more highly than 'accuracy'.

What's more, it helped that her near contemporary was having difficulty in getting the point—the limit point of fellow feeling, as it were—because he thus provided the foil, the setting, or ground upon which her divisions could be orchestrated, the plain style over which her fugue of comic insider-hood would stage the joke of Robinson's far older political idealism at bay. It was one that had once-upon-a-time, and which still might have been, even at this late hour, very much my own.

29

But why had his creator decided to pack his Robinson off, once he had been sacked from his academic job in *London*, to this riverside county town of all places? On a visit to the film-maker in Oxford made before the second of the three had been released, one of the cineaste's loyal supporters describes the 'cans of film and maps from his current project, *Robinson in Exile*, which will make a number of Defoe expeditions around the country', adding that the 'journey will begin in Reading: Beckett, Wilde.'

In the finished film, though, the second in the trilogy, Robinson is discovered, or better, said to be working at a language school in the town, and immediately after he has met his still concerned, though no longer romantically involved, narrator at the station he takes this disembodied voice to see the house where, it is still hard to believe, one of the greatest French Symbolist poets spent some months in the seventh decade of the nineteenth century—where this inveterate walker had done the very same thing, it would seem, worked in a language school, some one hundred and twenty-one years before.

In the final print of *Robinson in Space*, the *Exile* having hit the cutting room floor, the narrator makes no mention of the Paris-based Irish playwright, though; and nor does he reference the world-famous archive of his manuscripts, papers, and books which is now housed, surprisingly enough, in a part of the Museum of English Rural Life. Nor, just as surprisingly, given this Robinson's apparent sexual proclivities, does he allude to the two-year stay here of our most famous temporary resident.

In an interview with his collaborator, a text that appeared in the 1999 book of the film, *Robinson in Space*, the imaginary figure's originator remarks: 'Robinson had been sent to Reading, which is a very interesting place; there have been an unusually large number of television documentary series made about Reading. *The Family* was made in Reading, and the series about the Thames Valley Police. It also has a good art school, which has a respectability that Robinson might try and attach himself to.' Nothing, unfortunately, appears to have come of any attempts he might have made to make contact with this Art School, which was, by that stage, and still is, a department at the University.

'And it's also got that mixture', his interviewer adds, 'you describe as characteristic of present-day England: extreme dilapidation plus conspicuous wealth, a telling combination.'

'It's the fastest-growing region in the country', the cineaste continues. 'Berkshire has the fastest-growing population.'

'But how does wealth coincide with ruin in this theory?' the interviewer asks, and continues: 'In a town like Reading—actually you pick this up throughout the film—you've got dereliction and also this sense of emergent prosperity.'

'I think there's a distinction', he explains, 'between *new space* and *old space*. *New space* is so-called *market-driven* space—somewhere like the Thames Valley Park in Reading: a business park. Microsoft have built a big site at Thames Valley Park; you can see it from the train. There is a lot of *new space*—a lot of distribution estates, a lot of leisure parks.'

The cineaste goes on to expatiate on this theory of new and old space, commenting at length on the condition of the housing stock, and how this is as much a problem for the rich as the poor.

'House maintenance', he states, 'is a consumer's nightmare.' It was something I could have told him a thing or two about, believe you me.

He also notes that this 'isn't the same everywhere in the world—the Japanese economy produces technologically sophisticated artifacts, and one of the artifacts it produces is the industrialized house. House-replacement is quite common in Japan, but here, because we don't produce many artifacts or aren't very good at it or have to get other people to organize it for us, our housing is a mess.'

While reading those exchanges from the book of the film, I couldn't help remembering all the DIY shows there had been on British television in the weeks after we first returned, before the financial crisis of which I've spoken—television shows about plucky people buying up ruins and turning them into gentrified real estate which would produce very nice profits, thank you. Estate agents had also shown us some 'ripe for improvement' places when we had ourselves been looking around the town—and the place we eventually plumped for had needed a year's work doing to it too, for there was no central heating, and my dear Friday and our daughter had grown up in much warmer climes. What's more, the whole place had been the victim of cut-price, do-it-yourself home improvements which had wrecked the wooden floors with turquoise-blue gloss paint, while what would have to become our front room had been the previous owner's studio, which he'd subjected to Francis-Bacon-style creative neglect—though sadly not sufficiently famous to have it removed and reconstructed as a memorial to himself in an art gallery anywhere else but here.

The credit crunch had put paid to those property-ladder series as well—not least because the banks wouldn't loan people the funds to do the DIY, though it wasn't long before the escalation in house prices for this part of the world would again take on inflationary proportions and lenders were advertising their desire to keep us under their sway in the form of invitations to have our property valued free of charge by the local house traders eager to have us on the move once more.

Given, too, the particular stranding we'd experienced before our return to these shores, I couldn't help adding to that celebration of an East Asian capacity for house replacement that, in comparison to our bricks and mortar, the houses out there rarely have central heating, are painfully cold in the two months or so of bitter winter, often appear to be made out of ticky-tacky, and collapse around their inhabitants in any serious earthquake—such as the one whose aftermath we had witnessed in 1995, the very year that *London*, the first of the Robinson trilogy, was being made.

Still, there we were a few days after our visit to the Institute, those two young researchers and me, in the process of gathering some Robinson-style literary associations for the area in which we all three lived and, surprisingly perhaps, discovering that it was distinctly rich in them.

'*Wind in the Willows*, isn't that set around Mapledurham House?'

That's what the elder of them was saying as we set off in our walking boots for a bit of psycho-geography-inspired exploration of Whiteknights Park and environs, with its eighteenth-century satirical associations, its place in the network of Thames valley Catholic big houses, the estate where the poet of Binfield and Twickenham had first met those two sisters who would be in receipt of his letters and be dedicatees for poems.

Nor was it too difficult to picture him trotting on his pony down the hill from Mapledurham House, the original for Toad Hall perhaps, crossing the Thames at Caversham, passing through the little village in whose later developments we now live, nestled between its two main rivers, multiplying into as many as seven streams, I'm told, across its marshy plain, over the old stone bridge on London Street, then along the country lanes up the southern Berkshire downs to Whiteknights House on a slope above its artificial lake produced by damming a rivulet descending to the Thames.

The poet was quite a different outsider from the author of *Robinson Crusoe*, though a victim of the Test Acts too, for while the supposed inventor of the English novel was a Nonconformist, the great satirist was Catholic. That free-born Englishman pursued by debt, in and out of trouble, that pamphleteer and spy, was also pilloried by the Catholic poet in both his epic devoted to the dunces of his time where 'Earless on high, stood unabash'd De Foe', and in his anthology of bad lines and passages called *The Art of Sinking in Poetry* where he writes 'That the true Authors of the *Profound* are to imitate the Examples in their own Way, is not to be question'd, and that divers have by this Means attain'd to a Depth whereunto their own Weight could not have carried them, is evident by sundry Instances. Who sees not that *DeF*—was the Poetical Son of *Withers* ...'

The poet didn't only offer disparagement, though, for like most everyone else he could find it in him to say that the 'first part of *Robinson Crusoe* is very good—Defoe wrote a vast number of things; and none bad, though none excellent, except this', adding that there is 'something good in all that he has written.' Though it wouldn't do for a contemporary bit of jacket-cover 'plea-bargaining', that last phrase of the poet's is one which might be aspired to as a decent epitaph for many a writer.

On we would walk into the grounds of Leighton Park School, where a number of modern poets were educated in Quakerism. On the 23rd of October 1916, a Monday, there was a debate on conscientious objection there. The previous Saturday, the future poet whose name, it comes to me, sounds like the word for some coloured decorations—Bunting—had disappeared on 'an unauthorized trip into Reading'. The school was then on the far side of Whiteknights Park, not then a campus of the future University, in the vicinity of the rural village of Shinfield. The headmaster wrote of this unauthorized outing to the town: 'Glad he is safe' and 'there satisfaction ends', asking himself if for the sixteen-year-old new boy this was a 'juvenile escapade?' During the same term, the future poet, evidently homesick, complained that 'it's something indefinite that is in everything about Leighton & Reading, something poisonous in the atmosphere, something foreign and unfriendly in even the nicest of people'.

The three of us, in would-be-psycho-geographer-fashion, with our walking boots, notebooks and provisions, then continued our tour of the town's educational establishments by walking along beside the Abbey School, which, though no longer situated above the surviving part of the Abbey Gate, I liked to think is a descendent of the only official schooling that the great Georgian novelist 'enjoyed', she being sent with her sister out of her beloved Hampshire to receive it.

On we would go speaking of novelists such as the town's more recently noted practitioners who appears in print under the same name as the Hollywood actress who played the Queen of Egypt—you know, the one who ends up killing herself with the bite from a snake. But then, as we've seen, when it comes to names, everyone's somebody else, if not a very legion of them.

Back across the town we went by way of the University's London Road site, recalling its associations with the first woman professor in the country, and the Great War poet, whom she had encouraged in his study of verse while working as a lay assistant for a vicar in the nearby village of Dunsden. Her inscribed copy of his posthumously published poetry, sent by the poet's mother, is one of the rare objects held at the Museum of English Rural Life.

Next we dropped into *Great Expectations* on London Street for a bit of refreshment and to sip our beer in the pub's library, a perhaps fictional throwback to its hey-day as a popular education establishment, brick-built but with a pillared façade in Bath stone. It had been opened by the author of that novel himself—hence the current name. The great writer was present in the town during 1843 when he gave a reading in this very building, then called the Literary, Scientific and Mechanics' Institute. One of the exceptions that prove the rule, he was not a *Robinson Crusoe* fan, noting with a certain disgust its near complete lack of feeling or sentiment—which he particularly detected in the matter-of-fact account of Man Friday's eventual death in that skirmish with the savages.

The Thames valley was very much a part of the great serial novelist's territory. Around 1858 he had established his mistress, an actress (who later, I believe, married a man named Robinson), just down the A4 in Slough. *The George Inn*, in the middle of town, still advertises itself as the place he would stay when visiting here. The borough's local dignitaries were such admirers of the great writer that they invited him to become their MP, but he had declined the honour. As a consequence they made do with a now not very well known playwright, the man who had introduced the first copyright bill into parliament, a bill supported by the comic poet with the same name as the outlaw of Sherwood Forest in his 'Copyright and Copywrong'. Notwithstanding, the bill had failed.

And it was in the library of that noble hostelry, *Great Expectations*, that the three of us held our conversation about the town, a conversation overlooked by a large framed reproduction of the famous author himself.

'It's a transport hub,' I said, 'and has always been, thanks to its bridges across the two rivers, and the fact that the Kennet, once made into a canal'—about which, by the way, there is another dreamy film—'could connect the Thames valley to the Avon.'

'It's also the crossing point for a north–south line, and for Brunel's GWR,' our younger colleague added, 'and a line with its terminus at Reading that can take you into Waterloo, or down to Gatwick. It's accessible from all points of the compass, and thus an intersection, a cross section of transits, many of them literary, artistic and cultural ...'

'Yes, it's easy to get to, and so convenient for London,' I added.

'And to get away from,' our colleague interjected, with a certain wry twinkle in her eye.

30

There's another fiction writer, honoured in his homeland, the one who founded the Italian Department at the University, who would give the place its due in his bilingual memoir, *La material di Reading*: 'In a broadcast for the Italian Service of the BBC, at the time, I said that Reading was *una bruttina simpatica*, "a bit plain but quite charming": but that was because I wanted to sound like a man of the world; in reality I didn't think she was plain at all.' He was then working in the English Department at the London Road campus, when a future Nobel laureate visited the town, probably in June 1948, and subsequently wrote a little poem called 'La trota nera' ('The Black Trout'), translated for you here:

> Curved on the evening water
> graduates in Economics,
> Doctors of Divinity,
> the trout sniffs at and clears off,
> its carbuncular flash
> is a ringlet of yours undone
> in the bath, a sigh rising
> from your office catacombs.

The future Nobel prize winner sent his poem to the then Head of the Department of English Literature, with a note on his typescript that reads: 'Reading, 1948. Caversham Bridge. No trouts in the river! To Donald Gordon, this private poem of Eugenio.' The poem's being set at the Caversham Bridge makes a good deal of sense, but what are the graduates doing there, and then what is the significance of its appearing and disappearing in relation to the hair in the bath, suggesting that the addressee is a woman, and, for that matter, to the catacomb of her office?

This author's contributions to the Crusoe cult include an essay on his creator, where I first encountered the idea of my nickname-sake as a *homo economicus*. There's also a later poem of his called 'Sulla spiaggia' (On the Beach) in which the poet ponders the unlikely possibility, given the circumstances, of emulating Crusoe's exploit. And then there is, of course, his memory of Offenbach's eponymous operetta, which contributes the concluding detail to his poem entitled with the English word 'Keepsake', a poem he had published almost a decade before his visit to the town.

In that June 1948 the future laureate was visiting England at the behest of the British Council. There he apparently spent time with an Italian woman, known only by the initials G. B. H.—which inappropriately also stand for *grievous bodily harm*—whom he had met in Florence in 1945. In a piece of travel prose called 'Baffo e C' from *Fuori di casa* (which might be translated as 'Playing Away'), the poet returns to the occasion of this experience: 'Or else I follow the reflections of the bridge on the water, at Reading, beside Caversham Bridge, and the solitary, assiduous ruminations of the members of the Angling Club. I've never seen so many fishermen casting their lines into a river notoriously lacking in fish.' So perhaps the graduates of economics and the doctors of divinity are also members of the Reading University Angling Club? This poem too keeps its secret by telling you it's got one.

According to at least one critic, the poet is looking down into a pond on the campus at the University, surrounded by those awarded degrees in economics and divinity, when he sees a black trout come to the surface and then swim away—and the flash of its appearance reminds him of the hair curls of his current muse figure, maybe G. B. H. in her London flat and her perhaps underground travel agent's office—or, as likely, or condensed with it, his Clizia, a nickname too, one which she insistently repudiated, though she was then living in the United States. Then this association of the fish and a loved woman restores him to himself, or at least to his poetic self. It is one in a series of epiphany-like moments that he deemed worth keeping in the 'Flashes and Dedications' section of his third collection, *La bufera ed altro* (The Storm and Others) that eventually appeared in 1957.

This is what I was pondering as my two young friends and I went stalking back through the London Road campus, across its memorial garden for the Great War dead, where now a plaque records the period of study that the War Poet undertook, past the old library where I had bought some second-hand books left over from the period when the campus had been sold to a private Japanese university. It had been obliged to pull out when their bubble burst and the supply of rich businessmen's children dried up. They had sold the campus back to the University for something like a pound, just to be rid of its expense.

I can see him now, the future recipient of the Bounty of Sweden, meeting the future founder of the Italian department on his visit here— thinking it highly unlikely that he wouldn't have—perhaps in his office at London Road, with its weak floorboards in which the girl students' stilettos would get stuck in the cracks—something I would myself witness some years later in the early 1960s, but at the other end of the country, at a harvest festival dance in a dilapidated Victorian church hall.

Pondering 'La trota nera' and on the lookout for more psycho-geographical realities amongst its redbrick walkways, I could neither see a pond nor anything there that might have been a trout. In any case, the poet's note makes it clear that the trout, had there been one, would have been in the Thames, not on the campus—though admitting that there were no trout in the river either. But then that's a poet's imagination for you.

31

Robinson's cineaste is exercised by the inequalities in our shabby-genteel modesty, for, as he says, a 'town like Reading, with some of the fastest growth in the country (Microsoft, US Robotics, Digital, British Gas, Prudential Assurance) offers, albeit to a lesser degree, exactly the same contrasts between corporate wealth and urban deprivation: the UK does not look anything like as wealthy as it really is. The dilapidated appearance of the visible landscape, especially the urban landscape, masks its prosperity.'

The contrast between corporate wealth and individual difficulty was also visible in the stark contrast between the large amount of new-build office space and the rows of haphazardly improved terraces that had grown up around the old factories of the town. And the only thing reducing this contrast was the inflationary spiral in house prices that had made almost all the domestic housing in the town worth more on the market than its value as an experience of human habitation.

The existence of the massive Prudential Assurance buildings, occupying the ground where the Huntley & Palmers biscuit factory had once been, was, though, one of the things that had seemed to tidy up the town—a town which had done a lot to try and rid itself of its 'much-maligned' reputation, with respect, at least to its old industrial plant, and the worst of the housing stock that had sprung up in its shadows.

This meant the demolition of the Huntley & Palmers, the Simonds Brewery, which stood where the Oracle is now, and much of the poorest housing that had been built for their workers—but also of old country houses and neo-classical villas that has fallen into disrepair and were not, at the time, thought worth keeping or subjecting to renovation, repurposing, or gentrification.

The look of the place had changed, though hardly at all amongst the old spaces given over to its housing stock, or, if it had, usually to its detriment, as when institutions would demolish old red-brick sports pavilions to replace them with what looked like spaceships landed in playing fields, with all the temporality of such craft that would return to their home planets once they realized how inhospitable their landing grounds proved to be.

The cineaste's point was simple enough, though, for while the domestic architecture was very little changed in outward appearance, what 'has changed' he adds, 'is the distribution of wealth'—and, as frequently happens, what the vanguard film-makers and cultural commentators are saying in one decade, will become the *cri de cœur* of politicians, often of a contrary stripe, in the following years.

One difficulty with psycho-geographic localism is that it can seem painfully provincial, the locals clinging onto the slightest shred of cultural credibility, trying to revalue their much-maligned town, so much-maligned that a management consultancy firm was approached not that long ago to 'rebrand' the place—and such revaluation, the filmmaker has noted, and the author of *Rubbish Theory* first identified, would often go with the quite literal gentrification of the once working-class housing stock, something that the rapid rise in house prices had also effected whether those needing roofs above their heads were poets of the streets or not.

But I didn't mention any of those complications as the three of us finished our bite to eat in *Great Expectations*. For my companions' conversation had turned back to the mystique of the Robinson filmmaker's work, and the elder and more worldly-wise of those students was finding in her notes and quoting those very same taunting words.

'Robinson's decision to move to Reading', she reported, 'was reinforced by his hasty misreading of Michel de Certeau's *Practice of Everyday Life*: "Reading frees itself from the soil that determines it ..."'

'Oh no, not that pun again!' her younger companion exclaimed, 'and why is it that round here the places are so patently not pronounced the way they're spelled? You know—Slough, Sonning, Reading—none of them sound the way they're written?'

'Well, it did used to be written as *R-e-d-d-i-n-g*,' she said.

'I suppose that local academic, you know the one, the author of *Puns*,' he added, 'was doomed to write his book, seeing as he was living and writing here.'

Then, giving me another of her looks, she picked up her device and, commanding our attention, started to read once more.

'I did not think that Robinson's move to Reading was a good one', she quoted, with another of her arch and twinkling smiles. 'Despite his vision "that other people could become fellows and neighbours", the fact is that, as Lefebvre says, "The space which contains the realized preconditions of another life is the same one as prohibits what those preconditions make possible."'

'Which is as much as to say,' I said, 'that having people live next door is a precondition of being neighbourly— but who you and they are, and the compulsive privacy in which we must co-exist, means you don't, to all intents and purposes, have neighbours at all!'

The pair of them had their eyes firmly on me as I came to the end of my little aphoristic tirade.

'So there you are then—*Robinson in Reality*,' she laughed.

32

Robinson in Reality, indeed, and fair enough, I thought; but my place in reality, as had been so recently underlined by that viral collapse, was as a temporary fact among others—and, strange as it may seem, it was the one advantage you seemed to have over this other Robinson, the advantage that you would, for a time at least, have existed. No, I was not a fiction, I was a person—though given my sickness unto death that too might seem a dangerous and hubristic boast, and one, by the by, not that easy to prove in writings such as these.

But turning those memories of our conversations over in my mind, and pondering these thing in my heart I walked up from the station, leaving behind the statue of Edward the Seventh, around which the taxi rank must take its place, and passing the old Victorian town hall on the left found myself in the commercial heart of the town, in Broad Street, its main thoroughfare.

This is the site of the Skirmish, or, as it's sometimes called, the Second Battle of Reading—or, most evocatively for locals, the Battle of Broad Street. It is, I'm told, the last such military encounter to take place on English soil. The Boyne, after all, is in Ireland, and the French incursions of 1798 took place near Tenby in Wales, and the two Pretenders' marches into English territory, if I'm not mistaken, were not halted by engagements but by decisions of their commanders—and Culloden is, of course, in Scotland.

This so-called battle fought along the main street of the town was also the only actual fighting in the Glorious Revolution of 1688, when a small advance guard of William of Orange's forces drove back three times as many Irish troops defending London for James II, a matter of days before he realized that the game was up and escaped in an eastward direction across the Channel into exile.

The men of the town had fired on the retreating Irish from the upper windows of their half-timbered houses, a few of which do still remain at one end of Broad Street, where there is a clutch, appropriately enough, of estate agents and mortgage advice bureaus—those being the first premises that my Friday and I stepped into when first visiting the town to see what putting a roof above our heads might then require.

Those events, it would appear, the Battle of Broad Street and the collapse of his Irish defenders, were what had helped encourage James to realize that he would not be able to hold onto his throne, that he would be obliged to flee to France with Mary of Modena, his Italian wife, as he did by heading off into Kent and towards the Channel ports.

Then here before me, as if to underline the stability of the ruling dynasties since that far-off skirmish, at the top of the rise appeared the statue of Queen Victoria dated 1887, a step away from the offices of Blandy & Blandy— hit by a stray bomb during the Blitz, and next to them, St Laurence's, one of the Abbey Quarter churches, which, though not deconsecrated, has now largely been repurposed as an event space.

Now here is the row of estate agents' windows, their expanses full of houses, and their own real estate strangely heterogeneous—including a higgledy-piggledy half-timbered frontage that will have been here when those Dutch protestant soldiers drove out the retreating Irish Catholics, failing to keep the merry monarch's brother on the throne.

There are surviving gravestones for some of that skirmish's fatal casualties in the grassy mounds around the parish church of St Giles.

One of my regular destinations on these constitutionals, the Oxfam Bookshop, is still open on the left beyond the bus stops, located in what appears to have been part of a now long-abandoned Lloyds bank building. Among the many treasures I discovered there during the time of these convalescent perambulations is *El Robinson urbano* by an Iberian author whose name escapes me, his book published in Madrid in 1993. It begins with the temptingly suggestive sentence: 'La major literatura de la modernidad la han escrito grandes robinsones urbanos' (The major literature of modernity has been written by great urban Robinsons) and 'Robinson espía: mil ojos abiertos quisiera tener para percibir de un solo golpe todas las cosas que la ciudad le ofrece' (Robinson spy: a thousand open eyes I would need to perceive in a single glance all the things the city offers them). So despite our shortage of shelf-space, I succumbed and took it home.

Thus the *flâneur*, the man of the crowd, his epigone in the *Spleen de Paris*, and the wanderings of its main character through the masterpiece of that Irish Crusoe admirer are associated here, as indeed they should be, with the different wanderings of the shipwrecked sailor and his Friday—and this book written by a Spanish author unknown to me at almost exactly the same moment that the cineaste was preparing to film his slo-mo urban wanderings of a camera named Robinson.

Although those second-hand bookshops would prove a lifeline during that long convalescence, even I could get sick of them, of that withdrawn and compulsively contemplative existence. Nor could I feel myself immune from consumerist criticism just because my desires might look like the spiritualized kind—for when it comes to books, second hand or otherwise, bibliophiles are never done, for there is always more, and yet more.

It was also there that I came across, and immediately bought, another strange tale with a connection to the town, for in 1845 'a dullish bookseller' from round here 'ruined his life by falling in love with a painting'.

It tells the story of a resident of Minster Street and a modest local printer who discovers what he believes is a lost old master portrait of the future Charles I at the auction of lots from the closing down sale of a nearby boy's boarding school.

In the sale catalogue the painting had been listed as 'after Van Dyke', but the local bookseller was inclined to think that it derived from the Prince of Wales' 1623 attempt, made with his friend the Duke of Buckingham, to marry the Infanta of Spain, when the future royal martyr would have spent enough time in the Escorial to have granted a sitting to Spain's great court painter.

The art-lover, whose name seemed another case of *nomen est omen*, for now I recall it was something like 'Snare', is then caught up in a lifelong struggle to prove that the work he bought for £8 was indeed what he says it is. But the result turns out to be a spiral into debt, exacerbated by a series of Scottish court cases, and emigration—in which he takes the picture off to America—and to his solitary death somewhere in those United States.

The picture itself disappears from sight in 1898 and no engravings or photographs of it are said to exist. Nor is the author of this cross between art and local history able to track it down, making the entire story have the air of a magic realist fiction, or that portrait of Mr W. H. by this town's most famous temporary inhabitant in which nothing may have been quite what it seemed, but in which its protagonists are, nevertheless, embroiled in a fatal traffic with aspiration, passion, illusion, and fatality.

Yet in a number of ways the story of this snared character isn't quite the one its author tells—or, better, it keeps going out of focus as she switches to her real love, which is the art of the Spanish old master. Yet her glimpses of the town, and Minster Street, the bookshop and print works that he lost through bankruptcy indirectly resulting from his obsession with the painting, do conjure up what the humiliation of losing everything in this town must have felt like, of the bitterness in having your own brother-in-law take out a lawsuit against you for debt. This author also reports, from her researches in the local papers, the sale of all his property around an abandoned wife and children, organized by Haslams—a family firm that still has an estate agent business in the town.

But it was his legal persecution, and singular obsession, which kept going through my mind as I drifted about in the vicinity of the railway station, wondering what had happened to the supposed portrait of Charles (which the author reveals at the end of her book had not been the painting in Banff after all)—or, for that matter, the lost manuscript of *The Seven Pillars of Wisdom*—wondering if the latter would eventually turn up in some railway lost property office, or the former be found hung on the walls of an unwitting American collector.

And so I too, a Robinson spy, had been wandering along, taking in the spectacle, the pressure of the visual being endlessly deflected and displaced by my convalescent movement across that familiar ground, the signs and signals, the invitations to eat and drink, to take a train or a bus to an airport and be anywhere else but here, for business or pleasure, and not compelled to keep on at these constitutionals, for my own health, yes, and even perhaps for yours as well.

33

Once, on one of these reiterative rambles, I took a further detour west to try and find a much rumoured, and said-to-be unusually evocative, public art project commissioned in the early years of this century. It had been thought up, apparently, as if to make amends for earlier planning decisions of the Council's—which went some way to explaining the existence of two strange excrescences, one standing at a corner of Albert Street, the other in Chatham Place, over on the far side of the Inner Distribution Road, the IDR.

It will have been another of our equivocal English spring days, grey clouds gathered above the western end of Broad Street as I made my way through the flow and counter-flow of shoppers traipsing to and from the Oxford Road area of town, heading on over the wide bridge where, as in a cartoon, the place's land suddenly falls of a cliff, down into the grey ravine of that dual carriageway cutting like an arrow through the heart of its streets.

At that hour an endless stream of cars will have been careering below us in both directions, while up above on the bridge, surrounded by empty air, there was no built environment to protect us from the wind, which was buffeting the shoppers and others—though none of them, as far as I could see, on a detour to take in those twin, separated pieces of contemporary art.

Their creator's involvement in the 'Artists in Reading' scheme around what is called the Chatham Place Development appears to have been made public in November 2004. It was to be part of a regeneration of the entire area, an area which—I'm getting there now—lies just to the west of the IDR, and is manifestly blighted, at least spiritually, by the relief road's cutting it off from the centre of town, isolating it on the western cliff-edge of this man-made motor transport ravine.

The title of the work was to be 'Mirror Mirror', alluding, presumably, to the words of the wicked queen in *Snow White and the Seven Dwarfs*—which, if so, would make it not quite a compliment to the relation that this place's 'much-maligned' status has to its attempted regenerative civic pride, as it is still described on the webpage for The Chatham Place Project.

'My work is about public things,' the artist explains in the project update on the 11th of July 2005, 'about the social, the general, what is common, what is shared. I make art as a focus, a condenser, a complicator of social feeling.'

Whether the Chatham Place Project's timescale had been complicated by the credit crunch may be deduced from the fact that the initial capital for the scheme was raised from the Royal Bank of Scotland, and that before the project could be completed RBS's shareholding in it had to be bought out, which could only take place after repaying the 'senior' debt in full.

The stated aim of the project, part of what is called the town's 2020 vision—another hapless witticism waiting to happen—was to link into Reading's essential core, and extend the high street to the west, thus reducing, it was hoped, the chronic blight that can be felt immediately to that side of the IDR.

The Chatham Place Project appears to have been completed in 2016, some twelve years after these initial announcements; but approaching the area at the far end of the bridge beyond Broad Street that nondescript day in springtime, it didn't appear so much a blighted-space-transforming architectural intervention as another piece of international modernist glassy reflective anonymity parachuted in from the planning mindsets of global capital.

The style of the development, medium-rise car parks, flats, and commercial spaces—including a workout gym—appeared to be contributing next to nothing to the social space at ground level, a space with strategically placed benches straight from the architect's drawings that, as I passed through on this particular day, was all but deserted.

As if to underline the fact, when I was approaching the art—one of two vertical columns made in shiny steel with coloured images imprinted on their transparent panels—there was a clatter beside me and a man emerged from a door to retrieve what turned out to be his mobile phone. It had been left on the ledge of an open window on the first floor to what might have been an office, or flat's living room.

'You won't be doing that again,' said the tart voice of a colleague, or maybe a friend, leaning out of the window above.

The work is, when I reached it—the one on the corner of Albert Street first, then, eventually, after a deal of looking, the other in Chatham Place—a modernistic version of what is called a Morris Column. These pieces of street furniture first made their appearance in 1855 in Berlin, having been invented as a means for displaying advertising for *flâneurs* the previous year by a printer whose name I can't quite bring back to mind—though that is why, my sources all confirm, they are called *Litfaßsäule* in that country, and are to be found everywhere.

Although they are thus associated with Wilhelmine Berlin, they are perhaps more familiar as the street props to various Swinging Sixties films set in Paris—and indeed the name Morris Column comes from a Parisian printer, who gained the concession in 1868 and named them after himself, his surname that is. My source, the obvious one, also informs us that the familiar hoardings company of JC Decaux bought the original firm in 1986, the one that had been set up to build and paste them with posters.

Modelled more on those poster columns in Paris—where I can picture the pop singers and actresses of that era draping themselves for a snapshot to promote their latest products—they are the nearest this town gets to the radical ambience of the Situationists, and the Lettrists before them, or, back before them, the Surrealists too, as well as that great Frankfurt-School stroller through arcades, and all of their different attempts to interpret, challenge and transform by analysis and representation, such visual experiences—the endless spectacle of our ever more visual culture, and its apotheosis in the contemporary city.

Unlike the most familiar ones in photographs and films of Berlin and Paris, with their *Jugendstil*, their Art Nouveau ornamentation, these art columns are made of stainless steel without any ornamentation, but rather a functionalist brutality that may be as much a defence against defacement and vandalism as a statement of style-choice ... Still, they do blend well with the architectural mode of the development itself—though to have built them in a mock-Edwardian style would have made, in that particular built environment, more of a visibly visual statement.

For the 'advertising' content of these columns is distinctly 'heritage' in flavour, their artist having maybe spent time in the Museum of English Rural Life, and also, perhaps, the University's Ephemera Collection, housed in the Department of Typography and Graphic Communication.

This 'advertising content' consisted of a neatly rectangular patchwork collage of theatre bills, concert posters, variety cast lists, alongside public announcements about the punishment of criminals, all with a direct connection to the town, and ranging from the early years of printing — and John Snare's pre-old-master-obsession work as a jobbing artisan may have been among them, for all I knew.

So, unlike the original columns in Paris and Berlin, these don't have a changing repertoire of posted bills and notices—nor do they have the evocative texture of the torn and tattered papier-mâché over-layering of different epochs in their posters. They are intended art, after all, and not the hapless kind that contributes such a great deal to the texture of our lives.

So the posters have been sealed into the already smutted permanence of their stainless steel columns, as if a further reinforcement that in our culture a thing of beauty has to be a joy forever, or it isn't art—and they appear to be saying to the inhabitants of the shiny new Chatham Place apartment blocks and offices that this more homemade and *ad hoc* sort of visual experience is what constitutes their cherishable history.

Naturally, on that wind-swept day, nobody but me was cherishing it, and, while I did, a few stray persons did walk straight past the two columns—wondering what the heck that character standing there could possibly be doing, no doubt.

For what you were doing would have been difficult to explain, there on that *dérive*-like detour—privately assessing the scheme to address the blight caused by the IDR, suspecting that this grand attempt to put the poor town back together had itself been blighted by our very own credit crunch.

For of course I was also gathering, as you will have noticed, material for my constitutionals, discovering by happy chance and serendipity that one of the variety acts being commemorated on the Chatham Place column was the *Robinson Twins Twists and Twirls*—a high-wire tumbling act, like mine.

Nowadays, despite or because of the hegemony of visual culture, there were a great many urban spaces in our towns and cities that proved extremely difficult actually to see. They are much more cluttered than in the days when they would have been crowded with horse-drawn omnibuses, or, earlier, with the footpads and dodgers of the metropolitan crowd.

'Do you suppose,' I thought to myself, 'that the taste for public sculptures of national and local dignitaries, the royals in that Royal Berkshire town, or the other memorials to wars and suchlike, was what started the cluttering of these spaces?' But the historic street-phenomena of our parents and grandparents, their more straightforwardly urban lives, were only limitedly imposed on by the painting up of adverts and signs. The glitter and volume of our advertising and entertainment culture is forever in people's eye-lines. They are distracted from the aesthetic features of the spaces in which they live—and it is almost impossibly difficult to notice a great many of the beauties of our cities, whether from habituation, distraction, or using a mobile phone while walking. One task of art, then, might well be to alleviate such quotidian blindness.

For it was true that the artist's columns—and I could find no indication of who they'd been designed by and what for, no explanatory plaque or signature—were standing alone, isolated from each other so there was no eye-line that could include them both—except a helicopter's—in the stylish emptiness of those fresh architectural spaces. So were they meant to be *memento mori* for street clutter, or ironic instances of it?

Here the artfulness of their creator's art might even be said to have alerted us to the problem of that visibility. It might have created a pair of tombstones commemorating the kinds of visual clutter we used to experience, by contrast with the more streamlined type we're obliged to process now.

But was this art a sticking plaster placed upon the more savage reality of the urban planners? Or was it a nostalgic gesture remembering the detail of a social existence that has more or less vanished? Or, again, was it, as far as the columns' commissioners were concerned, a stylish bit of gestural heritage culture?

'It may complicate,' I thought to myself in that windy street of nondescript daylight, 'but could it clarify?'

And inevitably the Chatham Place columns had been used as appropriate sites for some contemporary fly-poster sticking—and there it was, an advert for a rave.

In the end, when it came to it, this troubled public art project had the air of a noble idea gone awry, one that could contribute little to linking together—except perhaps as an emblematic lack—the cruelly divided eastern and western sides of the town.

Standing there alone on that windy afternoon, I doubted—whatever its commissioners had believed—that its artist had ever thought it could. For it would appear, at least to my wandering attention, that there is little more invisible for us now, in the current scheme of things, than a stranded piece of public sculpture.

34

The terrain back down around the railway station undulates with man-made irregularities, and the real lie of the land as it once was can only be sensed down by the river—for the town, as you know, now spreads out athwart the flood-plain of the Thames, in the stretch of protected land and natural moat formed with its other main river, the Kennet, turned into a canal, which, as we've seen, enters the Thames to the east of the town.

These two main waterways are all that remain of what was a veritable marshland which, my sources tell, was transected by some six or seven muddy streams—and the town may well owe its existence to the simple wooden structures that were assembled to get across this area from the Berkshire downs in the south as far as what is now Caversham Heights and the Chilterns.

Like King's Meadow, now left some way behind, the land here ought naturally to have been flat and gently rising to the southern river cliffs, from which you can at least still look down into Hampshire. But here, coming back from the station, first of all I had to cross under the great embankment that Brunel had ordered to be heaped up by his navvies to carry the Great Western Railway on its route from the bridge at Maidenhead (site of that famous painting with the hare pursued by a train, the one called *Rain, Steam and Speed*, or something in that vicinity) and on towards Swindon, where the railway works were, the embankment naturally protecting his tracks from the incursion of the Thames in winter weather.

Then, as you recall, the railway station itself had to be built on an artificially raised hillock in the middle of the town—and it's down the slope of this mound that I am now walking from its latest station towards the Forbury Gardens.

Surrounded by a Victorian brick wall, this public parkland also rises from the flood plain in an artificial mound heaped up during the Middle Ages as the site of the Abbey, which would be an actively targeted object of that other Cromwell's disestablishment campaign, his dissolution of the monasteries between 1536 and 1541, the Gardens being laid out amid remnants of its ruins.

Perhaps this is what gives a curious air of trespass and sacrilege to stepping through the open lower entrance's wrought-iron gate, with its curiously nested feeling, as if setting off into a sensation novel, one in which I were about to be accosted by a woman dressed in white in need of my protection.

But no, I'm all alone going up the few littered steps that issue in among its trees, shrubs and flowerbeds, the Abbey mound to my left, a ceremonial bandstand beside it, and the great sculpted lion on its plinth right up ahead.

Today the Gardens are filled with people, sitting on the benches, eating their lunches, playing with children round the corporation flowerbeds, that no bees ever visit, planted out with a host of colour in their floral displays.

Here the townspeople not only sit on benches around the empty bandstand, with its plaque commemorating the fiftieth anniversary in June 1994 of the D-Day Landings that contributed most directly to the Liberation of Europe. This bandstand does sometimes still have summer concerts from the local brass ensembles—the musicians blowing fit to burst next to the gardens' central feature, that enormous sculpted lion. Today, I see, parents and toddlers have colonized the band's wooden-planked floor as a place to play in safety.

The Forbury Gardens' central feature is indeed that great imperial beast, the Maiwand Lion, a memorial to the soldiers from the Berkshire regiment killed in the second Afghanistan War of 1879–1880. It was produced by a member of the brewing family who combined this with an artistic inspiration that contributed a number of sculptures to the town, including biscuit Palmer in the park named after him, and the Queen Victoria dated 1887 which stands not far from the town hall in one of the town's commercial streets.

The sculptor is mythically reported not to have studied closely enough the way that lions move their four paws in walking (when in fact he'd been down to London Zoo with his sketchbook), because, it is said, this one has the front pair back to front, so that such a grand symbol of our imperial power, even at a moment of its more precarious weakness, would, had it tried to walk like that, fallen over in the dust. In another frequently repeated local myth, it is reported that on this design error being pointed out to him the sculptor promptly committed suicide. But these are two more urban myths.

His Lion was unveiled in 1886, and it further instances the way our public parks often have these reminders of a violently aggressive history, as well as, for that matter, the resilience of those who have opposed us—for the Battle of Maiwand, fought on the 27th of July 1880, was a disaster, with 967 killed and 177 wounded, though the British and Indian forces were able to beat an effective retreat to Kandahar over that and the following day:

> THIS MONUMENT RECORDS THE NAMES
> AND COMMEMORATES THE VALOUR AND
> DEVOTION OF THE OFFICERS AND MEN

OF THE LXVI BERKSHIRE REGIMENT WHO
GAVE THEIR LIVES FOR THEIR COUNTRY
AT GIRISHK MAIWAND AND KANDAHAR
MDCCCLXXIX–MDCCCLXXX

The lion's pediment has some rousing words cited from the British commanding officer at the battle, in which he notes the heroism of the ordinary privates caught up in this defeat. 'That Day' from *Barrack-Room Ballads* versifies upon this humiliating retreat—and there are other poems celebrating what, for them, is a victory in Pashtun and Afghan folklore. More recently, one of the town's local writers has published a poem linking the lion to this country's more recent attempts at nation-building in that country, and their similarly equivocal, compromised outcomes.

The Maiwand Lion also deserves a mention at the opening of *Robinson in Space* where, as described, it 'commemorates the battle after which Dr. John Watson was invalided *out of* the army and *into* his acquaintance with Sherlock Holmes.' Sadly, the illustrious detective and his chronicler don't ever seem to have ventured for their cases to the town where this grandiose memorial to his war wound might have occasioned a memory or two concerning what he suffered in that painful retreat.

The book of the film *Robinson in Space*, from which that quotation has been copied out, was published in 1999, just two or three years before it would be necessary to disambiguate those nineteenth-century imperial adventures in Afghanistan from the one that afflicted the first dozen years and more of the present century. But it had been those earlier military setbacks—and the other poem that the same author wrote about a British soldier saving his last bullet so as not to fall into the tribesmen's hands—that as good as reminded me of when these latest allies embarked on their most recent South-Asian adventure.

Its outcome, if the Russian experience of the 1980s weren't enough to foresee, could have been predicted by reading up on our imperial exploits 'up the Khyber', an idiom that still survives to mean *in awful trouble and as good as lost.*

No one, I imagine, would these days sculpt and cast in black iron such an enormously aggressive-looking imperial animal to commemorate not only a defeat, but our interventions, our attempts at nation-building, in which the funds were squandered, private firms improved their balance sheets, and the local people, oppressed by the radicals among their own, were compelled to endure yet more misery and strife.

Every November there will be a large red poppy wreath leaning against this great lion's grey granite plinth, its sides covered with the names of the as-good-as-forgotten dead, as-good-as-forgotten in that no one appears to remember now what their dying might have actually meant.

As I approached it today, there was a little South-Asian girl unsteadily running past the poppy wreath at the foot of a plaque naming the 'fallen', and on around the base of the plinth, the cast iron lion baring its long incisors at our nondescript, provincial air.

Beyond the lion, to one side of the path leading up to the surviving Abbey gateway, you might then pass by the refreshment kiosk, usually closed, and behind it, the public toilets, again so useful on my constitutionals from the attack on my system which had been so debilitating. Yet, unfortunately and sometimes agonizingly, those toilets would often be closed and locked as well.

Yes, the usually locked toilets were only too relevant to my convalescence, for, as mentioned when we were passing the riverside Tesco, one of the most difficult after-effects of that illness was the tendency to be caught painfully short, as a consequence requiring the further development of my private map showing the town's most out-of-the-way public conveniences—plotting the staging posts on the circular constitutionals with those very necessities ever in mind.

It's the sort of knowledge, once again, that could have given you a bad name, if you were caught haunting them as vicars used to be, but, in my defence, I wouldn't say I haunted them so much as usually found them locked, cursed under my breath, and set out as fast as possible (walking with my legs crossed, were that possible) towards the nearest available one—which would be among the shops and precincts of the town's commercial streets. You see my toilet haunting was not a sign of a sexual predicament, but the long-lasting aftermath of that stubbornly residual sickness.

Yet this too is how getting my health back came to be associated with the world I was walking through, with the public conveniences available to anyone who happened to be caught short, and the kind of society that would provide such amenities, but then not be able to protect them from vandals or provide sufficient funding or staff to allow their being kept open.

Crossing the road in the direction of the County Court building, I come to the dilapidated Abbey Gateway, then slated for heritage refurbishment, now all but complete, further evidence of the disestablishment of the monasteries, the town's being targeted especially because of the vast power it had, and so near to London too.

My namesake's filmmaker also notes in the book version of *Robinson in Space* that 'Jane Austen and her sister, Cassandra, were at the Abbey School during 1785-7. It occupied rooms above the surviving gateway of the ruined abbey and was run by Mrs. Latournelle, a French émigrée.' All the more reason, then, why the town council should get on with restoring this sadly dilapidated bit of local heritage, which sports, as I noticed walking under it again, no, not a blue plaque, but signs warning us not to climb on the stonework.

Many are the times I've speculated, as you know, passing this way to and from the railway station, for instance, that ours would be a less maligned town if its great mediaeval abbey—where the musical setting for the earliest English round of six-part polyphony, 'Summer is a cumin in', was found—were preserved in something resembling its pristine state. For the Abbey had been a centre of power, and as if to underline it, I'm told that long before Reading Gaol was constructed to the north-east of the Abbey site, there had been a prison for local villains within the confines of this religious establishment's walls.

Still, now, there is heritage lottery money and a matching grant from the council to restore the entire area and make the Abbey ruins safe for people to stroll among. They want to turn the area into the sort of place English Heritage is entrusted with preserving—and work has started on it as I write, though still there are the broken panes in the windows of the gate house, and space under the archway clad in scaffolding and boards to protect passers-through from the risk of falling masonry. And there is the sign warning them to BEWARE OF FALLING OBJECTS—a strangely portentous and yet vague notice, as if they really weren't quite sure what might tumble from the sky, perhaps the sky itself, as in that children's fable about a frightened chicken.

35

The New County Gaol is itself a victim of the town's mid-twentieth-century planning blight. When first constructed, the prison—always to be associated with the name of the author of that novel about a man whose painting ages and he doesn't (until that too ends badly)—had looked rather like King's College, Cambridge, with a crenellated gothic-revival perimeter wall and two mansion-like houses for its governor and chaplain. Bradshaw's Railway Guide, the 1866 edition, describes the Gaol as a 'model prison'. In a print that shows the edifice soon after its completion in 1844 the land looks as though it runs flat down to the Thames, though the railway embankment had been constructed by 1840; and there are the remains of the outer wall of the Abbey, for the prison had been built on the north-eastern end of the old religious centre's mound.

Those original crenellated walls were demolished and replaced in the 1970s so as to widen the road around its perimeter and improve the flow of traffic from the bridges across the Thames and Kennet, past the vast Huntley & Palmers biscuit factory, large enough to have its own fire-boats in case of incendiary incidents, also no longer there now, and down to the King's and Queen's Roads, leading east towards Cemetery Junction and the A4 to Maidenhead and London. I've also heard it said that the old entrance gate, like a castle doorway, was not wide enough for modern deliveries.

In their place, high, blank brick walls had been constructed, topped with lights shining inward onto what remained of the old exercise yard where that soldier and wife-murderer, the dedicatee of 'The Ballad', would walk in imposed silence. At about the same time, perhaps in that planning-blight decade, the prison had also been enlarged with a modern wing in nondescript international modernist style, like a fortified secondary-modern school building. I could see the top row of its windows from the mound in the Forbury Gardens.

Reading Gaol of literary fame is, of course, the place where you-know-who served his time from 1895 to 1897, where he wrote his letter to the boyfriend, *De Profundis*, on paper provided by the prison authorities, and which furnished him with the material, of another kind, for his last and most substantial poem. It is the work that contains those most famously questionable sentiments, ones I happen to think are simply not true, that each man kills the thing he loves, and that the brave man does it with a sword—a thrust doubtless aimed at his beloved and disappointing aristocratic friend.

'*You* should know', is what the author is said to have replied when asked by that very person what he had meant by the all-too-famous line.

It is also rumoured locally that the author of *An Ideal Husband* and *The Importance of Being Ernest*, both on in the West End in 1895, was transferred from Wandsworth to the Gaol here through the influence of Palmer; and it is likewise reported that he was allowed extra rations of biscuits—but these are only the kinds of local myth I've neither been able to confirm nor confute.

Certainly the playwright had met the biscuit king's family before his downfall, perhaps encountering them on his trips up along the Thames, trips designed to combine time to write with pleasure in the company of his aristocrat friend. There is then a strange dramatic irony and poetic justice, of a sort, in his being transferred to the prison here.

After all, in 1895 those two plays of his currently enjoying such a success in the West End have characters whose names are comically derived, sometimes with charming incongruity, from places in the hinterland of London, the Thames valley and environs. It's an area that had boomed with the advent of local railways, one aptly evoked in what's-his-name's *Three Men in a Boat*, published just six years before.

Lord Caversham is entitled after what was then a separate village on the northern bank of the Thames, now absorbed into the main part of the town on its opposite bank. Lord Goring derives his seat from another little village in the Thames Valley. Lady Chiltern would seem to be the dowager whose estates cover the entire area of delightful villages and chalk down woodland, while Lady Bracknell's pretentions, her *arrivisme*, are simultaneously underlined and punctured by the associations—worse now than a century ago, perhaps—for Bracknell has become a dormitory and commuter town, as well as providing that famous pantomime dame of a character with her married name.

Most likely, back in his gilded age, the important thing was for the playwright to make sure the characters' names didn't happen to coincide with any actual titles, created or inherited, so that he would not be subject to libel suits, something which he needed to defend *The Ballad of Reading Gaol* against in correspondence before its release by the publisher in 1897.

There has to be a tacit comedy in the author's entitling of such grandly class-conscious personages with the names of places that have precarious claims to grandeur themselves. Yet it is as if, by transferring him to this town, those gentle jokes upon the British aristocracy and ruling class are turned upon the joker.

Could this have been the reason, as if life were imitating art here too, why of all the prisons that he might have been sent to, it was decided that Wilde should be subject to two years of health-destroying hard labour here? It seems too much of a coincidence to have been an accident, and might have added to the sense in which the establishment was making a point about the risks that this writer had been taking, not in his sexual life, though there too of course, but rather in his faintly contemptuous treatment of English— and Anglo-Irish—aristocratic pride and self-esteem.

The town would see numerous waves of Irish immigrants right up into the 1950s, and it has a further connection with that country and its history—this playwright being only the most famous of the many Irish people confined here. For HM Prison Reading was also one of the places where captured Easter 1916 insurgents and internees were held. Even the founder of Sinn Fein had passed some six months of internment here, as did a number of other Irish journalists and poets. There are in fact quite a few ballads about this round of Irish imprisonments among the compositions they produced in Reading Gaol.

Nowadays, of course, the Gaol's most famous occupant and ballad writer is something the place as good as celebrates—and I have seen the town hall packed to the ceiling with people turned out on a chilly winter's night to witness that actor and personality, the one who personified Wilde in a film, conjure up the writer's witticisms, his place in the history of gay liberation, and recite some of his longest poem's most famous verses.

But walking down from the gateway now, the most noticeable part of the Abbey's remains, I might decide to cut through behind the fragments of stone wall, until recently too dangerous to be open to the public and in the process of being refurbished in the Abbey Quarter project, then down to a part of the Kennet canal, which is called—yes, I do remember—the Oscar Wilde Walk.

There you'll find its horridly kitsch gateway modelled on one of his most famous photographs—from his earlier youthfully costume-drama fashion period—picked out in the swirls of a green-painted iron fence. The council even went so far as to commission a poem by a contemporary Irish poet, which has been cast into the memorial fencing placed alongside the path. Walking there now, underneath the row of trees, I'm trying to make out what that poet's lines say, and what it might mean for them to be there—cut in metal on the memorial gate.

Pausing to read the explanation of how such well-turned verses got there, I found this: 'Commissioned by Reading Council, these poems were written to mark the centenary of Oscar Wilde's death on November 30, 1900. Three years earlier, he had been released from Reading Goal. The text of "The Gate" is incorporated into the new wrought-iron Oscar Wilde gates on a path near the former prison.' It's usually deserted—the Oscar Wilde Walk—but especially evocative in the autumnal leaf-fall, or in those springtime days when the buds would be bursting out upon my constitutionals.

The Oscar Wilde Walk does seem an appropriately quiet place to contemplate man's inhumanity to man, with the high walls and now deserted silence of the recently closed HM Prison on my left and the by-canal to my right, ahead the endless stream of traffic crossing on its way through the town, while over the peaceful stream, the little terrace houses, now gentrified and costly, stand along the waterside.

The town, much to its surprise, no doubt, has become the hapless victim of this playwright's celebrity. Transformed from imprisoned outcast to martyr and saint of sexual liberation and gay pride, he had taken over from Reading sauce, or Simonds beers, or Huntley & Palmers biscuits, as the only 'brand' that could possibly bring the world's attention to this modest-sized country town caught between the commercial shadow of London and the academic one of Oxford.

Yet just as the vilification of the playwright had been an injustice, so the idea of him as a great martyr to the ideal of same-sex love required a massaging of truth as well. After all, keeping up the merest pretence of a heterosexual family life while purchasing the services of working-class rent boys for the pleasure of himself and his aristocratic spendthrift hardly looks like an ideal at a time when it is possible for people of the same sex who love each other to be united in holy matrimony, and have the same rights as their other-inclined citizens.

So the town which happened to house him for those two years of incarceration had remained a place to be neglected and abused, only now the great and good would come and perform his *De Profundis* as part of a celebration of the Gaol—though it was only circumstantially this town that had inspired the letter. Nevertheless, if the prison governor hadn't granted its author that paper to write it on, this work of his detention could not have been produced, as perhaps it wouldn't too had he not been transferred from Wandsworth, where the regime was much harsher and the great writer's literal survival would have been in even greater doubt.

36

Before the closure of Reading Gaol, before they finally called time on time, an opportunity arose to go inside the prison itself and be introduced to some of its inmates. Those visits were connected with my long-term employment as a teacher of languages, and that profession did, as it would for the cineaste's Robinson, allow at least one surprising discovery.

This is why I can give you an idea of what the Gaol used to be like before it was closed, and tell how I went there and met the young people living inside in that lonely crowd. None of them, though, gave the impression that they thought of themselves as innocent or not to blame, quite the contrary, if anything, serving their time inside that famous prison with the sounds of the Great Western Railway in the distance, the London-bound trains going by.

The first problem, though, not unsurprisingly, was actually how to get in, for arriving at the guarded door it was made manifestly evident that the one thing I had to remember to bring had been left at home. There I was without any form of identity that had a photograph on it, nothing to prove to those efficient prison guards who this person asking to be allowed in to their jail for the purposes of verbal education might happen to be. But, thank goodness, there was no need to worry, for the dedicated lady who had invited my contribution to a reading group happened to have with her one of my books, and there, on the back, was sufficient indication for the prison guards of who this might be, and why he was trying to talk his way into their establishment.

Of course, in what follows, to protect the guilty, I've rearranged their faces and omitted to mention their names, could they even be called back to mind—only ever introduced to them by their given ones, and not vouchsafed information about why they happened to be inside. Nor would it have been appropriate or tactful to ask.

The request had come to talk to the inmates about the experience of isolation on our far-off island shore, experience that, without any prompting, they quickly began to associate with their own. Then, talking about what it had been like to come back home after all those years, further inspired them to volunteer that it resembled the feelings and difficulties they would have on being released.

My host for the session was a volunteer who had formed this *ad hoc* reading group among those prisoners—prisoners who by that stage in the Gaol's history were all aged between eighteen and twenty-one. This HM Prison had become a last chance for juvenile offenders, a last chance in that if they didn't reform this time, they would be transferred to the much harsher regimes of adult penitentiaries.

So it was I discovered that, before the closure of its famous Gaol, the town had what amounted to an alternative university, or, better, a training college, one that specialized in practical trades such as bricklaying, house decorating, woodwork, metalwork, and cookery, though visual art as well, and writing—which was where I came in. There was also a fully equipped professional kitchen, including sharp knives too, for each man kills the thing he loves, or so the poem says, and the man who had to swing had cut the throat of his beloved with a knife. But there in the prison kitchen each of those dangerous utensils had its unique place hanging on the wall, the place outlined in exactly the shape of that implement and blade, in white paint, showing the size and form of the knife—like the lines painted around the absent bodies at a crime scene.

The idea of this arrangement was that you could see at a glance if any of the implements had not been returned to their places—having, I imagined, been filched by one of those inmates for, doubtless, nefarious purposes. And my informant then regaled me with a few incidents of grievous bodily harm among that youthful prison population.

But before meeting some of them, I was taken on a tour of the solidly built Victorian institution, still, at least in its internal appearance, much as it had been in 1895. My guide led the way into C wing and took me to look inside C. 33's cell—*The Ballad of Reading Gaol* being attributed in its first edition to the person who had occupied that particular space of confinement—which, it transpired, though they had renumbered the cells in later years so his no longer bears that cypher, both had a little plaque on the wall by the reinforced door, and could not be seen because its current inhabitant was, at that very moment, in residence and locked inside.

'Amazing,' I exclaimed to my guide, 'to be incarcerated in the penitential equivalent of blue-plaque accommodation!'

Walking along the banks of the Kennet canal, as on so many of these constitutionals, I could see the prison's more recent bare walls, its central Victorian crenellated tower, the barred windows on the old wings, and more modern additions—secondary-modern classroom block—from where its inmates would hear the trains arrive and leave through our latest station.

Just like the *act gratuit* murderer in the song by that Country & Western artist, you know, the man in the long black coat, who sang in a gravelly voice about shooting a man Reno 'just to watch him die'—the inmates of our Gaol were able to hear the Great Western trains going in and out of Brunel's station, heading all the way down to the Cornish Riviera. Time, though, at least for one of them, wasn't dragging on—like it does in the chorus to what's his name's 'Folsom Prison Blues'.

'Inside, time goes quickly,' so one of those young offenders said, at a quiet point in the guided reading circle. And I asked him, surprised by his remark, how that could possibly be.

'It's the routine of being in here,' he replied. 'Here there's always something to do, and people to help you to do it; but outside you just don't know what to do with yourself from one day to the next. That's why it's so hard to keep out of trouble ...'

Things will have changed a lot since 'c.33' occupied his cell, and, as if to underline it, some large-headed sunflowers had been planted beside their exercise yard, the very yard where he had walked, kept incommunicado, on his daily round; but the idea of routine making time go quickly, that was what most arrested me.

And how it all comes back as I wander on beside the newer walls enclosing the now-closed Gaol ... Like an oubliette in the heart of the town, as I say, like a hidden sore in the midst of life, there stood the famous, the notorious Gaol—overlooked as it always has been by the outside population, all along the banks of the Kennet canal.

Yes, walking past the prison now, all along the banks of the Kennet canal—in an echo of that other prison song, and an Irish one at that, it came stealing over me once again, this feeling of the place being a void or gap at the dark heart of town, increased if anything by its redundancy and emptiness. For I couldn't help wondering what would become of it now, surrounded as it is by retail outlets and new high-rise office blocks in glass and steel. Would it be sold off to make way for more flats, or a boutique hotel in which you could pay top dollar to overnight in the exact same space where the author of *De Profundis* endured his two years of hard labour? Or would it, as poetic justice and historical irony might require, be converted into a prison-museum, C.33's heritage-industry cell preserved as a walk in, and out, attraction, with, attached to it, on the footprint of the imagined-as-pulled-down modern block, a new theatre, the Oscar Wilde Memorial Playhouse? And would they also demolish the 1970s brutally blank walls and open up the grounds where the hanged prisoners, including the one in the poem, were buried in quicklime in unmarked graves?

37

Such speculations about what would happen to the Gaol, owned not by the council but by HM Government, are common enough these days around town. Talking one time to another local artist, I listened as he outlined for me the lack of a creative centre in the town, an alternative, or supplement to the notion of renewing the Abbey quarter as a historical heritage site.

What he thought they needed was an international art venue, for installations and happenings, all the latest things in visual culture, with celebrities parachuted in from the global art scene, putting this little provincial place, caught in the financial and intellectual frost shadows of London and Oxford, firmly on the map. But no, no he didn't want a permanent collection where the local people could look at art, art such as the town already possessed (though lacking the space to have it on permanent display), but rather a performance and installations space: a place for the leading edge of art to come and show off its wares.

And no, he wasn't interested in what might happen to HM Prison here, didn't see its Victorian cell blocks as suitable for the exposure of contemporary art—for the only thing he felt about the local arts scene was that those Sunday painters needed to be shaken out of their complacency, which could only be done by bringing the very latest international artists to exhibit.

'Like another Biennale along our waterways,' I said, pronouncing the third word like a language-corrupting native English speaker, just to bring out the almost ambiguity.

'If you like,' he came back, not thinking it a forgivable pun.

'Yes,' I continued unabashed, 'it would be good if something arose out of the present situation, the local painter's guild, giving them somewhere to exhibit their works and reach a market for art.'

But then again he said: 'No, nothing good can come of that; they just need to see what's really going on, and to see how incorrigibly provincial they are, and why they simply need, if you ask me, to give up doing what they're doing.'

To which I replied: 'But then the local and the inter-national are like ships in the night'—and it was clear we would have to agree to differ on how the Gaol and town might be re-integrated in some future creative repurposing.

But now, what my interlocutor had envisaged, or foreseen, it seemed had come to pass, for the international art world would be coming to the town, beginning with an exhibition in the now-empty Gaol—so that celebrity art and artists could indeed be visited upon the local people.

There would be complete readings of *De Profundis* by famous actors and even a now silvery-haired doyenne of the New York punk rock scene. Though at least one of the celebrity readers was locked in C. 33's cell for the time it took, and could be peered at through the spy-hole while performing, his recitation broadcast into the old prison chapel—most of the readings would take place in the chapel itself, on a lightly raised stage with a white backdrop and the old door to you-know-who's cell placed upright behind the seat. From this minimally symbolic staging would issue the marathon non-stop recitals, for the text would be performed out loud without a break. It would take between four and five hours, and happen repeatedly— the whole thing being filmed, like a piece of performance art... and photography by the public would not be allowed.

The atmosphere had something of a religious rite about it, and the congregation would quietly arrive and leave throughout the performances, as in an Italian basilica, the performances, that is, of its less well-known, non-celebrity readers.

Within the old Victorian Gaol—the only part of those HMP (Her Majesty's Prison) structures that was used for the event, a curatorial combination called *Inside: Artists and Writers in Reading Prison*, which ran from the 4th of September to the 30th of October 2016—there were 'Letters of Separation' written by creative people who had a reason, whether sexual or political or both, to share experiences with C.33, artists such as that bearded Chinese dissident (sorry, can't bring his repeat-syllable name to mind), who had been interned without trial for eighty-one days. These could be read and listened to in individual cells, some of which were also decorated with artworks, prints of the night sky, pictures of water, said to be the Thames, and footnoted with many quotations or pieces of information in tiny text. The price of entry was £9 for adults—and one wag noted as I bought my ticket that the way to get in used to be to steal, but now you had to pay ...

Taking the show in on the first day as a minor detour from one of my recent constitutionals, revisiting the sites of those more painful early ones, I saw that they had stencilled on the brickwork about the entrance the word INSIDE, with the subtitle of the exhibitions and events in smaller letters, and at the corner of the modern walls where they turn towards the Homebase outlet on the other side of the road, had been stencilled: WITH FREEDOM, BOOKS, FLOWERS AND THE MOON, WHO COULD NOT BE HAPPY? The words are attributed to the town's most famous inmate, but the quotation doesn't mention relations with other people and has two words—the abstract noun and the adjective—that are both notoriously hard to define.

The guards in the art-prison were young volunteers wearing grey T-shirts with other examples of his wit and wisdom stencilled on them. One of these had the task of rolling up large posters, also printed in tasteful shades of grey, which showed a vast stretch of sky with a single bird in flight. That rolling up of posters was itself like a piece of performance art, the grey uniform, the cliché of the free bird, and the repetitious task all playing an oddly counterpointed variation on the Gaol's original function.

In the course of that perplexing visit, while I was traipsing from cell to cell, there came the loudly echoing sounds of a distressed child calling out 'mummy, mummy, mummy, mummy ...'

'Is this part of the art, or is it reality?' I asked one of those grey-clad attendants, leaning against the wrought-iron balustrade outside a cell up on the third floor.

'Good question,' she replied.

Some while later, I saw the boy that had been crying, who must have been about four or five years old, being carried up the central iron stairway by his mother. It had been the most expressive and evocative moment in the show—for here was someone who had really been upset by finding himself in that echoing place of solitary confinement and correction, and who had expressed his feelings about it without any of the pointed relevance and allusively conceptualized aphoristic perspicacity that so marked many of the artworks and writings on display.

No sooner had I got outside again, past the larger queue for tickets with just an hour to go before closing time, than a stranger in the street came up and asked: 'Is he still reading?'

I understood she must have meant the actor working his way through *De Profundis*, and replied that there was still a long way to go to the end—which had been clear enough from glancing at the lady sitting beside me in the old-church-hall-style wooden seats, with those places for the service and hymn book on their backs. She was following the reading in a Penguin edition, which sported heavy pencil underlining of significant passages.

'Are you something to do with this artists in the prison exhibition?' another woman asked as we were both crossing at the lights.

'No, I'm nothing to do with it,' I said, 'but I have just been there.'

'Is it still open?'

'For about another hour.'

'Oh dear,' she said. 'I have to go and get some shopping in Waitrose, and don't think I'll have enough time.'

Off she went in the opposite direction, heading back into the town, leaving me to wonder about that visitation of contemporary artists and writers to this provincial place located between those greater centres of commerce and learning upon the river Thames.

'It all happens in Reading,' as the lady said scrolling through photos on her mobile phone, the kind of mildly ironic remark that both acknowledges the town's historic reputation, and suggests it might be less true than assumed.

Yet how often it would appear thus, I thought to myself heading on towards Homebase, only to discover that it had just closed—and for ever now—how often the celebrity arts, such as our most famous temporary resident practised, would collaborate with commerce, fashion and remark—with speculation in reliable investments. For when the banks totter and the stock market plunges, art comes to the rescue of the pension schemes, and even of the national Treasury, strangely enough, as the seemingly even more arbitrary evaluations attached to portable works of art turn out to be copper-bottomed assets in the mayhem of precarious financial conditions. Then there is even more work, and commission, for the experts advising, yes, even the Chancellor of the Exchequer on what to buy for the protection of the national purse.

This is why the visual arts are so much more closely locked into the tastes of the times—I found myself speculating—and their radicalism can so often feel like a sop for the beneficiaries of zero-hours contracts and raids on pension schemes by absconding captains of merchandizing. It was as if, being visited upon the provincial folk of our medium-sized county town, contemporary art would accommodate the unacceptable face of capitalism, accept it by accidentally painting its portrait.

38

In the north-east corner of the maps of Wessex with which his publishers illustrated the endpapers of your man's novels, you can find the town of Aldbrickham. *Old-brick-town* (the place given that name in recognition of the then brick-making industry and its rapid red growth in the latter decades of the nineteenth century) is the scene of that most ghastly narrative climax in *Jude the Obscure*.

This novel, the last its author completed and one particularly disliked by his wife, not least, perhaps, because the couple had not been able to have children, was published and publicly burned by a bishop for its supposed immorality in the very same year that our notorious dramatist began his two-year stint at the Gaol. The 1890s moral backlash had set in.

It also came out the year before a baby farmer, who, it is speculated, may have killed for financial gain more than four hundred infants over a twenty-year period, was executed for her one proven child murder—though not, I think, in the Gaol. Given that she was rumoured to have done this over such a long time, it would occasionally cross my mind, as I wandered along, that the author of *Jude the Obscure* might have heard of these stories and built one of his novel's later catastrophes upon them. If not, the seeming link between, now her name does come back to me, Mrs, yes, Dyer—yet more *nomen est omen* there—and Little Father Time's suicide and child murder is a remarkable literary and historical coincidence.

No, Mrs Dyer wasn't executed in the Gaol, though, it being the place where the most famous person hanged at this time for murder, for murdering his wife, was the soldier commemorated by our dramatist in his poem— who in poetry goes to his execution wearing the wrong-coloured uniform, for it wasn't a scarlet, a red coat. It was, though it wouldn't have rhymed, a blue one.

In *Jude the Obscure*, Little Father Time's suicide after his murder of Sue and Jude's children, '*Done because we are too menny*', appears thus to foreshadow, or tacitly echo, real child killings in the town its author called Aldbrickham, killings also, though more indirectly and contortedly, brought about by illegitimacy and poverty. So could it be possible that rumours of infanticide in this area had reached the great author of Dorsetshire even before Mrs Dyer was apprehended, condemned and executed? I have never read anything in the scholarship that would confirm or confute such a possibility. But then again, perhaps such child murders were more widespread, and he could have got a hint from elsewhere—or, heaven forbid, he could have invented it himself.

Stepping on beside the island upon which the Huntley & Palmer biscuit factory had stood, again I was wondering if there might be any connection between these instances of children being killed in life and literature, though Little Father Time's Malthusian reasons for killing the children may very likely not have been the reason Mrs Dyer did her murdering, about whose psychological motivations nothing is known, at least by me—knowing only the theory that it was for the cupidity of taking the fees, then not spending them on the babies' upkeep, that she did it.

Amelia Dyer—her first name too comes to me now—also makes an unexpected and vivid appearance in *Love and War in the Apennines*, because the peasants of Pian di Sotto who are sheltering the young escaped POW in 1943 delight in discussing '*I mostri criminali inglesi*':

There was Mrs Dyer, the baby farmer, who used to drown the infants committed to her charge at Caversham Weir—I remembered Mrs Dyer very well—how could anyone forget her?—from visits to the chamber of horrors in the school holidays, a mad-looking pale wax figure, dressed in black bombazine, or what I imagined black bombazine to be, forever pushing the small black perambulator with which she went about her ghastly work ...

What I do now know is that she strangled them, then threw them into the Thames, and did so right where the outdoor ladies' swimming pool alongside Caversham Lock would be constructed—there beside the foaming drop of the weir over on its Oxfordshire side. Further downstream, one of those drowned babies was eventually fished out—as if by a real-life Gaffer Hexham—which is how she eventually came to be caught.

The town also figures as one of the gateways to the novelist's Wessex because the building of the Great Western Railway helped form a crucial creative tension in his artistic life. The first station here had been built in 1840, the year of his birth in a village near Dorchester. The county of Dorset retained its rural aspects at least in part because the decision was made to build a rival line—not along the 'coastal route' via Dorchester, but on a 'central' one through Salisbury and Yeovil, a line completed in 1860.

His life too was shaped by these networks of lines linking London, where he published and maintained a literary reputation, and rural Dorchester, around which much of his imaginative life would turn, and where he would build himself a house, settling with his wife there at Max Gate in 1883.

At least three of his published poems ('Midnight on The Great Western', 'At the Railway Station, Upway' and 'After a Romantic Day') show the direct inspiration he found in the new transport system's landscape and architecture. Other poems, such as 'Faintheart in a Railway Station' and 'On the Departure Platform', underline too the poetic promptings that its more strictly timetabled meetings and partings could occasion.

But while strolling in the vicinity of the Gaol and touching on the matter of crimes and punishments that have associations with this town, of our *'mostri criminali inglesi'*, there comes to mind the strangest case of all, the case of the post-impressionist painter (another one for Holmes and Watson), whose tenuous connections with the place had begun when he—like that great novelist and her sister before him—was sent here to get some schooling.

Having recovered from an outbreak of typhoid in Bedford, the future painter was not sent back to his day establishment, but away to 'a small boarding prep school at Reading'—an event which must have happened around 1869. According to his biographer, he 'felt banished from the comforts of home life' and his 'memories of the school were coloured with Dickensian horror.'

'Many years later,' the biographer goes on, 'he told Virginia Woolf how the place was run by a "drunken old woman" who, among her outrages, once beat a boy who had broken his arm while—as he put it—we thirty little wretches lay there cowed. The headmistress clearly took pleasure in such acts of cruelty, for it became one of Sickert's verbal tics, when undertaking some disagreeable task, to remark, "And 'what is more', as my horrible old schoolmistress in Reading used to say, 'I like it'".'

Some sixty or so years later, the University here may have made some amends for this early experience in the town, its renowned real and fictional cruelty to the young, by awarding him a second Honorary Doctorate. A photograph survives recording the occasion. It shows the painter present at the ceremony, presumably in the Great Hall on the London Road campus, with a spade-like white beard that doesn't entirely conceal his bohemian open-necked shirt. What this particular photograph doesn't reveal, though, is that, as my local art-world informants tell me, the great painter received his honorary degree in carpet slippers.

After his death in 1942, this post-impressionist settled into the benign semi-obscurity that is the fate of most artists— remembered by enthusiasts for that period of British painting and to be found represented by a murky canvas or two in many of the country's galleries and museums (but by no means a household name).

All this was to change, at least up to a point, when, through the blathering of a fantasist who had claimed to be his illegitimate son, he was embroiled in a far-fetched and thoroughly disproven royal conspiracy theory regarding the identity of Jack the Ripper. This was then followed by a series of speculations, climaxing in the work of an American detective novelist, including her gruesome re-enactment of the murders with thrift-shop clothing and butcher's offal, to the effect that our honorary doctor was himself the Ripper and that, at last, the case could be closed.

Now the painter, like many another 'true crime' fan and dedicated follower of the art of the English murder, had taken an interest in the series of prostitute mutilations—

which occurred between, it is suggested, the 3rd of April 1888 and the 13th of February 1891, most of them during an eight-week period (while he happened to be summering with his family on the Normandy coast).

Back in London that October 1888, walking home one night he passed a group of what have been called 'Copenhagen Street tarts' who ran from him calling out 'Jack the Ripper, Jack the Ripper.'

This, his biographer notes, 'was the only time during his life that anyone suggested that he was the killer.' And the only way that this detail can have been known is also—evidently—because the painter himself told the story, indicating, among other things, that the girls weren't actually suggesting he was Jack, or accusing him of the crimes, but were venting their anxiety and stress with some gallows-like mockery, some humour-in-distress.

About fifteen years later, in 1905, he had again returned to London and begun working in Camden Town on a series of nudes in poor bedrooms, sometimes with a single male figure seated on the bed.

His landlady at this time believed that one of her earlier tenants, a young medical student, might have been this very Jack the Ripper—another story that the painter himself would tell. At that time, too, there had been a never-solved murder—a suspect was tried, but acquitted—in the same area of London; and the painter, as ghoulishly interested as ever in 'true crime', gave a number of his canvases names associating them with this 'Mornington Crescent Murder'. The crime-novel-funded tittle-tattle that had attached itself posthumously to the painter drew some 'evidence' from these artworks.

That famous and vastly successful American whodunit author had spent a deal of her vast wealth on the research required to 'prove' that this British post-impressionist was the Ripper, gathering a large amount of material about the hoax letters that were sent to the police, including, of course, the one from the two journalists who had given the murderer his name.

This supposedly proved that some of the painter's own letters had been written on paper from the same source as these forgeries—the evidence sufficient to prompt an art historian at the University here to accuse the painter not of being Jack the Ripper, no, but of being one of the many who must have showered the police with forged correspondence supposedly from the serial murderer himself.

So my question for Holmes and Watson is not whether the painter was or was not Jack the Ripper—for there is absolutely no doubt, according to the postscript to his recent biography, that he was not; no, my question rather is why ever was this bearded post-impressionist, who in any case had a cast-iron alibi, why was he so obviously accused of things he could not possibly have done? Why ever was he posthumously framed?

39

Then down to the Kennet I would once again descend, down the concealed steps by the road, with their graffiti, their dead leaves and garbage blown into the corners—sodden, so often, from the wind and rain. Once down there, again I'll encounter for the thousandth time the life of the old river bank, the rusted fencing opposite the space once filled by the monstrous Huntley & Palmers factory, now the equally vast but rather more sterile-looking headquarters of an insurance company—and yet more waving buddleia spears.

There you might happen to notice a few office workers standing outside for a smoke, or someone fishing in the slow canal. Walking past an empty and abandoned development, currently clad in polythene, being readied for its much-deserved demolishing, to be replaced by further high-rise flats, I would reflect that so long as you were faintly depressed, everything would look as it should do; but here, passing these derelicts, if that day you happened, for whatever reason, to have been struck with an unexpected access of happiness, the state of the domestic architecture, and other people living in its shadows, would inevitably strike you as painfully wrong.

Then from the trodden iron bridge's black arc over that canal, there came a clamorous wing beats' clumsy rhythm, a great swan striving to take off and climb steeply above the further stone parapets—then I would see again that same swan slow to land this time, to break the skin of sluggish water and ride on its incoming wave.

Here too would appear, before it was painted out, that attention-seeking slogan, if ever there were one—for 'This is a photo opportunity' had been scrawled in red paint on the side of a wharf. But it was not to be the only one, for now they have built yet more luxury apartments, new urban living for the fresh transients with jobs in the metropolis, perhaps, those unable to meet the cost of property rents or ownership in our absentee-capital city.

And now, this ironic—if it is ironic—graffiti has first been overshadowed by that greater opportunity, the fancy apartments rising above it, and the building contractors, who were just then finishing off the site for handover, have doubtless effaced it, ironic or not.

Still, I could at least pause a moment before *Reading Piece* of 1982, another work of public art—in the form of a rusty half turbine-wheel, or junk-sculpture sunburst, could pause a moment to ponder its appropriateness as a memorial to the town's disappeared industrial era.

I might stop and notice it this once, as usually doesn't happen. For, as mentioned when paying a visit to 'Mirror Mirror', there really is nothing like a piece of public art for hiding in full view—as if in perpetual fulfilment of that other American writer's *The Purloined Letter*, being spotted right now not only by his detective, but by this very imitator of his, this 'Man of the Crowd' as well.

You see the place is itself becoming a dormitory town, and the areas that were once sites of heavy industrial plant are, as in so many other places, being converted into, or replaced by, inner city domestic housing stock in convenient reach of its transport-hub connections.

An initial assumption might have been that these developments were to house the new population of service industry providers, of office workers and their young families, but now it's clear they're being built and marketed as convenient for London commuters too.

The property prices, if they're high here, are of course astronomical in the capital, just twenty-five minutes down the Great Western Railway, as, like St Petersburg, it has been renamed, with a revival of its original brand logo as the cherry on the cake. All of which will accelerate as soon as the Elizabeth Line, the Crossrail project through London, is completed, since the capital's housing crisis is making it difficult for the middle station of wealth creators actually to live in the place where that wealth must be created.

Here then I might hesitate a moment, and consider going on past what was the Huntley & Palmers factory, up towards Blake's Lock, finding myself in yet another dilemma about which way to go—which habits to reinforce by the regularity of walking, and which ones to try and break before it's too late.

By this stage, too, I'll again be in desperate need of another toilet, so will more than likely drop into *The Jolly Anglers*, a free house rescued from closure when the brewery decided to withdraw, and another memorial to the power of public action in preserving a trace of community among these ever-more corporate, and corporatist times.

While pondering on that matter too, I'll notice again all the different types of pigeons lined up on the fences by the water, fences drip-painted white with their droppings, and see today's clutch of drinkers muttering to each other on the waterside benches, notice how well the row of willow trees—fiercely pollarded during the winter—are beginning to sprout with their whitish-green leaves, and, beyond them, will marvel once more at the row of little domestic houses on the wharf opposite, an ice cream van permanently parked outside, a row of houses so precariously near to the canal that they must be in perpetual risk of flooding out.

'So what would the insurance premiums be like on those places,' I might wonder out loud while passing by on the opposite bank.

40

But this time what you do is turn and head up to the remnants of the grand Bath stone town, rambling on past Montpelier House, with its English-spelt, French-sounding name. This is the place that—as has been mused upon already—back in the later nineteenth century, used to contain a French language school, across the road, now, at number 165.

The diary of that French Symbolist poet's younger sister reports that on Wednesday the 29th of July 1874 at 9 a.m. her brother, in a serious and tense mood, announces that he is going out and that he won't return until lunchtime. And it can be deduced from what then happens that he has gone to be interviewed for—or to be appointed by an agency to—a job. This isn't something the poet is known to have done before: hence, perhaps, his state of mind.

When he returns, he announces to his mother and sister that he is leaving London the following day. This is treated with great surprise, and the diary describes the sister as astonished. She then mends his trousers and overcoat, the sort of thing you might do for someone who is about to attempt to hold down a respectable position.

However, he doesn't leave on Thursday the 30th, because the laundry woman hasn't returned his shirts—another sign that his departure is for some purpose that would require him to look neat and tidy, while it appears that they are making purchases to improve the state of his wardrobe.

On Friday the 31st of July at 4:30 a.m. the poet leaves the Argyle Square address where he was staying in London with his mother and sister. They had come across the Channel to be with him after he too had fallen ill with a fever, and there followed a number of weeks of something quite other than his season in hell in the same city with that other abandoned poet, a poet lost to drink as much as anything else. For this period in London resembled, rather, a domesticated bit of family tourism, in which they see the sights of the English capital and visit an exhibition related to Abyssinia (of all places) at the British Museum, the place for which he also has a reader's ticket.

His sister's journal reports of his departure on the 31st: 'He was sad.' The exact causes of his feelings are not noted, but may have been a combination of the departure from his family (though in one who had made it a habit to set off on his own this seems less likely). The other reason could be that he must give up his life of private study, writing, and *flânerie* in order to earn some money.

At half past two that afternoon, his sister again reports in her diary that she and her mother will be leaving London in an hour. Her nervousness increases and becomes anxiety. She asks herself if it is because she has grown attached to London without realizing it. She thinks of her brother and his sadness, and of her mother who cries and writes.

Then they leave, and she will never again see their room, nor the familiar landscape, nor London. She is to die of tuberculosis the following year, on the 18th of December 1875, aged just seventeen. Her brother would attend her funeral, and was drawn in profile at the time by a friend of his, with head shaved in proto-skin-head fashion—but, actually, in what is now understood to have been a sign of mourning.

Another source for this curious moment in Reading's history, a book on the poet's later life in Africa called *Somebody Else*, notes how when he left London early that morning he enters one of 'those shadowy periods that will increasingly predominate his life'. For, although his doomed sister's journal suggests that she received a letter from her brother and sent him a long reply on the 1st of December that same year, the poet's published correspondence has a lacuna here which lasts until we pick up his traces once more in Stuttgart in 1875.

Its author then dismisses the ill-informed suggestion that he had taken up a teaching post in Scotland, but entertains the possibility that he may have gone to Scarborough, a place whose 'façades circulaire des "Royals" et du "Grands" de Scarbro' ou de Brooklyn' figure in 'Promontoire' from *Les Illuminations*—and he even goes so far as to suggest that he may have worked in these hotels or, more likely, at one of the seaside town's French language schools advertised in the local papers. The biographer supports this speculation by noting, incorrectly, that the Grand is built on a promontory. Also, sad to say, neither of these hotels has a circular façade. Rimbaud's wording, associating the Yorkshire seaside town and the borough of New York, all suggest, and from the young man who had written 'Le bateau ivre' without ever having seen the sea, that rather than autobiographically inspired, documentary reportage, this is, once again, an inrush of his characteristic improvisation.

The poet's most recent biographer dismisses the Scarborough suggestion and attributes its appearance in *Les Illuminations* to the role of newspaper adverts and other illuminated plates in the poet's work. He then speculates, again in the light of what is to be documented about the poet's location in November, that this future famous French author would have been aiming to catch a 6 a.m. Great Western Railway train from Paddington.

According to his earliest English biography, written by the sailor-suit-wearing Oxford academic who was the first to make this connection, a M. Camille Le Clair, perhaps, had opened a new language school on the 25th of July 1874, and announced his move to the 165 King's Road address in the *Reading Mercury*. Robinson's cineaste writes of this address that the 'size of the house and the number of courses offered suggest that he employed several teachers.' He would then have appointed the Symbolist poet, who had already completed the vast majority of his classic works, through the agency in the British capital that the young writer was using to try and find work as a teacher of French.

165 King's Road is described as 'an immodest, three-storey Georgian mansion called Montpelier House (now converted into flats). It stood in the nicer part of Reading, though not far from Reading Gaol'—forming thus a curious ley line between two of the town's most famous literary inhabitants with their, as chance would have it, not entirely dissimilar sexual proclivities.

His recent biographer also speculates that the poet whose name, it comes to me, sounds like it would have been pronounced by his London neighbours as 'Half-a-Rainbow', might have made a trip to Oxford at this time, and notes that he was still working on *Les Illuminations*, his book of mostly prose poems, at this point too. Might the references to canals—'The sound of the locks covers my footsteps'—be a tacit homage to the vicinity of Blake's Lock at the rear of Montpelier House?

In *The Times* for 7–8 Nov 1874 there appeared the following announcement: 'A PARISIAN (20), of high literary and linguistic attainments, excellent conversation, will be glad to ACCOMPANY a GENTLEMAN (artists preferred), or a family wishing to travel in southern or in eastern countries. Good references—A. R. No. 165, King's road, Reading.'

This could easily have been overlooked, for after all, it had to be conjectured that this 'A. R.' is the poet himself, and if it is the writer then he is concealing his northern provincial French background. Nevertheless, confirmation came with the discovery of a hand-written draft for the advertisement, with its English corrected by another hand, perhaps that of a fellow teacher, among the poet's literary remains.

This manuscript contains two drafts of the eventual *Times* notice. In the first, the phrase 'of high literary aptitudes' is adjusted by the deletion of 'aptitudes' and the insertion above of '& linguistic attainments', while in the second the phrase 'of high linguistic social & entertaining conversation' is adjusted with the insertion of 'literary and' between 'high' and 'linguistic'. And oh how familiar, O 'Crusoe', you were in youth with that very same hesitation between including the fact of literary production, or else leaving it with the language proficiency that might serve as well, or better, on its own!

Nevertheless, a person fiddling with the details of his achievements in such a fashion might well have not yet made the decision to abandon poetry—if indeed he ever did make such a decision, as opposed, that is, to merely stopping because he was doing other things and no longer felt the urge, or no longer thought it could help him escape his physically and emotionally claustrophobic environment.

Yet, still, in the space of three months, the great poet had tired—or so it would appear—of his life in the county town of Royal Berkshire, and was anxious to take off on his travels, as the cultural companion to a travelling artist of the Edward Lear variety, or a wealthy family doing some grand touring.

His announcement most probably went unanswered, and he must have written that lost letter to his family only a week or so after the notice was published in the *Times* if he was to cross the Channel and arrive home by the 1st of December. He is reported to be back in Charleville on the 29th of that month, right at the end of 1874, having returned, some think, though it is not confirmed, for Christmas— and, while both of his poetic companions on these visits to London would return, as the Robinson film maker also adds, the great Symbolist 'never went back to England.'

Thus, one of France's greatest poets, very near the end of his brief creative period, may have spent as much as five months in what his biographer calls 'a small industrial town'. It is even conceivable that he found himself losing his inspiration and giving up writing poetry, whether in verse or prose, while living in this much-maligned place.

What's more, it was tantalizing to think, as I drifted along, that this inveterate walker might have taken more or less exactly the constitutionals repeated here, that he too could have followed the course of the Kennet and the Thames.

So it wasn't at all hard to picture him, as I frequently would, with pipe in mouth and a soft bonnet on his head wandering out along the King's Road in the direction of London and pausing for a drink at the Marquis of Granby— to down a pint of foaming English beer, to eye the barmaid's figure, eat a ham sandwich, and plan his next escape?

Then he would make his way back to the attic room at the top of Montpelier house that I imagine him inhabiting, on no evidence at all, turning up and back the way that would become part of our neighbourhood, heading through more open land, with the latest building developments taking shape, up towards the private grounds of Whiteknights Park.

But why did he make wordlists of names for kinds of specialist pigeons in what appeared to be the same moment that he had been teaching here? Was he planning a prose poem about pigeons? Would his interest in their names suggest he had made the acquaintance of a local pigeon fancier? Such questions might never be answered, but one could always try.

41

Then the instinctive researcher in me had murmured that it might be worth the trouble to read through the local newspapers for the entire time the poet appears to have lived here, evoking the life of the town, the products advertised, the crimes reported, to see what might have caught his eye or invited transformation into the phantasmagoria of *Les Illuminations*—and a bibliophile near neighbour of ours had done precisely this.

It was doubtful that the poet would have been listed in the police records, or those of the local magistrates, not least because one of his biographers would surely have found him out if he had—but on the time-honoured biographical model that when you have no evidential trace of your subject, then the next best thing is to describe the circumstances in which the person is thought to have lived, and since the topic might indeed, as our neighbour suggested, be *Rimbaud's Reading*—with apologies for that same pun yet again—the local newspapers would surely be a primary resource.

'Elementary, my dear Watson,' as I didn't say, for newspapers such as the *Reading Mercury* could well furnish potentially illuminating elements, far beyond the humble skills displayed by Inspector Lestrade of the Yard.

Emerging from an opium dream, or from a *deréglement de tous les sens*, after strumming a few chords on our discarded church-hall piano, I had taken myself round to the book-lined abode of this retired colleague with more time on his hands, who had recently spent those few hours at the Berkshire Record Office, with the rates for 1873 (though not, it turned out, 1874), which do not have an entry for any Monsieur Le Mons, nor for 165, but—they come piecemeal unfortunately, in spurts and only occasionally sequentially (the King's Road is in the 'Parish of St Giles' section)—some charming details of residents and their commercial activities in the lower numbers of the road, closer to the town centre. There are also some choice names to note, some names of pubs on or near the road that our poet might have frequented, which for whatever reason are not given a number, so there is no way of knowing exactly where they were.

Asking for the 1869 Directory my colleague had found Le Mons earlier in the week from the open shelves behind the desk, but he must have been given a different directory, as no Le Mons appeared in this one. And, he joked, I will naturally soon be writing 'The Case of the Vanishing Mons' with Mr Conan Doyle's help.

'In short,' as far as his researches in the footsteps of the man with soles of wind were concerned, my colleague concluded, somewhat crestfallen, 'I've got pretty much nowhere.'

'But there's no such thing as negative research,' I suggested. 'It's really just a matter of how one presents what one has not got.'

And he congratulated me on the suggestion, already noted, that a reading of the local newspapers might prove useful.

'I'm presuming they're no longer locally housed, however,' he added. 'Oh and I tried getting the census data off the Net, but 1873–4 is awkwardly situated between 1871 and 1881.'

He had been convincing himself, more and more, as of course you do largely to keep up morale, that something could be concocted about the five months that the great poet might have spent here, and was heartened to find a confirmation that, even so, it might be worthwhile taking these researches further.

He then promised to re-read *Les Illuminations* over the Bank Holiday weekend and see if he couldn't torture something Redingensian—yes, that's the unlikely adjective—out of them.

'Right you are,' I said, as we parted at his door.

And, good as his word, he did deliver in the form of the following phrase: 'En quelque soir, par example, que se trouve le touriste naïf, retiré de nos horreurs économiques ...' (Some evening, for example, that the naïf tourist finds himself, withdrawn from our economic horrors)—as, indeed, you find me now.

Here, then, in King's Road, was the house that he'd used as a post box address in *The Times*, when he may have been working as a French language teacher, and so I would imagine him sleeping for a few months in one of the rooms, the *chambre-de-bonne* attics with their mansard windows, perhaps, at whose panes he might 'Robinsonne' among a few borrowed books, or have stood and dreamed of his future travels in southern or in eastern climes.

While here, you recall, he had also mysteriously studied those names of pigeon types. But perhaps that was just another part of his RSI, no, not his repetitive stress injury, but, as an old friend of mine would have it, his relentless self-improvement? You can imagine him learning and teaching languages because he imagined a future for himself as a gentleman's companion on a sort of grand tour, fantasizing again about his position in life, as writers naturally do.

But the more cynical might want to say that it was coming to this town that finally snuffed out his interest in writing poetry, that it was coming here to this much-maligned town that had murdered his muse. *Les Illuminations*, his last book, has very little indication that the surroundings here had given any obvious prompts, and nothing that he couldn't also have got from wandering around the Paddington area and the canal at Little Venice.

There are just two references to canals in his illuminations book, and there's no saying that they are references to the Kennet. Nevertheless, it is believed that he was still working on those prose poems during his months in this county town of ours.

And after all, he was living just around the corner from the enormous Huntley & Palmers biscuit factory, less than a couple of decades before one of its biscuit tins would figure so significantly in *Heart of Darkness*, being used, as already mentioned, to mend the hull of the boat that will transport Marlow and the others up the Congo in search of Mr Kurtz.

Though Montpelier House is a grand neoclassical building, fronted in what is now, it having been sandblasted, light cream Bath stone, during the poet's sojourn here it will had been blackened from the industrial pollution all around.

However, despite what may be your cynicism, such evidence as there is doesn't point in the direction of our town's doing his muse to death. Rather, their curiously English colouring, all the way down to the anglicized pronunciation of the title, the *Illuminashuns*, or so his fellow-poet had it, suggests that the decidedly *fin-de-siècle* town of Reading may have left a faint mark on this high point of French literature too.

Nor was I the first Robinson to have been captivated by the

thought of the poet living among these very streets, for my cinematic namesake had been here too—'Robinson met me at the station', the narrator of *Robinson in Space* reports:

> and immediately took me to King's Road, where he had identified the building which had been the 'coaching establishment' where Rimbaud was employed as a teacher of French in 1874. Robinson was very excited by this and the other literary associations of the town, which he praised with a euphoria reminiscent of that of Nietzsche for Turin, so much so that I was concerned for his well-being and the extent of his commitment to *the derangement of the senses.*

The filmic shot then cuts to an empty glass lying in a bit of what looks like parkland grass. So his auteur was concerned for the 'mad heart' of Robinson, as was I, and the fear that he might be suffering from manic-depressive bouts that would one day tip him over the edge—*ecce homo!*—into the madness that had befallen that philosopher, who embraced a humiliated horse in Turin, he being another compulsive walker who thought that his ideas, his best ones at least, were the result of peripatetic habits, especially over higher ground.

By the time in 1995 that the film-maker and his Robinson were taking an interest in the town and its famous poet inhabitant, 165 and 167 King's Road were in a terrible state of disrepair—and there is a still photograph, taken on a rainy day in what looks like late winter, but is given as the 28th of March 1995, of the building's empty and roofless shell. Over the glistening asphalt a British-made car is driving, already half out of shot.

At that point in time—as people will say—the two addresses were known collectively as Palladio House, and seem to have been called this, the cineaste speculates, 'before they were gutted.' Yet this was not to be their fate, for by the time we had come to live in the place, the building had been given a face-lift, its façade fiercely cleaned, and its interiors converted into luxurious-looking offices or flats.

It had been given back its old title, Montpelier House, with that trace of its previous existence in the French associations of the name. For the moment, though, sadly enough, civic pride and culture has not stretched to the mounting of a plaque on the front of the building noting its association with that unlikeliest location for one of the high points in the history of French Symbolist poetry.

Along those very roads, some of the old cobblestones survive where a 'désert de bitume', as the poet puts it in 'Métropolitain', has fallen away. There too you could see the old streets erupting through its more recent layers of black stuff, and they would offer the momentary illusion that I really could be walking in the footsteps of the 'voyant' poet, could tread upon the very stones where those 'semelles de vent', the feet with soles of wind had, for those months in 1874, also trod 'among these dark, satanic mills.'

42

Here in Eldon Square, and the George the Fifth Memorial Gardens, there is a white statue—my local informant tells me, for the inscription is in rubbish Latin—of Rufus Isaacs, Marquess of Reading (1860-1935), who was a QC, an MP, Solicitor-General, Attorney-General, Lord Chief Justice, Viceroy of India, and Foreign Secretary. Thin-lipped, much decorated, with a hand raised to his collar, he stares out across his little park with his robe's train hanging down right over the whole of his pedestal, in its patch of grass, with memories of summer days, and of grander times, and the student parties, too, from yet another era.

It's also, especially in good weather, a haunt of the unemployed and those who pass their time by blurring the day with cans of drink or smokes—smokes whose telltale aroma you can frequently catch wafting towards you, passing under that heavy-laden apple tree with its boughs hanging over the black railings at the corner where the lights on Eldon Road pause traffic wanting to cross or enter the flow on London Road.

And not far away, too, there's the recently closed Eldon Arms, another little hostelry where our poet could have downed a pint after the stresses and strains of language teaching. Further along is the Dom Polski Centre, set up there on London Road by the first Polish immigration—the one that had followed from Danzig and the Polish Corridor, that had fought heroically against the Nazis, from the Battle of Britain all the way to crossing the Rhine. In this area too is the Polish Catholic Church, also recently cleaned, down on Watlington Street—another church taken over by a more recently devout denomination.

Sometimes I would pass by as an evening gathering

was spilling from its church hall. There they were, that latest young community all speaking their own language, teenagers together, women and children, wearing their finest clothes and doing their best, or so it seemed, to advance the interests of the coming generations. I couldn't help being reminded of life in the middle of the previous century, when a boy, and a witness of how the young wives' groups and such would collaborate to help each other through their mutual difficulties. Those were the years of the early National Health Service, when free milk, orange juice and cod liver oil were in the first flush of their youth as well.

Pausing at the corner of Eldon Road and the London Road, under those laden apple boughs, I would be standing opposite the premises of A. B. Walker and Son, Ltd., Funeral Directors and Memorial Masons, with their Union Jack hanging limp on its pole. It's only too conveniently placed for the Royal Berkshire Hospital, whose old, grimy, yellowed frontage dominates the opposite side of the crossroads—the place that I've mentioned more than once, if not mistaken, as where the fighter-ace-to-be had undergone the life-saving removal of his legs. It is also the place where the consort of our future king was born.

And it was another location where I had been provided with an occasion—a painful one at that—to see what it looks like inside. The Royal Berkshire Hospital, a great rambling extension with its own multi-storey car park, which had developed piecemeal, it would seem, behind the grand Victorian façade on London Road, had a make-do-and-mend feel to its interior—as if the latest equipment which crammed its wards and theatres had somehow overfilled the space, the public areas having an air of partial renovation, or of institutional scuffing, like yet one more secondary-modern school building.

And all these signs, like a half-hearted effort at reform, were the outward visible sign, familiar enough to anyone who has needed to frequent them at all, of the credit-squeezed and cash-strapped public institutions in this extraordinarily ill-distributing un-commonwealth of ours.

My first reason for having to frequent the Royal Berkshire Hospital had been during that viral collapse. As if the years of staring towards the horizon in search of a ship or a sail had finally got to them, I had also been obliged to undergo a series of tests for my bothersome eyes.

In the ophthalmic clinic, at the reception desk, you could still see heaps of paper records behind the reception desks, the transfer of this patient material to electronic data a long way off still. And the amenities inside the Royal Berkshire Hospital reminded me of nothing so much as motorway services, except for the uneasy looks of patients and visitors, and the hurrying staff.

That visit to the eye clinic had also turned into something of a farce, though a happy one at that, for, yet again, after the long wait for an interview with a consultant, I was informed that there was nothing they could do for my naturally strained, my troubled and troubling eyesight. Indeed, the specialist simply complimented me on how I was coping as well as was possible with what he could see to be a permanent condition. In fact, he asked why this patient had been referred to him, to which the only thing I could say—and couldn't even say that—is how somebody must have blundered.

That mirage-like difficulty with my eyes was what provided a first opportunity to see what the hospital looked like inside, followed by an efficient and complication-free removal of a wisdom tooth.

But then, while I was away from this town of ours, visiting the north, the land of my ancestors, my dear Friday—I'm sorry—had gone down with what also seemed like a violent stomach upset, but proved to be far worse.

Perhaps that illness had been caused by the climate here, inhospitable for one of her sensitive nature, someone who had grown up where it is so much warmer all year round. She would feel the cold perpetually, like that Mimi in the opera *La Bohème*, if you like—and compelled to be an angel of the house, for which she felt so little aptitude, and an angel who has to have reasons—and you've seen how I do too—to get out of the house as well.

Then, remember, just as I was arriving back from that brief sojourn up north, how Friday was rushed into the hospital with a swollen and inflamed, an infected appendix—the kind that, if not treated with urgency, can turn into peritonitis—and the thing had been removed in an emergency operation that very same evening.

My Friday had then been moved onto an intensive care ward and her case overseen by an overworked junior doctor, one of the ones who would find themselves compelled to strike over working conditions and the imposition of a new contract just a few years later. I had visited her in her immediately post-operative state, on the ward, and even had a quiet word with the young doctor herself.

But the next time, come in and gone round to where I thought my Friday was, the nurse in charge told me that, no longer needing intensive care, she'd had to be transferred onto one of the long-stay chronic condition wards, way over on the far side of the hospital.

When I eventually found her, there she lay, in a six-bed bay, surrounded by extremely old people, the majority of them barely conscious. Many were hardly able to recognize they had visitors, and their relatives would be checking their email on smartphones—and fair enough if it helped them get through those vigils with their loved ones, still not gone and not forgotten, lying there in their sorry states and maybe dreamless sleeps.

And I suppose it didn't help that, now as you know, I'm so allergic to hospitals, having had a serious dose of them myself. During my long period of convalescence and constitutional-taking, I would be obliged by the medical profession to keep delivering blood and other samples to them so that they could try and find out whatever could be wrong.

The results would come back, and because they were inconclusive and there was nothing to say, the GP wouldn't even make contact to say they had come back, would never say what the matter was, which they never did; and because they had no evidence of anything or any success to report, they didn't report anything, just leaving me, as so often, dependent upon them, and feeling once more the loss of control over our own lives—which is a further reason why I've been taking these constitutionals—to get back a little autonomy.

No, the problem was that illness and the loss of bodily control would make you feel abject, would bring back other feelings of helplessness that had inflicted or been inflicted upon you, and the experience of hospitals would not mitigate this feeling of abjection, but rather exacerbate it. And, yet, as you can see, it had been so much the worse for—sorry—my dear Friday. It had underlined once more how we are, all of us, alone in the end, alone and obliged to deal with our ghosts, too, alone.

There in that ward for the chronically sick she would stay for the following week, developing a post-operative infection and a fever too, which would leave her weakened, debilitated and yet more depressed for a good few years to come.

'I can't eat any of the food they have here,' she'd say, and I gathered from the way she waved the ward menu that she wasn't referring to the effects of having had an appendectomy. You could think she was about to be murdered by savages, ones she was only trying to talk to and calm down.

Those days would be difficult for her because she simply had no experience of such a Health Service as the British one to use as a guide—for in any institutional setting there is a form of native know-how and cunning that can be deployed to get the best out of whatever it has to offer. This involves, as anywhere, befriending those in power with a combination of helplessness, common-sense humour, and carefully modulated deference.

But such a tricky combination would require far greater skills with the language, and the customs of the country, than my dear Friday—as she doesn't like me calling her— could have had at her command. No, I was not that good a language teacher, and, in the end it's not only a question of language. For just like anywhere else, and experience shows, a hospital ward is a place that the more pragmatically gifted among us can work with, and work upon the employees so as to get what they need, and their way.

But my own dear Friday was unable to do more than tell them that she didn't want to eat any of their food, because it was so unlike anything she had ever eaten before, and it was so obviously bad for you, which she was unable to refrain from saying—as could obviously be seen from the terribly overweight state of most of the other patients sleeping round about her there.

So my dear Friday expected that I would be allowed to come into the hospital and bring her the meals she wanted to eat, expected that since the nurses and auxiliaries didn't seem to have the time to wash her or take her to the toilet, then they wouldn't at all mind if her Crusoe came into the hospital and, being her companion through life, performed those duties for them. This is, after all, the way things are frequently managed elsewhere.

Which was only the beginning of the problem, because one of the things she didn't realize is that when you go into hospital in this country you as good as hand over your life to the institution—because if anything should happen to you once you've been admitted, it would be their fault, they would be legally responsible, so health and safety would be involved, and they wouldn't want to confess that they had been obliged to hand over the feeding of someone whose life was in their hands to a member of the public—even if that anxious soul happened to be a relative of the patient. So, of course, I couldn't bring cooked meals in for her to eat; and they didn't much like the idea of my performing the daily care duties for one of their patients either.

Naturally enough, and you can understand why, they didn't want to have members of the public, even if they were their nearest and dearest, being involved with the care and treatment of one of their patients. You never knew what might happen. It was another of those no-win situations. They didn't seem to have the staff—and it was a weekend after all—even to perform the basic essentials. Nor was I going to be allowed to do anything about it.

But that Sunday it had proved impossible for my dear Friday to find anyone who would take her to the toilet and give her a wash. So she phoned me at home on that autumn weekend morning.

'Can you bring me some edible food,' she asked, 'and some soya milk, and if you could come and take me to have a bath, because I can't find anyone who'll do it. No one will help me out of bed, and down the ward.'

She had sounded so terribly weak and upset, and, naturally, I was already angry about the situation when finally stepping onto her ward once more.

Arriving at reception, though, when I took a deep breath and asked as politely as possible in the circumstances if I could bathe my wife, the staff-nurse there just sent me away with a flea in my ear.

'I don't know who your wife is,' she said, 'and I have a ward-full of patients to consider. So if you wouldn't mind ...'

When eventually she found an auxiliary to come and do it, the girl could hardly speak, although evidently a native speaker—seeing as she was so young, so shy and inexperienced. She seemed unable to answer or understand what my Friday was trying to say.

That stay in the hospital intended to relieve her of a dangerous appendix had turned into an alienating nightmare, a nightmare that reproduced my age-old fear of hospitals, one that had doubtless been passed down through the family, closely associated with the fear of losing control over your body and life, not so much of the illness, though of course that didn't help, but of the medical profession. And, what's more, I'm sorry to say, I couldn't help blaming my dear Friday's illness on having brought her to this inhospitable climate of ours.

But then oh my dear, my dear Friday, how would I ever have survived here without you!

43

Crossing back over the London Road will take you once more into the area of town in which we decided, and decided in a hurry, to live when we first came here to settle and work. Walking this route once more, I could remember the sensation as we were first driven one early July morning along the Erleigh Road. An estate agent was bringing us to view one of those houses they show you with little or no hope you'll like it, one that had been on the market for a good long time, a little overpriced perhaps, and one you won't like—but, while we're passing this way, he might as well show us—and it did in fact have two FOR SALE boards from different firms, one of them Haslams, in its trampled patch of garden.

We had been shown a great many such properties, none of them seeming in the least bit possible. They were either too small, or too large, too far from my future place of work, on a main road, or in a very dilapidated condition. They were the sorts of property that the estate agents would call 'an opportunity', an opportunity we didn't have the funds, time, or patience to undertake.

But then when we drove along the tree-lined Erleigh Road, its overarching canopies of leaves creating oases of shade from that sweltering July, there came a playing field opening beyond green railings to the right, a field laid out for cricket at that time of year; and what I later discovered was a local boys school beyond it—the lanterns and pinnacles of its mock-gothic roofline clearly visible through the summer leaves. Our daughter had said it looked like Hogwarts, the school, as you know, which that boy magician attends—and I would discover that it had been considered a possible location for the series of films, and that the painter John Minton had been taught for three years here in the Thirties.

'This is more like it,' I thought to myself, at the exact same moment the estate agent was replying to my misunderstood question:

'So what's the town like at night?'

But the young man driving us hadn't for a moment thought I might be asking about the drunkenness, the street violence, or disorderly behaviour, replying immediately to a supposed question about the vitality of the night life. There were indeed, he said, a great many bars and clubs, plenty to do—as we were to find out in the small hours of the morning when inebriated students would make their way back to their halls of residence past the house we did, in that hurry, decide to buy. Their bizarrely rowdy states of excitement and aggression would come echoing through the bathroom window, or across the backs of houses, punctuating sleep or insomnia alike.

Still, you had to admit, and even so, that this was much more like it. For the scene opening up before us as we were driven on under the leafage of summer, on past the sold-off old vicarage, and health clinic opposite, the unfolding scene manifested the spatial coordination that you might identify with a real place—a place with a name and perhaps even some self-esteem. It was doubtless something to do with the mixture of brick red and leaf green, the architectural styles, that heavy grandeur of Edwardian-era shop-buildings— even when the ground floor levels have been modernized with non-period frontages that give the impression of heavy, polychrome, brickwork perched unsupported and precariously on a sheet of plate glass.

Crossing what I would eventually know to be Alexandra Road, passing the orthodontic clinic on the left and the GP practice where I would go for my viral diagnosis on the right, the property values took a slight but distinct dip, coinciding as they almost did with a curious shed-like bar called the Fruit Bat, and then an off-licence, a few take-away emporia for various global foods, a halal grocers, a fish-and-chip shop, a second-hand car dealer with 1960s sports-car-racing pedigree, some rental agencies aimed at the student market, and, what would come to be its social centre for us, a local branch of the Co-op.

From there it settled into the mixed status area I was trying to describe when first setting out on these constitutionals—which was just as well, for it had quickly become evident that our budget and the house-prices at that precarious moment on the cusp of boom and bust were by no means tipping at that illusion-driven moment in our favour.

Returning sometimes, though, and by way of a change, for a further drifting variation, and another way of escaping my compulsive routines, I would occasionally walk a little further along London Road beyond Eldon Square to the corner where the BUPA Health Centre appears, the Royal Berkshire Hospital's vicinity making this the medical district of town, and would then cut up along Denmark Road—a quietly residential street lined mostly with large houses, though there are some bits of old estate infill, punctuations of mid-century semis or town houses. This is one of the grander addresses in the locality, so much so that I have even heard it described, exaggeratedly enough, as 'our Hampstead', which it might be in so far as some of its largest single occupancies may be inhabited by bourgeois bohemians of the wealthiest kind.

But that day, as I was walking in a southerly direction, up towards Erleigh Road, though knowing the side-street had been named in light of the then recent marriage of the

Prince of Wales to a member of the Danish royal family, I found myself preferring to imagine that the name of this wealthy enclave had derived from the incursions of my northern ancestors, the Earls from the Danelaw and their attendant warrior cohorts. Attempting to extend their realm as far as the south coast, they had ventured beyond the Thames, and, as already encountered, had fought the first Battle of Tesco nearby—though that is not, of course, how it's known in the *Anglo-Saxon Chronicle*.

And it further dawned on me that my faint feeling of being a perpetual interloper around here might derive from the fact that King Alfred had eventually driven those ancestors of mine firmly back up north, and that the future rulers of the kingdom, the Normans, had been decisively aided in their unification of the kingdom by their enemy, Harold, of that tapestry, who had finished off all those northern claims to the kingdom at the Battle of Stamford Bridge, only a matter of weeks before that arrow in the eye had done for his own.

44

Cutting up this way, in that springtime, I was greeted by another acquaintance, a fellow teacher, who offered to accompany me as far as the end of Denmark Road.

'So how have you been?' he began. 'We haven't seen anything of you in a while.'

'No, I've been ill,' I explained, and gave him as brief an account as possible of what you already well know, for people don't really want to hear an itemized list of ailments when they politely ask after your health—at the end of which I reciprocated by inquiring how things had been going during my absence.

'Oh, we're all just hanging on,' he was saying, taking it to be a request for an update on our mutual place of employment. 'We're all fearful that the need to make savings will be turned upon us next, afraid to find the most vulnerable of us left out to dry—afraid we'll discover them hanging from frozen posts!'

As you see, he had a lively line in conversation, and so naturally I didn't resent being interrupted in my solitary divagations. Being one of the spiritually enlightened, and only too sceptical of merely monetary motivations, he could see plenty that was wrong with the way we live now, but seemed unable or unwilling to imagine an alternative beyond the urgent moralization of contemporary business practice. Doubtful but intrigued, I asked him to explain what he had in mind as we were mooching along.

'The point is,' he began, 'that there's nothing in itself wrong with the business world and the making of profits. It's just the way people go about doing it nowadays that causes the problems.'

'Really?' I said. 'How so?'

And, all ears, I was wondering if I had ever said there was—though with those old phrases, 'the acceptable face of capitalism' and 'the accumulation of surplus capital', echoing remotely in my memory banks. This young colleague, who could have been born perhaps in the lead up to the Iron Lady's first success at the polls, had begun almost to hector, religiously, as it were, with an apology for an ethical version of the very neoliberal economics that I had set out on these walks to overthrow.

'So why then do good companies do bad things?' I enquired.

'Well, they have to be free to act,' he began, 'in the interests of their shareholders—but they also have to exist in a society, and be constrained by a culture, and that requires education, and an ethical education too.'

'But doesn't that merely bring us round in a circle?' I suggested. 'After all, once you've said that culture and education should check rapacious freedom without legal constraint you are also confronted with problems like the fragility of goodness—'

'Indeed,' he added, 'and that only goes to show the difficulty in being good if being good means not doing any harm, when this is impossible, because every minute of every day you have failed to do some possible good deed, and you yourself, or others in your name, are bound to have perpetrated some local or international injustice, so what can you do?'

It seemed that now he was singing from my own hymn-sheet, but there under the bursting buds of spring, I heard myself say—reaching for a slogan from my large collection—that there was always the attempt to act locally and think globally, to do what we can, however small.

'Easier said than done,' he interrupted.

'But doing some good in your own small sphere without any expectation of virtuousness,' I came back, 'is as much as any one of us can hope for.'

There seemed no reason to quarrel as we walked along that fine spring morning, and I imagined my responses would be construed as conciliations, but that wasn't how he appeared to take them, as the direction of our exchanges immediately revealed.

'I know I'm not going to persuade you,' he said, 'but I don't see that you really have an alternative to mine, you know. After all, I'm only asking that the religious and moral values of the society we already live in are applied and sustained through everything we do, including business.'

'But isn't one of the challenges of Jesus' teachings—casting the money changers from the temple, forgiving the woman taken in adultery—that it's so at odds with the way we live now ... and the ways we have always done?'

He could of course see what I meant, and admitted the point, a point insisted on by my asking how he imagined the Department of Trade and Industry, or whatever it happens to be called these days, might suddenly conduct its business by considering the lilies of the field.

'Well,' he came back, 'we must render unto Caesar the things that are Caesar's and unto God the things that are God's', and then added with a winning smile, 'we mustn't bury our Talent in the ground, but return it five-fold to our Master upon his return.'

'But then if we are, as your faith tells you, born into sin and unable to amend ourselves without the grace of God, then it follows,' I found myself saying, 'that the only way to approach such a state of affairs as you prefer is to contain the effects of greed and the six other deadly sins by enlightened legislation, effective oversight, and vigilant policing.'

'But then you're putting the responsibility of surviving virtuously on the institutions of society, and not upon the individual souls themselves—and, as it says, you should judge not that ye be not judged.'

With the playing fields of that mock-gothic crenellated boy's school before us, it seemed a parting of the ways.

'Take care of yourself then,' he smiled.

'You too!' I said.

He had left me at the top of Denmark Road, having turned towards the roundabout and hospital. So on I walked, brooding slowly, taking in the sky and clouds, the clouds forming and dissolving, and that very day, as if a bolt from the blue, a scheme for the reform of the entire world began to take shape in my convalescent head.

'Well then,' I practically thought out loud, continuing our debate even though he had taken the road not taken, for I was continuing on towards Alexandra Road, 'can you even begin to reform the world if you haven't first reformed yourself?'

'But, physician,' another of me said, 'if thou art to heal thyself before getting down to work on the world, then nothing will ever change, because you'll never be well enough,' as that me ended up supposing in my weakness, 'even to make a start.'

'Yet if you start without being sufficiently well to keep going or to have enough balance, then surely,' my other self came back, 'it will miscarry and there won't be good or appropriate change—which produces one of those convenient binds in which you'll fail if you try the one, and you'll fail if you try the other—the sort of argument which gives no guidance when it comes to crossroads, and there is no road not taken because you haven't even gone down the other ...'

Which is how it was that, pulling myself together, there at the corner of Erleigh and Alexandra Roads, with the surgery opposite, at least three thoughts, a trivia if ever there was one, came to me all at once.

The first of them was that if you wait to reform yourself before you have a go at reforming the world, then you'll never begin; the other was that the only thing you have much control over, and then not very much at that, is your own small sphere; and the third that it is a mistake to think these two things are actually separate, as if the public and the private were hermetically sealed—which is an illusion that everything and everyone, it appears, would prefer us to believe.

After all, if solipsism is correct and the world is only known in perception, then not only is the world of the unhappy man different from that of the happy one, but so it is for the sick man and the healthy one too. And this world, the only world in which you can be that solipsist, if it is your language and ideas and perceptions—which will be extinguished when you die—this world can certainly be changed by going for a walk. For, look, you can see all around you people getting on with changing the world any Sunday afternoon, or, as we say, any day of the week.

Almost all year round, if you set off yourself after lunch and head down to the Thames Path, you'll encounter the canoeists wearing their boats like hats upon their heads, the cyclists pounding along towards Sonning, and more leisurely strollers crossing those wide open green spaces, model airplanes looping the loop above them, out beyond the edge of town, in the vicinity of the new technology park and environs—the area that had so engaged the cineaste and Robinson.

Those strollers would be heading for the tea-rooms set up around the lock-gates, whether to lure the summertime canal-barge folk out for some refreshment, or to catch a penny or two from the populations out on their own constitutionals, all of them changing the world as they go—if by 'the world' is meant the one that each of us constructs in consciousness and will die when we do, and all of them changing within the one world that has to exist in its evolutions for those separate ones to have any meaning at all.

Yet such a solipsistic sense of 'the world' isn't enough for many of us, and especially given, as you'll recall, that the philosophers have used Robinson as a test case for their quarrels over the possibility, or not, of inventing a private language. Nor is it enough for all those who sign online petitions and engage in politics at whatever level; nor is it good enough for all the writers who are at this moment working to shape their senses of the world as not merely 'their own' but as one that can be shared with and understood by others, that can have a shaping role in those 'other worlds'—a learned native or second or further language, in such a sense, being once again a living disproof of the strict form of the solipsism thesis.

Age, of course, will reconcile you to many things, and it's part of being healthy and mature that you are not overwhelmed by grief as you realize that the world you imagined yourself to be progressing towards has been definitively diverted from that imagined course—as by an unnecessary plebiscite, for instance. But then, however mature, on these constitutional walks of mine, healthy I clearly was not.

Yet it was only yesterday that an old acquaintance, a Dominican priest and avant-garde poet, had pointed out that the period of recent history, since the first election victory of the Iron Lady to the present day, is now longer than that from the founding of the Welfare State and the post-war promise that came with it, to that moment in May 1979 when a grocer's daughter from Grantham set out to put the poor back in their place, and keep them there—just as the local shopkeepers back in the 'good old days' of the 1920s and 1930s could keep the locals in theirs by granting or denying them their 'tick', the credit their wives needed on weekly shopping bills when they were out of work or out on strike.

Indeed, the problem with thinking that Margaret-from-Grantham's era was a temporary setback to the post-war settlement is that the period of 'late' capitalism from the end of the 1970s until now is longer than that from victory in Europe until the advent of her and her friend the B-movie American president's neoliberalism. Yet there remained, looking around, a niggling sense that all such successes are failures too, for they shape the terms upon which the doctrine of unforeseen consequences will create the conditions that eventually oblige later generations to abandon their so cherished, so equivocal solutions. We might even be living through that painful adjustment as I similarly wandered along.

45

Now as I continue along Erleigh Road, the intangible urban village that has borrowed its name from this street takes shape under trees to left and right. Erleigh village is not to be muddled up, of course, with the adjacent suburb of Earley—though it may, perhaps, have evolved from the same older place name. Returning among its familiar lineaments, I might be as good as pondering these things in my heart, almost saying them out loud, my lips moving to the arguments, so that if there had been anyone there to see I would have appeared like yet one more of those harmless, or harmless you hope, idiots that the cutbacks in social services have left to wander the streets muttering and murmuring to themselves, or addressing the empty air.

Had the banking collapses at the end of this century's opening decade been the first real sign of a crisis in that neoliberal replacement of the post-war settlement? Were the grotesque global inequalities it had helped to exacerbate—and make so perpetually visible, commented on daily in tweeted aphorisms and slogans thanks to our new technologies—beginning to create the pressures that would oblige the world to be reshaped on a more equable model? To achieve interrelated stable economies that will discourage all those who have been born equal in nature but created unequal by culture from wanting to up sticks and migrate to the other side of this world?

Or more grimly, I reflected, was all this turmoil yet another maladjustment that is currently being addressed by policies that claim to be simply better forms of house-keeping, more responsible bits of accountancy, more efficient versions of that same economic outlook and its attendant worldview of vicious self-betterment?

Such were the thoughts that came as I would pace along

in search of the health that had eluded me, and had eluded—
even the most sanguine of venture capitalists would surely
have to admit—the current global economic system too.

Now I was entering the area that, hereabouts, is graced with
the courtesy name of Erleigh village—that gathering of
shops, cafés, bars, and letting agents for students, clustered
together in the stretch of road that gives it its name. From
the crossing with Alexandra Road to the branching off to
the left of Junction Road, I had to admit that these tree-lined
streets and roads had taken on the lineaments of home.

And, as I mentioned, at the heart of this enclave is a
well-stocked, and recently refurbished, branch of the Co-op
coming up now on my left. Passing by, I would often hesitate
and drop in to pick up some milk, eggs, cereal, or the like;
and it really does amount to the social hub of our little intra-
urban, and our global, village too.

There I would, now and then, encounter fellow travellers
in the struggle to maintain the area around Cemetery
Junction as a home for socialism and an outpost of bohemia,
those who populate the local community groups, ones which
my Friday now attended, and had come to feel she almost as
much as belonged to, despite her chronic loneliness.

To mitigate it, she had even tried her hand at Scottish
dancing, but quickly had to give it up, whether because of
the mournful drone of the music, or the clumsiness of the
old folk who never got beyond being beginners when it
came to the steps and who were her only partners, I don't
know. But now, since that appendectomy—sad to say—my
Friday dances no more.

There she encountered and befriended people who will
write self-published local histories of the street in which
they live, some of which I have of course read in researching

these constitutionals—and one in particular, another relentlessly self-improving bookworm who happens to live right opposite the Co-op, one who has also devoted his life to decoding the implications in local phrase and fable.

'You must change your life,' he might say among the fruit and vegetables, or picking out a moderately priced Rioja for the evening.

'Another allusion there!' I would reply.

'You can say that again,' he'd say, and smile a sympathetic smile, neither of us exactly sure how the reading of a sonnet about a headless torso of the god Apollo, pagan deity of poetry at that, might encourage you to change your life, or facilitate its happening.

The people who work stocking shelves and on the tills at the Co-op—though it has recently introduced an automated self-checkout system that we try never to use on principle—are a cross-section of the district's population, and that's why our urban village is, as I say, a global one too.

The people employed here are from all over, from Nepal and the Philippines, India and the near East, and their friendliness to us is often reassuring and uplifting—when you're tired at the end of another day's work, when the ticking bombs have gone off again, or, as I happened to be through those long days of a spring not long ago, off from work and trying to recover.

No, they're not from everywhere, but they do seem to originate in practically anywhere over the world. Doubtless, though, some of them will have been born in, or in the vicinity of, these very streets.

'That'll be nineteen eighty-nine,' a headscarf-wearing young woman might say, reading the figures from the screen on her till.

'Interesting year,' I might reply, searching in my pocket for the money, remembering the Russian Premier's speech in Paris on the bicentenary of the storming of the Bastille.

'Really,' says the lady on the till, and I'll be wondering if she was even born when those events unfolded and the Berlin Wall came down.

'Nineteen thirteen,' she'd say another time: ah yes, the year before the end of the world, I'll have thought, but didn't dare say.

And yet if I should happen to pass by any of them on one of those constitutionals of mine, the friendliness we show in that specific situation over the exchanging of money, the jokes I might make about the times or histories when the price in pounds and pennies comes to a number that is also a salient date, might not reach to the casual spaces of actual acquaintance.

'Fourteen ninety-two', my wife's Nepalese friend would say, and of course I don't need to tell you what that year had brought.

'Ten sixty-six,' she would say.

'—and all that,' I'd be mysteriously reply, and quickly hand over a brown note with some change to get beyond the awkwardness.

But it would hardly stretch as far as the public space outside those specific, and economically conditioned exchanges, which we would at least mitigate by as much sociability as could be mustered.

For the truth is that it's a minor instance of what is now ubiquitous in this post-colonial, multi-cultural place, that people are able to inhabit the same space, and to be close to each other physically, on cheerful speaking terms—ones that they may be trained to perform for the good of business, though, I fear—and yet to appear to live in what the language allows us to call 'different worlds'.

For the experience of going by a young woman with her head almost completely covered, a woman who would never so much as catch your eye in passing, one who is pushing a pushchair and walking a toddler, this experience of being so totally ignored in your own physical existence, even as you carefully adjust your stride so as to give way on the narrow unevenly patched pavement, this experience is one, not of separation in those so-called 'different worlds', but of a cruelly alienated sharing in the world of each other's historically compromised humanity.

Still, it couldn't not cross my mind as I slipped my receipt into the overflowing litterbin outside, that my long training as a 'Crusoe' had prepared me, as nothing else could, not only to survive my solitude, but also to find myself as near as damn it at home among strangers, strangers cooperating in a local shop.

46

The calamitous calm and nervous anxiety of recent events has become palpable among multi-cultural communities such as those in Erleigh village. Their fear is palpable at desks and counters of service providers, and has only increased with the decision to leave—to leave because the so-called 'will of the people' wanted those others to leave—or not to have come in the first place.

'Oh where will it all end!' I would exclaim, beneath my breath, while I trudged back home with the shopping.

Still now, as I kept on walking, reaching almost to where the recycling bins for clothes, shoes, and different-coloured glass are to be found, my attention would keep drifting back to the rooftops and sky. It would alight for a moment on passers-by across the way from the hoardings—for there are so few signs around here of the sorts of mutual recognition that a lonely soul returned to his home country might hope to find in the encounters of everyday outings to the post office or the shops.

In comparison to the black-and-white footage of old twentieth-century urban areas there are so few people around—which is odd when you think of the increased populations since then—but there are very few indications of people popping in and out of shops, doing their com-missions, or running their errands, as it used to be called.

There are almost no signs of children playing out in the street, marking the paving slabs with hop-scotch squares, at skip-rope or football, and it makes you wonder what has happened to the idea of shared or communal spaces. Have they become deserted through a species of social fear? Is it because playing out in the road is now the equivalent of jaywalking in a rat-run? Or are there too many fearful strangers around, strangers lurking under the yew trees?

No, there's hardly anyone; but these days you wouldn't dare speak to a child for fear of being taken for one of those very strangers you yourself were warned against when young.

Or is it that the populations have been trained only to do such things in a municipal park, such as the one nearby with the statue of the local biscuit king, transferred from the town because it was in the way of the traffic, criticized at the time of its unveiling because he appeared to be wearing un-pressed trousers—a park laid out for them at about the time that the rows of terrace houses round here were built? It could only make you feel more strangely alone, even among the habitations of so many people—people complexly and yet separately interrelated.

For this is indeed an international community, one to which people come to change their lives or become who they feel themselves to be—and walking along I would think of the young Polish Catholic families at Mass on Sundays, the group of local Japanese mothers, or the survivors of the Irish immigrations down through a hundred years from the famine to the economic miracle.

Then there were the incomers from pogroms and totalitarian regimes in the middle of the last century, the Belgian refugees of 1914, the kinder-transports of the 1930s, and therapists from German-speaking lands … Now migrants had followed them from the countries of southern and eastern Europe whose economies have been in precarious states for some years now—and all of them coming here to make lives for themselves, and make our lives more variously inflected with something resembling a proto-world-culture.

For as long as this world is an unequal place (and it's difficult to see an end to such global inequality), and as long as the world becomes more interconnected by trade, so that the inequalities grow ever more visible to the people who form, or are meant to form, the docile markets for those global producers, so will they continue to imagine better lives elsewhere.

They will want to travel nearer to the point of production, or, more likely these days, to the point where the management of investment capital, or technological research and development, has generated a vast secondary service sector of bar and restaurant staff—but not now to the point of production, where, however unequal the economic structure of those countries, they will be less unequal than those between the successful producers and the target populations for convenient imports or exports.

Because if change will happen whatever we do, then we are presented with the challenge of making decisions, boycotts and choices, thinking about the differences, differences which will guide the changes in such a way that the world becomes the one we have made, and not merely the one that has made us, nor the one that happened to happen by a species of unintended consequence, a world unwittingly malformed in our own image.

That marvellously insightful eighteenth-century Anglophile aphorist, who was also and understandably an enthusiast for the masterstroke work that is at all times with me, would write: 'Most of our writers possess, I do not say insufficient genius, but insufficient sense to write a *Robinson Crusoe*.' Yet this admirer of a work that combines so relentlessly a confidence of agency and belief in Providence—was not inclined to give too much credence to the idea of freedom and free will.

'How did men arrive at the concept of *freedom*?' he asks, and adds: 'It was a great idea.'

'Many are obscurely aware', he also notes in one of his

pennyworths of wisdom, 'of how mechanical man is in all his so-called acts of free will ... In regard to the body we are quite obviously slaves ... What if belief we are acting freely consists merely in the feeling that now the clock is working properly?'

Naturally enough, in my present convalescent state, the bosom returned an echo to that intuition of his—adding, as I could and he couldn't because of predating the philosopher of the *Zeitgeist*, that if we are slaves to our bodies, then the master–slave dialectic must be internalized in us too.

And again, as if he were a follower of the great Dutch philosopher, our aphorist reflects:

> That a false hypothesis is sometimes to be preferred to the correct one can be seen in the case of the doctrine of the freedom of man. Man is certainly not free, but not to be misled by this idea requires a very profound study of philosophy ... Freedom is thus really the most convenient and comfortable way of picturing the matter to oneself and, since it has appearance so very much on its side, will for all time remain the most usual one.

But speaking of that famous Dutchman, thinking of him at his lens grinding as I wandered along, it had always puzzled me how a strict determinist such as him, a non-believer in free will, could also be an early libertarian in his political thought. He was such a logical thinker that the latter couldn't have been merely the fact that he had been brought up in the free-thinking city of Amsterdam, and had been early excommunicated from the Jewish faith for what sounded like the taint of heresy and atheism that would unfairly haunt him through his life, requiring him to publish his works anonymously.

But might this Robinson, this Crusoe of the suburbs that I'm doomed to impersonate, might he with some justification not claim to be a follower, too, of that determinist who argued for libertarian politics? If so, it will be because, as the argument might go, people cannot help being what they are, all being determined, and they should therefore be allowed to live in communities that do not prevent them, in so far as is compatible with respect for others, being what they can't help being whether the laws of the land happened to criminalize it or not. It was only too likely that, had I lived in the seventeenth century, I too would have had to keep my thoughts to myself, and to publish whatever works might be produced under a pseudonym—one like Jack Robinson, for instance—and to publish them elsewhere.

But you can see immediately that this is not what the 'mission' of these constitutionals had exactly been. The plan, rather, was to make a difference to more than myself and my physical health by going for these walks, which I've been calling constitutionals because of the way in which the language happily catches an embedded metaphor in the idea of taking the body politic for a walk as well.

Nor would these have been the first, or last times, that people had thought you could make a difference to the political life of the world by going for a walk, though they would more usually call it a march, and—as the March on Rome of 1922 reminded me right then—you can't be sure that going for a walk is going to do yourself or anyone else any good.

Then walking along, I would be thinking about the hunger marches, the Jarrow March, all the way down from the North East to the centre of power in London, or of the so-called Great Trespass, when a crowd of hill walkers climbed Kinder Scout to take back the countryside, or the great CND marches which set off from the nuclear weapons establishment not far from here, or the Long March itself, which eventually resulted in the founding of the present Chinese Communist state.

Merely thinking of those examples could lead you to accept that two out of three of these famous marches had changed things substantially—though evidently not always for the better. So even when going for a walk, it is necessary to be careful what you wish for.

The Great Trespass, it's true, had led to the protection of public rights of way across the owned countryside. The Long March established power structures that have, for better and worse, richer and poorer, altered yet once more the dynastic history of among the world's oldest, and certainly its oldest-surviving, civilizations.

Those hunger marches and the great CND parades at the height of the Cold War, while they can't be said to have directly changed policy in ways that would have satisfied their constitutional walkers, who's to say that they didn't keep alive values that would have died altogether had they not set out?

Who indeed is to say that those walks went or got nowhere? They have certainly remained examples of values that were preserved in the culture and are remembered as such, even as the powers-that-were then failed to take sufficient note—sufficient note of those only too rational and sensible human needs for sustenance and survival.

And, for that matter, as I was aimlessly walking along, while the dogs continued to live their doggy lives, or so it might seem, on a day like today, a local taxi happened to go past with a lurid red advert, its logo containing the three scallops of the town's coat of arms.

Those three shells are the heraldic reminder that this place had once been, like Canterbury and Compostela, a destination for pilgrimages—in this case to St Anne's Well, where pilgrims would, until the English Reformation, set out with the scallop shells on spiritual-health-granting constitutionals to pay tribute to those values and make differences to their health and welfare.

But now, finally, thinking these things, the clocks gone forward just a week before, I didn't know where to put myself, so light was the sky, and me there walking home again alone. Seeing too as we're all the things we do, here bound again to this same route, this same routine, reassuring at blossom time, with the magnolia-sprinkled pavements beyond, along Erleigh Road towards Eastern Avenue, how could I be different if I weren't doing something else?

The area at this time of year is re-coloured by ground-cover plants at garden walls and corners, bursting forth, a roused squirrel rustling in its undergrowth, birds' arias punctuating the air's fresh currents, the re-sown lawns sprouting their thin grass crowns. And it's at such moments that I would reflect on having come through yet another difficult winter, that at last my health appeared to be slowly on the mend, my weariness and fret miraculously lifting.

Now we were all able to look forward to the coming months of warmer weather, even if punctuated as they are here by the showers of rain that do so much for the lushness of our greenery, the sense of burgeoning possibility, swelling with what might be the illusion of more time created by the longer days, the daylight stretching on toward ten o'clock of those light future nights at the height of June.

I could hope that my health would return completely, and the art of the possible could be re-established, even to our devastated politics. We could do it. And all we would have to do is go for constitutionals. All of us, I mean.

For in spring even an ageing man's fancy can lightly turn to thoughts of love, of his old loves and more recent ones, and of how right now would be the time, if ever there was one, to be starting over.

47

It has been said by a philosopher of walking that taking such exercise is a means for suspending or dispersing your personality—but, if some philosophers are anything to go by, then all good philosophy is peripatetic, though maybe they only get their thoughts when out on a mountainside or brooding on being and having time alone along some woodland way.

But perhaps, quite unthinkingly, I had hit upon just the right method for dispersing that Crusoe-fixated self, that bogeyman of the Protestant ethic, the rise of capitalism, and all its consequent global ills ... I had, in my feigned madness, followed that German romantic poet in 'Der Spaziergang' where he would be repaid for every thorn in his bosom and the darkness of his mind and heart, put there from the beginning as grief for thought and art.

Or I may have followed, at the same time, another work in the German language by a writer who, it has seemed at least to me, may have been putting on madness in his sequestered later life—I mean that prose with the same name, *Der Spaziergang*, whose author would die from what may have been a heart attack when out on a walk in the snow on Christmas Day 1956, if I remember rightly.

For the idea, if I indeed understand it aright, is that by going for a walk, and what is meant by this is a purposeless drifting—as you might toss a coin at each corner so as not to decide yourself what would be the road not taken—going for a walk means abandoning, at least for the time of that excursion, the habits and habituations essential to the holding down of a job, and the accumulating of such capital as steady work and regular habits, going early to bed and rising early, which would constitute a compensation for the loss—or the never gaining—of wealth, health, and wisdom.

Naturally, I have doubts about such a theory, not least because putting it into action requires the walker self-consciously to bracket out the workaday self, that reference point in a network of digital information exchange, which is to be refreshed or displaced by the peripatetic activity. Yet the very self-consciousness in that bracketing out, like making a point of being off-line for a weekend, points to the presence of the monitory entity—for that very self-consciousness, an indispensable element in a modern identity, would surely be standing guard so as to prevent the possibility of the changes that it has conjured into illusory existence for the purposes of a little rest and relaxation.

Thus would it so often transpire in theoretical writing, that the price of the proffered potential for freedom from the anxieties associated with getting and spending would be isolation from the culture and community where that freedom from economic constraint was most needed—and because you couldn't have it both ways, have your cake and eat it too, well, it seemed, you couldn't really have either the confectionery or the digestive issue at all.

Just so would the wandering poets manage to establish a suitably dispersed lyric subjectivity and an endlessly receding horizon of imagined community only by finding themselves first detached from any sphere of political action, of the ideally preferred kind (for our famous visitor's gun-running would surely not count)—and, as that same temporarily resident Symbolist's subsequent career choices suggest, to be driven either to abandon poetry, or be confined as of unsound mind.

Thus the wanderings of any such poetic 'I'—as it might be yourself or another—would always already, as the hackneyed jargon has it, be a return over the ground broken by those originating explorers, who had been compelled to separate their drifting from the marching feet of citizen armies, and to distinguish the summer clouds in the sunset from the distant firestorms, lighting up the undersides of those very clouds, with the man-made *Götterdämmerungs* of bombing campaigns and other futuristic sublimities.

Put another way, what they were saying is that any attempt by a single individual to overthrow neoliberal economics by going for a walk would have to be Quixotic, because its very terms would separate the walker from the sphere in which the required changes would need to take place.

'But don't for a minute be taken in by all those poetical histories,' I said to myself, on returning now, 'after all, the same is true for the sorts of politicians who wear duffle coats or have Crusoe-like beards. They're just as likely to be granted the freedom to hold their more outlandish— as they'll be characterized—opinions, just so long as they accept that they'll be called "unelectable".'

There was, after all, that other old boy of the local Leighton Park School, who, if I'm not mistaken, had included the nationalization of the banks as part of his election manifesto, one characterized as the longest suicide note in political history—ah, you of the duffle-coat and no tie, thou shouldst be living at this hour!

For walking these very streets, I had reflected that the flooding of taxpayer's money into the banking system so as to prevent it from collapsing that weekend when the then prime minister committed his memorable moment of parliamentary slip-of-the-tongue-hubris, and had gone at least some way to achieving the nationalization that his predecessor as party leader, at least, had seriously proposed as a remedy for our economic woes.

Only the PM and that other Darling—no, not the lifeboat-woman, Grace, or the family of Peter Pan's girlfriend, Wendy—but what's-his-name had failed to take the control that 'our' majority shareholding would suggest, and then in effect failed to direct the banks to work for the benefit of the productive economy, the small-sum taxpayers whose lives would be generally diminished and greyed by the austerity that ensued from the financial meltdown coterminous with my debilitation, the consequences of which, a little further down the line, would be the protest vote that further isolated and impoverished those very same 'left behind' voters.

For the pun upon which my epoch-changing walks have been constructed—that a personal change of air, a constitutional around this middle-sized county town, its place-name a hapless and inescapable pun into the bargain, could change the constitution—was nothing more than that, a play upon words. Yet, still, when I thought of the pun on my first name in Greek that had been used to found a religion, or the pun on the angelic hosts and the name for its inhabitants that had sent a saint to convert this country, when I thought of them it made me wonder if that local writer who had produced a book called *Puns* might not have been on to something after all.

48

'You just go for a walk and then write about it,' as my family used to say, and it's true, though how I got into this habit is yet another story—though, come to think of it, one I've probably in effect told by reporting on this need to get away, and the need to get back again. Yet what I had attempted all those years ago might not have been so different in its stubborn resistance to the traditional supports of faith and belief, another way in which I might have been a 'Crusoe', despite my having been called that only for spite.

Coming back past the doctor's surgery on another of those constitutionals, I would recall with yet another twinge of conscience how, on a later visit when the symptoms were weakening and I had listened to the dispiritingly limited diagnoses, I had also lost my temper with a particularly unfeeling doctor.

What had been so exasperating, after all, was the way in which this particular member of the medical profession had nothing to offer in explanation for what had produced that long-drawn-out collapse, nor did he have any remedies for the aches and pains, the other humiliations to be suffered and endured, that, in short, he had nothing to give—which didn't prevent him from asserting his rights over my body, from calling me in for tests, subjecting me to scans and other invasive explorations, dispossessing me, if temporarily, during that illness, of my own life.

But that too I had to forgive and forget, to be grateful for the small mercy that even though they couldn't do anything, and never did come to any useful conclusions from all the procedures they put me through, that, still, thank Providence, whatever that is, I did eventually recover, recover enough to be taking this walk on beyond that very same doctor's door.

So on I would tread, extremely tired now, and hurrying too, as I will have needed to relieve myself yet again, past the local car dealer, the recently opened street corner café... and noticing, there on the pavement, those bluebottles swarming on a remnant of dead blackbird.

For by now it seemed the spring too was enduring its climacteric.

This way I would come walking again, making a visual audit of the litter-bins, the gardens' FOR SALE and TO LET signs, signs whose eventual removal a few years later would reduce the petty crime rate round here by some fifty per cent, and the graffiti—or counting the cost of the house-price inflation, still in that taciturn street's silences to which by slow habituation I had begun to feel that we belonged— beside the phalanxes of buddleia, the Japanese knotweed, and pink magnolia blossom.

Then again it might strike such a contemporary outside the halal shop's vegetable stall, one obsessed by wars in this martial country, and by war's memory, something that again was brought home in the reverse culture shock of return, yes, might strike you just how obsessed we are with our twentieth-century's wars, our military prowess, our successes and failures of arms—something else that will have to change if we are ever to put aside our delusions of grandeur and become equal members of a continental or a global civility.

Yet how hard that will be for us to do, it being part of our vanity-nationalism, our nostalgic cult of greatness, that grotesque global power that some of us want to get back, a fantasy of independence from the mutually inter-determining processes out of which none of us can extricate ourselves except in death, and, even then, only as far as our consciousness is concerned—for all the matter of ourselves, which cannot be created or destroyed, remains as part of the great ongoing mass of it all.

And I could see how here in Erleigh village our lives lived in parallel, with a mutual-seeming tolerant non-understanding, are so frailly and vulnerably subject to fracture in times of downturn, austerity, and the threat of unemployment.

That's how it is for this makeshift population of ours, acquainted with the hairline cracks in the neighbourhood pavement by St Luke's church hall where we mauled those songs and dances with lots of lads and lasses, all with smiling faces, and all gone down the Scotswood Road, to see the 'Blaydon Races'. But even that happened only the once. No, as I say, these days my Friday dances no more.

Then, towards the end of this walking day, the church hall's painterly brickwork being picked out in late raking sun, inside the church hall, remember, there's a brass plaque that says the building was used as a clearing station for stretcher cases with a Blighty one—our remnants repatriated from Calais about a hundred years ago. It was, doubtless, an overflow located here because it was so near to the Royal Berkshire Hospital where the mutilated would be taken to be patched up as best as the medical profession of that time could manage.

Going past the church hall, remembering the dance where I first saw that plaque acknowledging its role during the Great War, I was once again reminded of the future modernist poet—yes, Bunting—who passed through here too, and how he might have wandered this way on his unauthorized escapade from Leighton Park School—that trip into town made during his first term here on Saturday

the 21st of October 1916, the Battle of the Somme with still
a month to run as it petered out in a stalemate of mud and
blood.

Once again, too, I would sense that the pain of the past
had been absorbed into the brickwork, the built environment
as if like the blood on palace walls in that poem called
'London'—which would explain why the place can feel so
anguished, the sort of anguish that had led me to find out
about the local hostel for Belgian refugees, the POW camp
on Newbury race course, and the role played by HM Prison
after Easter 1916 in the incarceration of yet more famous
Irishmen, such as the then leader of the Sinn Fein party. I
would assuage my guilty feelings by going and looking up
information about them in the Berkshire Records Office on
the western side of town.

And passing by St Luke's church, I would imagine the
rector from his pulpit, as if in imitation of Christ driving out
the money changers from the temple, hear him intoning
for his parishioners: 'For we have regulated what we ought
not to have regulated, and deregulated what we ought not
to have deregulated, and there is no wealth in us ...'—his
congregation piously nodding at their vicar's imagined
aphoristic sagacity. But, then again, now that the current
Archbishop of Canterbury is an ex-businessman, and the
Church Commissioners are one of the largest landowners
and investors in the country, why couldn't the church take
a lead in the de-monetizing of the data?

But, then again, if you really do think that, then there
is nothing else for it but to keep on trying, and celebrating
the fact that the Kennet mouth hadn't been ruined by the
building of another link road, or yet spoiled with a park-
and-ride scheme, that the capacity of the inhabitants of a

place to shape its destiny, at least under such threats, had not been forfeited for ever to the largely unpredictable fluctuations of international capital.

Like those who are undefeated because they have gone on walking, in whatever long march or constitutional, I had no other choice than to get out of the house, to recover my health, to get myself back to fitness, all in aid of returning to face the struggle once more.

And yet walking along on that day of all days, I found myself imagining how in the past everything will have been different—such as at Cemetery Junction, with not a single car in sight—and, by that same token, how everything will be unrecognizably different in the future, and that the only thing you can say for sure about those times to come is that however they are, it won't be anything like, walking along here now, anything like you could ever imagine it to be.

49

Painfully slowly, home along Addington Road, was the way my convalescent Friday had decided to walk when finally discharged from the Royal Berkshire Hospital after that appendicitis operation, the one that had gone so terribly wrong in its after-care. It had been a much more dangerous situation, with the threat of peritonitis, than I had taken it to be at the time.

This street might well be named after a doctor and his son, the father having been a prime minister's physician, who also went on to treat that mad king of ours, the one who suffered from purple-pee disease, which is what had caused him to greet an oak tree as if it were a foreign ambassador—though it appears the man who may have given his name to our street had predicted his monarch would 'enjoy some remission from his mental problems', and he was proved right.

The doctor's son would grow up to become a Prime Minister in his turn, and be made a viscount, whose adopted name is memorialized by Sidmouth Street, not far away either, and one of the routes into town I would sometimes take on these constitutionals. This same personage had been Home Secretary at the time of Manchester's Peterloo Massacre in 1819, in which, by not playing a very noble part, he could also figure among the then contemporary politicians lambasted by that Romantic poet—who drowned off the coast from Leghorn, and was cremated on the beach—lambasted in his sonnet which addresses, from exile, the state of England in that very year.

My local informant also says that it is 'debatable' whether his father, the doctor, 'deserves to be honoured' in the town, since 'he kept a private madhouse, and is alleged to have claimed that the town contained an unusually large number of lunatics.'

'One is reminded', he adds, 'of the gravedigger in *Hamlet*, who similarly slandered the whole of England', saying that they think the Prince is mad and has been sent here because they're all mad in that country and so nobody will notice.

Wandering along this street at whose far end our little house sits, I would be reminded of that play's author— now how could I forget *that* name?—sitting in his London lodgings, rewriting and revising the whole of *Hamlet* in order to make use of that joke, and would be reminded of that thought again whenever I passed outside 2b Addington Road, which, as my local informant also writes, 'bears the name of the Prince of Denmark'—calling it, as he does, a 'pardonable pun'; and indeed from the name of this town to the title of this book there are activating puns aplenty to pardon and forgive.

Passing outside Gravel Pit Lodge on a day like today I'll notice again how the owners have made improvements, changing the doors and windows to the ubiquitous white plastic ones, and re-roofing it not in slate but fired-clay tiles. Gravel Pit Lodge is a tiny bungalow at the eastern end of the northern side of Addington Road. It stands out proud from the building line of the terrace-row that starts immediately west of it—yet the little cottage also appears to cower behind the JC Decaux hoardings that stand tall and bold, in their bright colours and larger than life-size celebrity faces, all around the corner where Addington meets Erleigh Road.

The little one-story dwelling's name suggests that it may have been constructed when this area was on the still-rural eastern edges of the town, before being built up into its capital-wards ribbon development sprawl. There must have been a gravel pit falling immediately behind it, for the land drops mysteriously at that point into a shallow depression, a depression now filled with a housing development.

These quite recent stints of home-building are, in effect, masked by the hoardings advertising a world of pleasures so contrastive in their textures and colours to the building materials, the patched asphalt road coverings, and the remnant nature of trees, knotweed, and surviving gardens (the ones not concreted or bricked over to form parking spaces) around this end of Addington and Erleigh Road— where it looks as though there must have been a two-pronged terminus point, opposite the crescent of shops, for the far end of an old tram line.

Gravel Pit Lodge is the most intriguing structure hereabouts, to my mind, and yet I've still never seen any sign of life in it, anyone arriving or leaving. But how true this is of so many houses and homes around here. You can see the lighted windows of an evening, and can occasionally glimpse people walking down the street, though more frequently you only notice cars and buses—but, as I say, what you don't see much of is people going in and out of their houses, or dropping into their neighbours' for a chat. It is as if the people live in hiding, or are ever in danger of being burgled, being always at work or socializing elsewhere, and so never here.

For public space, as suggested, is a no-place now, a no man's land, like the little patches of ground around cash-dispensing machines—there's one on the side of the Co-op—where nobody stays for long, and everyone is suspiciously glancing around to make sure there's nobody encroaching too closely upon them, as they punch in their secret codes, remembering always to conceal the key pad as they punch.

Thereabouts, and especially on Saturday nights and Sunday mornings, the ground is littered with abandoned receipts, like leaves swept into this no-place in autumn, and that dingy, wind-blown corner, it looks so all forlorn.

More often than not, as now, I'll return home along Erleigh Road, by way of the Co-op, coming back past the further crescent of businesses, with a betting shop that posts the prospects for the football teams in that week's games—so I can note how frequently the outcomes that they post, odds on, do not occur.

And that's how this place of unlikely poetry and inspiration will impinge, an inspiration from the most ordinary of things in its vicinity, the tops of trees stirring in the slightest of breezes, for instance, and celebrated, if celebrated at all, by relentlessly keeping going, by a dogged refusal to be put off by misfortunes, and all of it a reverberation of what has been involved in taking into myself that schoolyard taunt and nickname.

It must have been the sight, yet once more, of that betting shop with the odds for the weekend's matches in its windows, and the promises of what you would earn on a £10 bet that had done it.

Suddenly, passing there, it dawned on me: just as compulsive gamblers who ruin their own and their families' lives in such betting shops, with online devices, or traditionally at dog or horse racing tracks, or who are ruined because they are responsible for their own losses, all those who work in financial institutions, and who are given large bonuses whether their firms make profits or not, using others' hard-earned pension funds, all of them should be made, by law, *personally* liable for losses on any and every market trade they made.

That's what would, at a stroke, slow the madness down! For what employee who could be personally bankrupted any day at work would continue to serve the company as they do? What executive, who had to reach into his—or still rarely now her—own pocket to refund all the little investors' losses, would allow their traders the freedom they currently enjoy? The freedom to bring down long established companies like the Queen's own bank, for instance...and it's something of a personal triumph that the rogue trader who achieved this feat single-handedly is now brought out from time to time as a commentator on the state of the world's banking systems and trading environments!

Such a requirement to personal liability, if put into practice, might even bring all this speculative gambling on the future to a halt; but then, I immediately reflected, as the clouds above were cut with a tinge of sunset in the west, bringing such speculation on the future to a halt might also bring the future itself to a stand-still, or the future at least as currently imagined.

But as I struggled on to the end of this particular constitutional through the last outlets that make up the eastern edge of Erleigh village, I felt again the solitude and isolation that comes with the discovery of hair-brained or high-minded solutions to present predicaments, solutions that are unlikely ever to be put into practice. So too was I brought back to the signs of community and collaboration, to the notion of a polis, and the fundamental contradiction that an individual could remain just that and yet also do what is required of her or him—let alone to do so by such a thing as going for a walk.

And as I stumbled on into the gloaming there came towards me other strollers, talking out loud to themselves, or so it seemed, or with their faces up-lit by the screens of their devices. They do say, I was thinking at the sight of it, that the new technologies, screens and tablets, smart phones and laptops, or our addiction to them at least, have formed a concerted attack on 'solitude'—but I ask you, what have they done for loneliness?

50

Continuing to put one foot in front of the other, on another mad March evening, I might notice the wind funnelling through the grasses and flowerbeds of the remaining gardens, the ones not sacrificed to the exigencies of the internal combustion engine as a ubiquitous mode of personal transport—for, what's more, some of the concreted over front gardens are now, in effect, overnight parking for the vehicles of the town's taxi firms.

It was then, noticing those surviving flowerbeds, yet once more as I passed the graffiti-daubed electricity sub-station, that it suddenly dawned how you had yourself changed, had changed yourself, how these constitutionals really must have made a difference, that this was, for better or worse, another person than the one who had set out on them at one ambiguous beginning of spring. Yet, peculiarly coloured by these circumstances, the circumstances that help form a contrast between my surroundings and my self, this person appeared to have got sharper too, making me even more like a Robinson returned to his home world.

For, after all, Crusoe was himself a poet, as is revealed in the third and final volume of his autobiography, where he gives us his *Serious Reflections during the Life and Surprizing Adventures*—on that life of wanderings looked over at all times by a providential God. Nor is Robinson's poetry any worse than that of his creator. Pilloried for his pamphlet *The Shortest Way with the Dissenters*, and ever the projector, the man on the lookout for a new point of sale, he had his friends sell the large crowd of gathered spectators— who threw flowers at the future inventor of Crusoe, not the usual rotten vegetables—had them sell copies of 'A Hymn to the Pillory', which, as I mentioned, he composed and had printed for this very occasion.

Whether the poet was active during the composition of *Robinson Crusoe* is not something everyone agrees on. About sixty years after its publication, one critic whose name escapes me wrote, for instance, that 'our Author's energy runs into harshness, and his sweetness is to be tasted in his prose more than in his poesy.' However, he then adds that if 'we regard the adventures of Crusoe, like the adventures of Telemachus, as a poem, his moral, his incidents, and his language, must lift him high on the poet's scale.'

And perhaps it's this that makes the book so useful a guide, being poetry in the form of prose, and a novel pretending to be an autobiography, or a fabrication that sounds like the factual history of a man talking to himself and us, one describing how he survived—writing it down in order to survive. About a hundred years ago, yet another admirer of its author praises the great novel by reassuring his readers that when 'a new language is invented, *Robinson Crusoe* is one of the first books published in it'.

For, despite its inevitable denigrators, whether the Nobel-Prize-winners or the Jack Robinsons of this world, what an extraordinary work this *Robinson Crusoe* is! There must have been a time, though I can hardly recover it, when I wasn't aware of its existence, but now, as I glance along my bookshelves at the variously coloured spines in my carefully cellophane-wrapped collection of first editions, it seems as if the children's reductions had forever been at my side to guide me.

At first, as you can imagine, they were the illustrated ones with a shipwreck, the man in his goatskin suit and sunshade, with the footprint in the sand, and his black manservant and faithful companion. There I read of his confrontation with the cannibals and pirates, and his return

273

home, finally, to an England he had been dreaming about through all those years of exile and isolation.

The time when I wasn't aware of it must have been the almost irrecoverable dawning of the child in me, the little boy who hadn't yet learned to read, couldn't read the great classic that has formed such a recourse to innumerable people, real and imagined, both in life and literature.

Back then, with the idea of making something out of my unwanted isolation, I had begun collecting a dossier of the more famous instances to be used in the never completed *Crusoe and the Poets*—though my love of what is said to be the first novel doesn't quite extend to that of perhaps *Robinson Crusoe*'s greatest fan, or at least his greatest fictional one, namely Gabriel Betteredge, the house-steward to Julia, Lady Verinder, in *The Moonstone*. I have the book before me now.

'When my spirits are bad', he will always turn, he says, to '*Robinson Crusoe*.' And when he wants advice he will always resort to '*Robinson Crusoe*'. 'I have worn out', he reports, 'six stout *Robinson Crusoes* with hard work in my service. On my lady's last birthday she gave me a seventh. I took a drop too much on the strength of it; and *Robinson Crusoe* put me right again. Price four shillings and sixpence, bound in blue, with a picture into the bargain.' The house-steward's character, and mine too, as you have seen, is thus fixed by his almost addicted belief that *Robinson Crusoe* will 'put me right again.'

Still, though not able to compete with this fictional character, *Robinson Crusoe* had, at least, taught me how to try and be stubbornly resilient and to convert the misfortunes of life into a source of strength to resist them—and what more could a book be expected to do?

So when, a little while ago, a struggling local bookseller set out to get more people into his shop by inviting them to be professionally photographed there among the shelves, holding 'The Book of my Life'—as the project was called—I naturally answered his call and took along a tome from my collection of rare and illustrated editions.

There I am with my straggly uncut beard and long silver hair, thinning on top now to almost nothing, wearing some tatters of old clothes, the kind aged parents can't throw away out of sentimental attachments invisible to others, and clutching a mid-nineteenth-century edition of—you guessed it—the book of my entire existence, *The Life and Surprizing Adventures of Robinson Crusoe, &c.*

It had, indeed, been a Quixotic project—this attempt to change the world and institute an honest politics by going for these constitutionals. Yet, the time it took, and the conditions in which they had been taken, those constitutionals too had helped me think and realize what such an honest politics would involve, or how, unlikely as it may seem, and especially now, such a politics could evolve.

There were, as I walked, three main points emerging: for whatever you should criticize, diagnose, complain about or oppose, you should always include yourself, and your own complicity, in the state of things that you claim to hate.

And before you set out on a career of complaint and opposition, whether as something you undertake while getting your health back or not, before you heckle and barrack the state of things, be sure you have a plan for what to do should you succeed, a plan that includes the recognition of your own sickness in the symptoms you're setting out to treat.

And whatever plan you put forward, insofar as possible, make sure it is achievable, and that its costs are realistically calculated too. That way you won't be blaming others for creating the conditions you have a hand in yourself, and won't be making things worse by stirring up expectations of change that you can't then deliver—and won't either be attempting to bring such changes into being without having a sense of the costs involved, or, again, a sense of your own complicity in the incurring of those costs.

And all the rest isn't literature, Monsieur What-Was-Your-Name, it's politics—which so often seems the art of blaming others for what you've done yourself, and of failing even to do the possible (which, as doubtless already noted elsewhere, no longer seems to be, if it ever was, the realm of the political arts). For, come to think of it, however much they traffic in impossibilities, even literature and poetry are not as bad as that.

So it was, then, that my not quite aimless drifting from one point of interest to the next had simultaneously been recouping my forces, re-establishing my habits, and subjecting them to a gentle deviation. For if habit as good as foretells us who or where we'll be, however late, then by deciding on impulse to cross over to the far side of the street, the route almost never taken, you would thus subject yourself to a change of viewpoint and the promise of a different set of coordinates.

Or, just a little more consciously, I could make a point of disturbing my routines and habits. I could, with a Francophile inflection to the words, subject my entire being to an enlivening derivation, and thus, by homeopathic doses of renewal, might even go so far as to change my life; and, for that matter, if we all of us did so, attending to our carelessness, our carelessness for self or others, perhaps with us the entirety would change as well. For this is how, by going for a walk, and altering your route and your attention, you might contribute, believe it or not, not to the ends or end, but to the demise of neoliberal capitalism.

So on I would go, having first to cross the road before turning the corner, past the high, shaped hedges of our neighbour's front garden, a form of blank topiary expressing her obsession with being overlooked by making it impossible to be so overlooked, a desire of hers that we naturally respected—though, as I write, or, better, revise, she has now had them cut down.

Then up the path I must turn, the path, you remember, made of seaside pebbles—reminding me every time I step onto it of these surprising and further adventures, those years of beach combing on our remote ocean-lapped island with my Friday, I'm sorry, my own dear wife.

Down the path the steps would be taken so that finally I'd arrive at our front door, its original wood also dated 1929, the year of that earlier crash, a little rotten at the edges now, its many coverings of gloss paint matted by the weather through more than ninety winters, and flaking to reveal the layers of what might be called *pentimenti* as well.

I'll place the key in the lock, and thus, as I step across the WELCOME mat, and call out that I'm home, receiving from an upper floor or out the back, a returning echo, there and then I will feel in my bosom, here in my heart of hearts, will feel that I have indeed become somebody else!

51

But the last time I happened to go that way again, there was somebody accompanying me. Our daughter, also smitten with the sea, despite all our warnings, like those of Crusoe's father before him, that time she had come along too—to talk about her future. No, our daughter hadn't yet decided quite how she might sail away, but that was where she was heading. As if she could only feel at home when casting off from shore, with the boom swinging as the boat turned to take advantage of the wind, as if it were in the blood, she had settled on a maritime existence.

But now, here in this Thames valley town, she was tied up for the winter, the hatches battened down, wondering what to do with herself, landlocked, as it were. So we had gone out for another of my constitutionals, in aid of a father and daughter heart-to-heart.

Beyond the Thames Promenade, on that nondescript weekday, we were trying to find a way across town from that western point on the Thames, to get back across to the Kennet canal; but, not fully appreciating the degree of their divergence on the western side of the town, had got ourselves lost among its industrial cul-de-sac developments, its small business constructions and technology park roundabouts.

Emerging by the relief-road's under- and over-pass complexes that cut the town in half, we had found ourselves beside the blank-walled flow, the flow and counter-flow of traffic lanes, verges, and their exhausted dust. And I didn't know if it was the Holy Brook, this backwater stream, a remnant of the many that flowed across this once marshy terrain, running through undergrowth by a starter-home estate, its dwellings screened from ring-road asphalt by the ground cover's greying leaves.

Above one edge of the thunderous gulf were sheared-off end walls showing how the town's grand streets were orphaned, were blighted. And that was the road we decided to take.

But this was where my daughter effectively turned the tables on me. I had set off on the walk thinking that we would be discussing her future, her career ambitions, her difficulties with others, whether it be friends or relations, the people at work—yes, she was working as a receptionist at a local GP's surgery until the weather turned and she could cast off and get back to sea once more.

Instead, I found myself defending this habit of mine, the habit of writing down things that happen, changing them as I do so that the contours stay true—or that's what I was arguing—though the detail was selected and shifted so as to align differently and to suggest possibilities that might not have been evident in the originally prompting experience at all.

Though they might have been, and it was always an open question as to whether I had simply invented the meaning of events, or had teased out of them a significance which lay within—but one overlaid with the full flood of experiential detail which meant that you couldn't see the wood for the trees, as it were, and you couldn't see the meaning because there was too much material to be its bearer in the encounter with phenomena at eye level in the street, or on such repeated constitutionals as mine.

It's a moot point as to whether our ability to select out detail, not so much to forget as never to notice, is one of the ways in which we survive as a species, or one of the things that threatens us as one. Would we be better noticing more?

Is writing like this a way of preserving more than is usually noticed, or a way of giving prominence to a tiny fraction of what was actually experienced, and then almost as quickly forgotten?

I didn't know the answers to such questions, which kept coming up as we walked and talked that day in earliest springtime, before the weather changed.

'But isn't the point of writing just to get your own back on the world, or to justify a groundless sense of superiority?' she asked.

'No, surely not,' I replied, humiliated by the whole performance once more. 'I don't think it can be—because if the motivation is that kind of selfishness, then the writing won't come out anyway. Nor can it be done as a form of compensation for things that you can't get or do in life.'

'Oh come on,' she came back. 'Isn't that exactly what you've been doing all this time?'

'I hope not,' I said, and went on to explain, at least to my own satisfaction, that this kind of thing couldn't be done because you needed to increase your self-esteem, or your standing in others' eyes. After all, as I have known to my cost, it as good as risked the opposite.

So it all came down—I was trying to explain—to the theory of beneficial side effects, a version of unintended consequences, that you can't aim to get beauty or affect, but only have it as a side effect of trying to communicate something—where the unintended is by no means as bad as it's usually painted, or at least not always as bad.

'This curious calling of yours to have life relived in a representation,' she interrupted, 'are you just saying that it can't be any kind of excuse for failing to face up to what you would anyway need or have to be?'

'I'm saying that if you don't expect anything of it, this writing, and the writing life can reward you in all sorts of unexpected ways—but if you need it to do that for you, it most assuredly won't.'

'Oh,' she said, and left me standing there staring at a flaked brick wall.

'But don't you sometimes feel the world's unreal,' her nineteen-year-old self returned. We were crossing a super-market car park, making our way between the vehicles and recently planted trees, rising thin from the freshly laid asphalt.

At which I said that, yes, of course I did. In fact that same sensation would befall me all the time, but the only thing to do was to get on with it, to try and direct the dream, as you sometimes can when its shallow and near waking, in the hour or so before and after the dawn chorus sounds.

And, there and then, I tried to account for it in such a way as to reassure her that it was normal, and to tell her how she might lessen the sensation if it was oppressive—by sharing it with others, for instance—or to indulge it as a comedy, if that might be helpful.

'La vida es sueño', I said, to reassure her it wasn't, like, a new idea.

'Doubtless,' she said, in her teen-drama voice, 'but frankly it's more like a nightmare.'

'A lonely one as well,' I couldn't help adding.

'Oh Dad, cut that Crusoe-back-in-England stuff, would you?' That's what she said, and quite right too.

So life was, as the song would have it, but a dream and, come on now, you might think it true on such an afternoon of slant breeze and sunshine. I knew as much, though the doubt would have it this could be a dream too, as the slogans from our working lives fluttered from all the tattered banners of ambition—which I like to think will pass as all things must, like wind-gusts through the canal-side trees.

On the better spring days those surviving gardens would be intermittently crossed with shafts of sunlight playing over the strawberry plants and sprouting leaves, the latest stripes of tulip. Then my daughter's conversation would replay itself, the one as to whether—again in the words of that song—life is but a dream.

Though, yes indeed, you can never be sure that you aren't asleep and dreaming your life, like those slogans with their patently untrue boasts and claims, still I can dare to dream, can't I?—and put my trust, at least for a moment, in the devices and desires of our own hearts.

But, no, life couldn't be a dream, as I woke again to find it true, for despite those who claim that you can train yourself beneficially to direct your dreaming, I would keep coming back to the evident fact that the world didn't move at my will, that I couldn't move the world because I didn't know where to put the fulcrum, and couldn't move it whether I knew where to put the fulcrum or not, because my mind could not provide that sort of leverage.

Yet this is perhaps one of the reasons why life can seem a dream—simply because you can't direct it by acts of will, so it seems to be living itself, a relief at times and a terror at others.

Did I have to accept, then, that it was just an illusion? Like a help with my convalescence, my attempt to get back the ordinary powers of locomotion and bodily self-regulation, but metaphorically exaggerated by means of a pun, had I merely been trying imaginatively to adumbrate powers to myself, powers over my own life, in their at least temporary absence?

Though there are plenty who will tell you it's the bottom line that rules the world, you would only have to reflect for a moment on what is now called 'the bank of mum and dad' to see that economic imperatives and their mathematical or algebraic formulas—for the relation of currency circulation speed to volume of economic activity, for instance—such calculations are for ever compromised by the fact that people will not always act, and so cannot be relied upon to act, according to their supposedly strictest financial interests.

This is especially so when the managers of 'Mum and Dad PLC' are discussing the terms for a possible loan to their children, for their children too, especially when young and needing to establish themselves in life, will, like Robinson Crusoe, not only disobey their fathers but act in what isn't their best financial interests either.

Because, you see, as I've already mentioned, and as if to cap it all, like taking after her father, our daughter had gone and run away to sea. She had fallen in love with the ocean wave, taken ship, yacht in fact, and found herself, in more than one sense, in the western Mediterranean, where she had managed to persuade the crew to employ her as a ship's cook on a rich man's folly.

After many adventures, which included accidently having her skipper walk the plank and take a dip in that vessel's French port's murky waters, she had eventually jumped ship after a dreadful storm in the Cape Verde Islands, and made her way back to this Thames valley town, where here and now she would regale us with her adventures—recuperate a while as well—and plan a more permanent escape from this island home in which once more she found she had been stranded.

52

Imagine yourself, then, taking your children to school first thing on an early spring morning, coming up Eastern Avenue, climbing, as you are, the southern slope of our river valley formed by the Kennet and the Thames—walking in the opposite direction to all these repeated constitutionals of mine.

You're taking your girls to kindergarten and the entry class of primary school, dropping them off so that you and your husband can get into work on time, to earn the dual-salary living that will meet the astronomical mortgage and the ever-rising household bills. After all, keeping the wolf from the door also requires you to have a door to keep him away from, and that means being in debt to a mortgage provider, a bank, and to the overnight interbank lending rate.

Then imagine yourself pausing to cross Crescent Road with your children at your coat tails, for the rat run has already started and the cars and white vans are tailing back past the crescent on Erleigh Road, past the betting shop, the chemists, appliance-fixers, the hairdressers, and South-Asian women's fashion outlet, past the JC Decaux hoardings with their further invitations to enjoy and benefit from all the good things on offer, almost as far as the Co-op.

Now one of those stuck cars will do the responsible thing and let you cross to the other side. It's another chilly English spring morning, with a threat of rain in the air, and those east winds of March don't so much make the heart a dancer as make the last of winter seem interminable, especially to a convalescent.

Then as you pause at the mini-roundabouts, you'll notice again across the way, and with some exasperation—exasperation reaching to a mild curse under your breath—a light on in that front window there, where a table has been moved into the over-priced semi's shallow bay.

'So how come he's allowed to work away at this hour,' I imagine you mumbling under your breath, 'while I'm on the school run, then off to a morning of answering emails?'

What you can see is a reading lamp arching above the head of an aged figure, with wispy white hair and beard, perhaps even wearing a fur hat of some kind, a figure hunched under its pool of light. He's typing furiously at the keyboard of a laptop computer, intent on the words filling up the electronic pages before his straining eyes.

Absorbed in what he's doing, this figure doesn't look up or round, and doesn't appear to notice you and the kids at your skirts. After a moment's irritated glance into that tiny un-curtained front room lined with books, you turn back to the street and shepherd your offspring away up this car-infested avenue.

What's so irritating, as you repeat (and would repeat to him), is that he's able to work at such an ungodly hour—while you're out taking the children to school. Yes, there he is, the spitting image of an unencumbered writer, *Il Penseroso*'s Platonist in his solitude, enviably able to concentrate a while on whatever is forming itself, forming itself under his eyes—before the demands of another working day will doubtless press in upon him too, ship-wrecking him as well with its seemingly endless demands on our time that now tie us to this whole great island that is the world.

Those demands and their exorbitant costs will soon enough take the pair of us away from this page. They will oblige one or other, or both, to put the book down, or switch of the backlighting.

We'll be required to get on with answering the messages that will have piled up in our inboxes, even as we were devoting a few moments to ourselves, giving ourselves a little time to think and even dream.

There will be the paying of bills by online direct debt, the arranging of meetings, the answering of questions, the preparation of documents and accounts, the balancing of books and expectations—all the exchanging of attachments, as we call them, around the points of our electronic networks and social media venues.

'I envy you sitting there with the time to write in the circle of your lamplight. I envy you,' she might well be saying to herself with her lovely kids in tow. I know she will, because she will repeat it to my face.

But please, no, dear reader, whatever you do, don't envy me. I don't envy myself, as you ought to know by now. I don't, and can't see why you would, envy what has compelled me to fill these pages with the account of these exasperated, and exasperating constitutionals, my attempts to get my health back, my health broken by overwork and stress, by the burdens of responsibility and their inevitable frustrations.

Don't envy this compulsion to find in the darkening dream that passes outside this window traces of an alternative to what had broken my health, as if thus to save the world, when all I was doing was recovering the strength to be overcome by it yet once more. Surely there's nothing to envy in that?

For the trace left by going for a walk, and then writing about it, is what plenty of people would call ludicrous anyway. To give your life a sense of purpose by producing these fragile tracks of significance, a sense so wedded to an illusion, what could be enviable in that?

So you see, goaded on by being the subject of a schoolyard nickname again after all these years, out of my weakness and recovery, the solitude and privacy of those repeated long walks down those very same paths, as you see, I found myself compelled to write it down.

For it wasn't the constitutionals themselves that would get my health back, or so I might think, but the positive sign that the circling around of those walks might eventually turn into works.

Every day, as the song goes, I write the book. And what would I be trying to achieve by such an obsessional and compulsive habit? Overthrowing an oppressive way of life, of course, as I've been saying all along. So while every day I write the book, it's as if what I do is realize that this self-justification of so Quixotic a variety would only further bemire me in the implications of the need, the humiliating need, to be forever doing it.

Although, as I've said, you might think inhabiting a cliché would prove difficult, I've found it comes quite naturally. It was, after all, the thing that made me feel like I belonged, belonged to the idea of being somebody, being able to survive extremes of isolation and lack of social support, something I could at least aspire to—and at least to the extent of being a Robinson, or a Pilgrim for that matter.

And so I could find myself in books, and in those around me, could find myself precariously a part of the remnant of what passes for community in a place driven forward by a competitiveness that would make the world your punching bag, if you would only let it.

Still I might wonder if any of us had a choice, being born into a hierarchy that still required its human sacrifices to placate the gods that control it, an order in which to have the time of our lives we would have to sell that time, so that others may have the time of theirs and ours a well.

'What more do they want?' I heard someone in a managerial suit say to his competitively dressed companion, as they hurried past me in the street. 'What more do they want?'

Of course, I didn't know who 'they' were, but somehow now 'they' are everywhere, as if ourselves in disguise, for I couldn't help wondering who it might be that was above those managerial types, the ever higher managers, the controllers of destinies and fates, the gods of institutional continuance.

Yet, now, for these few moments, before the economic imperatives are at your throat again, before the demands of paymasters kick in, put aside your envy, your weariness and fret, and let your thoughts drift, drift with those of the writer, the writer back home in his front room, his parlour, here in the present moment where 'we are', as that experimental cineaste who has so inspired me through these wanderings, as he puts it in his 'Robinson Institute': 'inescapably stranded, ship-wrecked almost, in our present'. For like everyone else here, yes, even my own dear country, I may not be sick now—no—but I'm not well.

Editor's Note

It is with considerable sadness that I report here how, no sooner had the typescript of *The Constitutionals* been placed in my hands, than the state of mind which its author haplessly reveals in this work would worsen, his overall health and mental stability decline, while his memory for names, as for other things present and remote, would further mist over, to the extent of having now all but vanished. Though reporting Robinson's current constitutional condition, then, with much regret, I am fortunately able to add that he is being cared for by those nearest to him, including the person that he will insist on calling 'my dear Friday', despite appearing to acknowledge how much it could irritate; and in such pairs of safe hands he will almost certainly come to no harm—beyond the harm that time will do to us all.

In light of these sorry developments, it has not proved possible in every case to ascertain exactly from whom the author has been borrowing, whose words and which texts he has cited in every case. Some of these are clear enough from his circumlocutory essays at identifying the figures to whom he pathetically attempts to refer, but whose names more often than not he cannot for the life of him remember. Others are embedded, allusion-fashion, in the texture of his prose, whether consciously or not there is no way of knowing.

So although it has proved impossible to provide a complete set of notes and annotations to his sources, I have been able, with help from others close to him, and from the deciphering of manuscript remains related to this project—completed or abandoned—to at least list some of the more evident bibliographical contributions made by those whose names escape the writer here. Naturally, for readers who prefer to identify these by intuition from what I've called

Robinson's own sorry circumlocutions, the following paragraphs may be skipped; while, since they have no need of them, I'm sure such readers will not begrudge them to those who prefer the kinds of assurance that they may provide.

The most evident contribution to this book is made by Daniel Defoe; without his three volumes devoted to the *Life*, *Farther Adventures*, and *Serious Reflections* of Robinson Crusoe—both in their original and complete versions from 1719, and many of the various subsequent pirated editions or adaptations of it, whether for adults or children—this book could not have taken its form. To these can be added the innumerable responses to the books from Charles Gilden's satirical parody, through comments on the work and its author by Alexander Pope, William Cowper's use of the story in his Alexander Selkirk poem (whose title is given as 'Robinson Crusoe' in one draft), to the comments on Defoe and his most famous creation by Samuel Johnson, William Wordsworth, Samuel Taylor Coleridge, and John Clare, then on to Elisabeth Gaskell's use of the work in *North and South*, Wilkie Collins' homage in *The Moonstone*, Virginia Woolf's opinions and many more besides.

Further, there are the rewritings of Defoe's originals for other purposes, to which his texts have been subjected over the centuries since its publication three hundred years ago. These evidently include Jacques Offenbach's opera *Robinson Crusoé* (1867), Michel Tournier's *Vendredi ou les Limbes du Pacifique* (1967), Jane Gardam's *Crusoe's Daughter* (1985), J. M. Coetzee's *Foe* (1986), and Antonio Muñoz Molina's *El Robinson urbano* (1993). Among the critical works setting him going on this obsessional quest may have been *The Robinson Crusoe Story* by Martin Green, a book first published in 1991, which details many of the possible sources contributing to *The Constitutionals*.

Its author's compulsive collecting of poetical writings, not much touched on by Green, which refer either to Crusoe or other Robinsons, probably include Else Lasker-Schüler's becoming a Robinson and living in the East, Ingeborg Bachmann's radio play *Die Zikaden*, Elizabeth Bishop's 'Crusoe in England', Peter Bland's *The Crusoe Factor*, Iain Crichton-Smith's *The Notebooks of Robinson Crusoe*, Carlos Drummond de Andrade's 'Infância', Durs Grünbein's 'Robinson in der Stadt', the five Robinson poems of Weldon Kees (plus a host of imitations by Simon Armitage, Antony Dunn, Michael Hofmann, and Kathleen Rooney), Malcolm Lowry's poem alluding to 'Friday's print', Eugenio Montale's relevantly allusive 'Keepsake' and 'Sulla spiaggia', St-John Perse's 'Images à Crusoë', Maria Luisa Spaziani's 'Utilità della memoria', Paul Valéry's 'Robinson' from his *Histoires brisées*, Derek Walcott's 'The Castaway', 'Crusoe's Island' and 'Crusoe's Journal', and doubtless many more besides. Passing allusions might also be detected to the appearance of his obsessional figure in the writings of Roy Fisher, Karl Kraus, and G. C. Lichtenberg.

Other Robinsons not necessarily derived directly from Defoe's original and alluded to here would have to include Muriel Spark's novel *Robinson*, Chris Petit's work of the same name, and the 2017 work by Jack Robinson (aka Charles Boyle), with that very same title and an evidently helpful literature review. First among these other Robinsons is the never-encountered figure in Patrick Keiller's trilogy of films, *London* (1994), *Robinson in Space* (1997), and *Robinson in Ruins* (2010), as well as related publications by the same auteur, and, as can be detected, the commendatory writings of Iain Sinclair, who had first scouted materials our author finds so compelling in this figure's psycho-geographical writings.

Along with Keiller, and W. G. Sebald in *The Rings of Saturn* especially, Sinclair must also surely be among sources for the idea of doing something useful by going for a walk. Nevertheless, the Robinson-narrator here was at least intermittently aware of the Peripatetic School of Aristotelian philosophy, the *Philosophenweg* in Heidelberg, the *Tetsugakunomichi* in Kyoto, and the benefit that his hikes in the mountains contributed to the philosophizing of Nietzsche. Our author mentions, and will have doubtless read, at least two of the many works called *Der Spaziergang*, namely the poem by Friedrich Hölderlin and the short prose by Robert Walser. Much of this aspect to *The Constitutionals*, despite its author's niggling disagreement on a couple of points, is explored in *A Philosophy of Walking* by Frederic Gros (2015).

Of the writers and artists connected with the town of Reading that he variously forgets, half-remembers or garbles, the most prominent are evidently Jane Austen, Basil Bunting, Marion Coutts, Charles Dickens, Thomas Hardy, Jerome K. Jerome, Nicholas Moore, Paul Muldoon, Alexander Pope, Arthur Rimbaud, Walter Sickert, Sergeant Talfourd, Elizabeth Taylor and, of course, Oscar Wilde. Less familiarly, perhaps, our author was clearly aware of Christopher Salvesen, who wrote the poem about Cemetery Junction, the Italian novelist Luigi Meneghello's writings on the town, and the Reading bookseller John Snare's sad obsession with a painting he thought by Velázquez as related by Laura Cumming in *The Vanishing Man* (2016). He is also evidently heartened to recall, late in these peregrinations, a critical book called *Puns* by Walter Redfern.

Other writers not connected with Reading but alluded to here include the Henry James of *The Princess Casamassima* in the section on Robinson's time in York, Rudyard Kipling and Arthur Conan Doyle, as well as André Breton's proto-psycho-geographical *Nadja* in the encounter with the typographic designer who happens to have the same name. Joseph Conrad before he had adopted that pen name in the pages devoted to Stoke Newington, Calderón de la Barca in the conversation with his seafaring daughter, and the second of John Milton's paired poems in the final chapter's reflections on the writer back home at his writing table also make an appearance—though the last of these may in fact be a multiple allusion also recalling the second stanza of Yeats' poem (itself about the writer at home) called 'My House'—in 'Meditations in Time of Civil War'.

One of the things that I and my editorial advisors have not done in preparing this typescript for the press is attempt any further identification of the numerous living people that the narrating figure happens to encounter, have conversations with, or refer to in the course of these overlapping and intersected constitutionals of his. The book is described by its author in the formulaic prefatory disclaimer as a work of fiction in which 'any resemblance to people living or dead is fortuitous'. In this we hope to have acted in accord with our writer's wishes in protecting the identities of those he may evoke, occasionally cite, or to whom he seems unable to prevent himself from referring.

My apologies, and doubtless those of my author, go to any other writers whose works have been alluded to, cited, or in any way referred to here, but who, owing to the unfortunate circumstances in which *The Constitutionals* was drafted over a number of difficult years, and difficult of course not only for its author, I have—despite the best efforts of myself and other friends of Robinson—not been able to track down or trace. It remains only, then, to hope that those readers who find their way to this work may draw such benefit from it as its author had hoped, by its writing, to offer for the salve of his own damaged self and for that of the world.

Two Rivers Press has been publishing in and about Reading since 1994. Founded by the artist Peter Hay (1951–2003), the press continues to delight readers, local and further afield, with its varied list of individually designed, thought-provoking books.